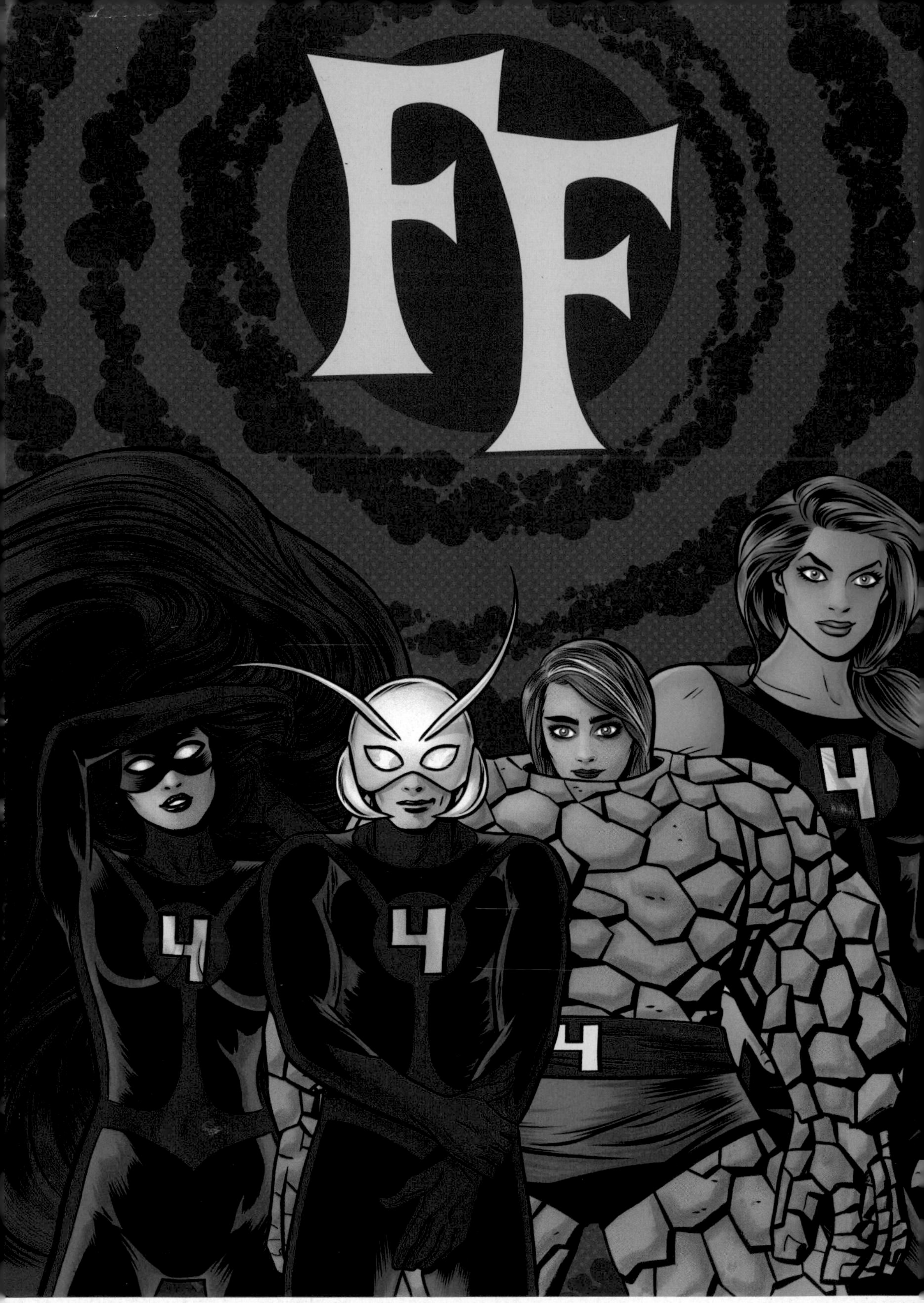
FF
4
4
4
4

FANTASTIC FAUX

DuBOIS

SCOTT LANG — ANT-MAN

DARLA DEERING — MS. THING

MEDUSALITH AMAQUELIN — MEDUSA

JENNIFER WALTERS — SHE-HULK

ALEX POWER • LEECH • ARTIE MADDICKS • BENTLEY-23 • DRAGON MAN • ONOME

VIL • WU • MIK • KORR • TURG • TONG

While away on their cosmic family vacation, the Fantastic Four left the young and brilliant children of the Future Foundation in the care of Ant-Man, Darla Deering, Medusa and She-Hulk.

Things did not go as planned. The Fantastic Four didn't return when they were supposed to. Then an older Johnny Storm came back, claiming that the rest of the Fantastic Four had died, and the only way to prevent it was to kill Victor Von Doom! But is this battle-scarred figure really Johnny? Scott and Wyatt Wingfoot, an old friend of She-Hulk and the Fantastic family, think so, but the rest of the FF aren't so sure...

WRITER
MATT FRACTION

ARTIST, #4-5 & #7-8
MICHAEL ALLRED

ARTIST, #6
JOE QUINONES

COLOR ARTIST
LAURA ALLRED

LETTERS
VC'S CLAYTON COWLES

COVER ART
MICHAEL ALLRED & LAURA ALLRED

ASSISTANT EDITOR
JAKE THOMAS

EDITOR
TOM BREVOORT

Collection Editor: Jennifer Grünwald • Assistant Editors: Alex Starbuck & Nelson Ribeiro • Editor, Special Projects: Mark D. Beazley
Senior Editor, Special Projects: Jeff Youngquist • Senior Vice President of Sales: David Gabriel • Book Design: Jeff Powell

Editor in Chief: Axel Alonso • Chief Creative Officer: Joe Quesada • Publisher: Dan Buckley • Executive Producer: Alan Fine

L. 1: FANTASTIC FAUX. Contains material originally published in magazine form as FF #4-8. First printing 2013. ISBN# 978-0-7851-6663-4. Published by MARVEL WORLDWIDE, INC., a subsidiary of MARVEL
RTAINMENT, LLC. OFFICE OF PUBLICATION: 135 West 50th Street, New York, NY 10020. Copyright © 2013 Marvel Characters, Inc. All rights reserved. All characters featured in this issue and the distinctive names
kenesses thereof, and all related indicia are trademarks of Marvel Characters, Inc. No similarity between any of the names, characters, persons, and/or institutions in this magazine with those of any living or dead
n or institution is intended, and any such similarity which may exist is purely coincidental. **Printed in the U.S.A.** ALAN FINE, EVP - Office of the President, Marvel Worldwide, Inc. and EVP & CMO Marvel Characters
DAN BUCKLEY, Publisher & President - Print, Animation & Digital Divisions; JOE QUESADA, Chief Creative Officer; TOM BREVOORT, SVP of Publishing; DAVID BOGART, SVP of Operations & Procurement, Publishing;
EBULSKI, SVP of Creator & Content Development; DAVID GABRIEL, SVP of Print & Digital Publishing Sales; JIM O'KEEFE, VP of Operations & Logistics; DAN CARR, Executive Director of Publishing Technology; SUSAN
PI, Editorial Operations Manager; ALEX MORALES, Publishing Operations Manager; STAN LEE, Chairman Emeritus. For information regarding advertising in Marvel Comics or on Marvel.com, please contact Niza Disla,
or of Marvel Partnerships, at ndisla@marvel.com. For Marvel subscription inquiries, please call 800-217-9158. **Manufactured between 5/22/2013 and 6/24/2013 by QUAD/GRAPHICS, VERSAILLES, KY, USA.**

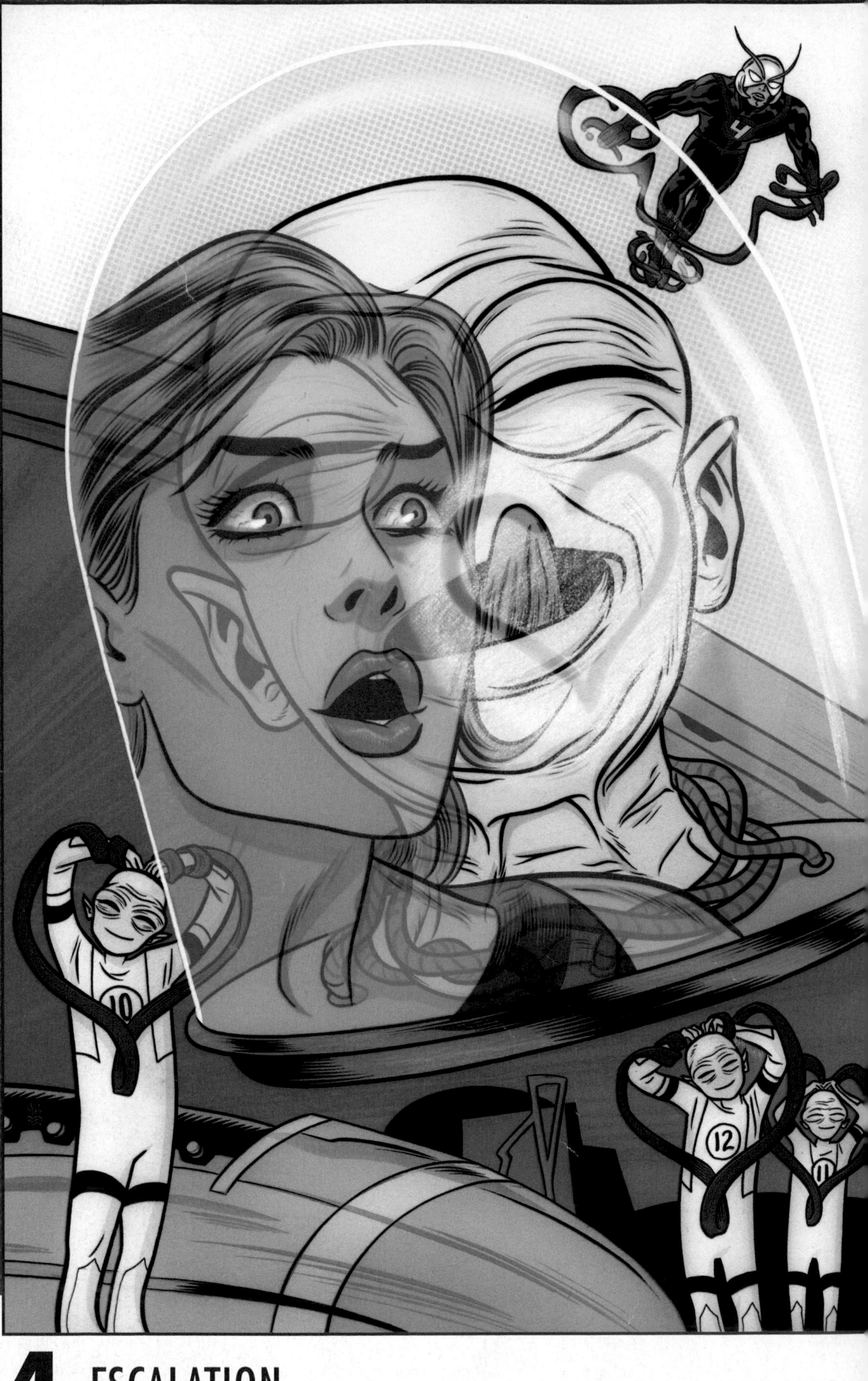
4
10
12
11

4 ESCALATION

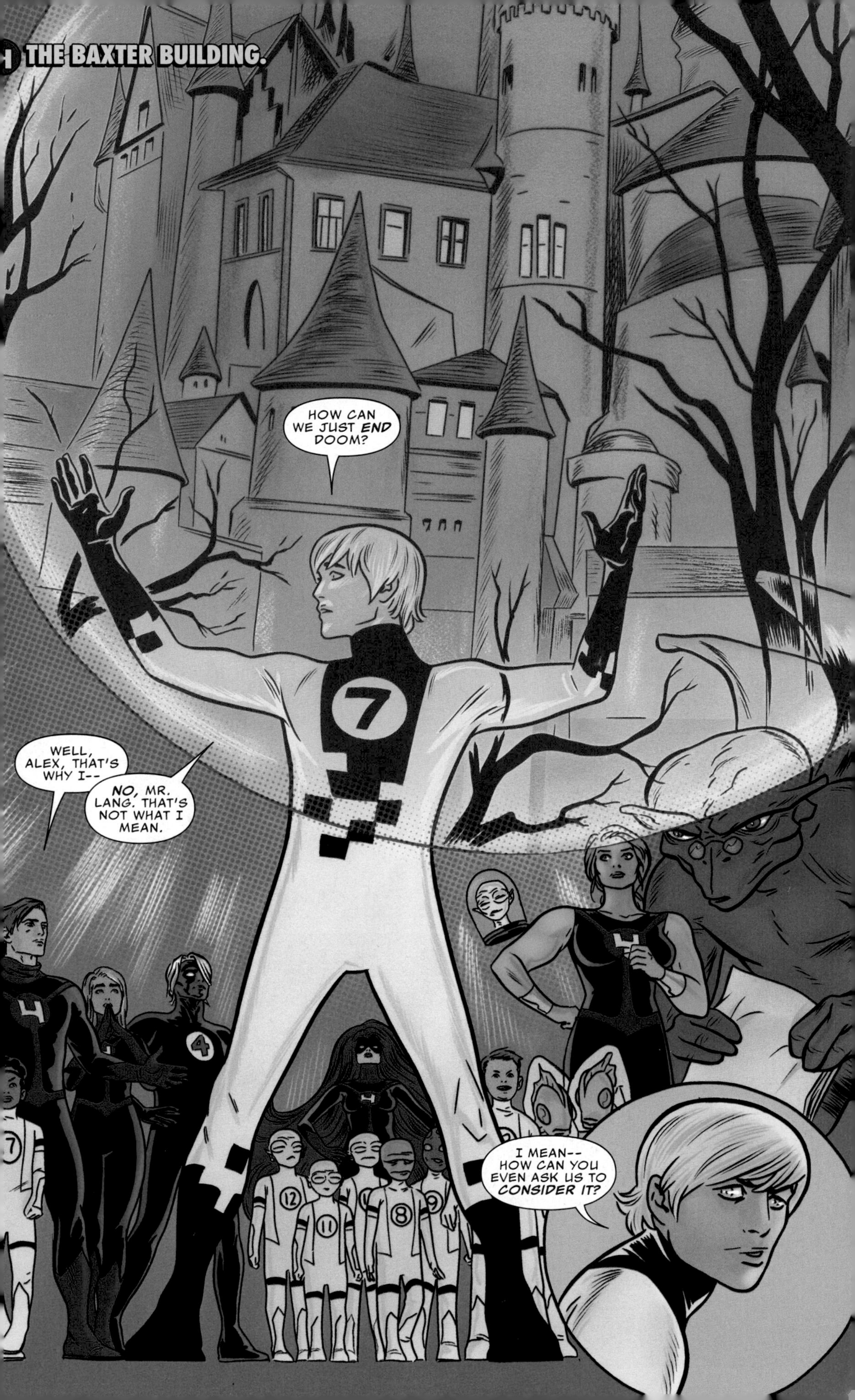

THE BAXTER BUILDING.
HOW CAN WE JUST END DOOM?
WELL, ALEX, THAT'S WHY I--
NO, MR. LANG. THAT'S NOT WHAT I MEAN.
I MEAN-- HOW CAN YOU EVEN ASK US TO CONSIDER IT?

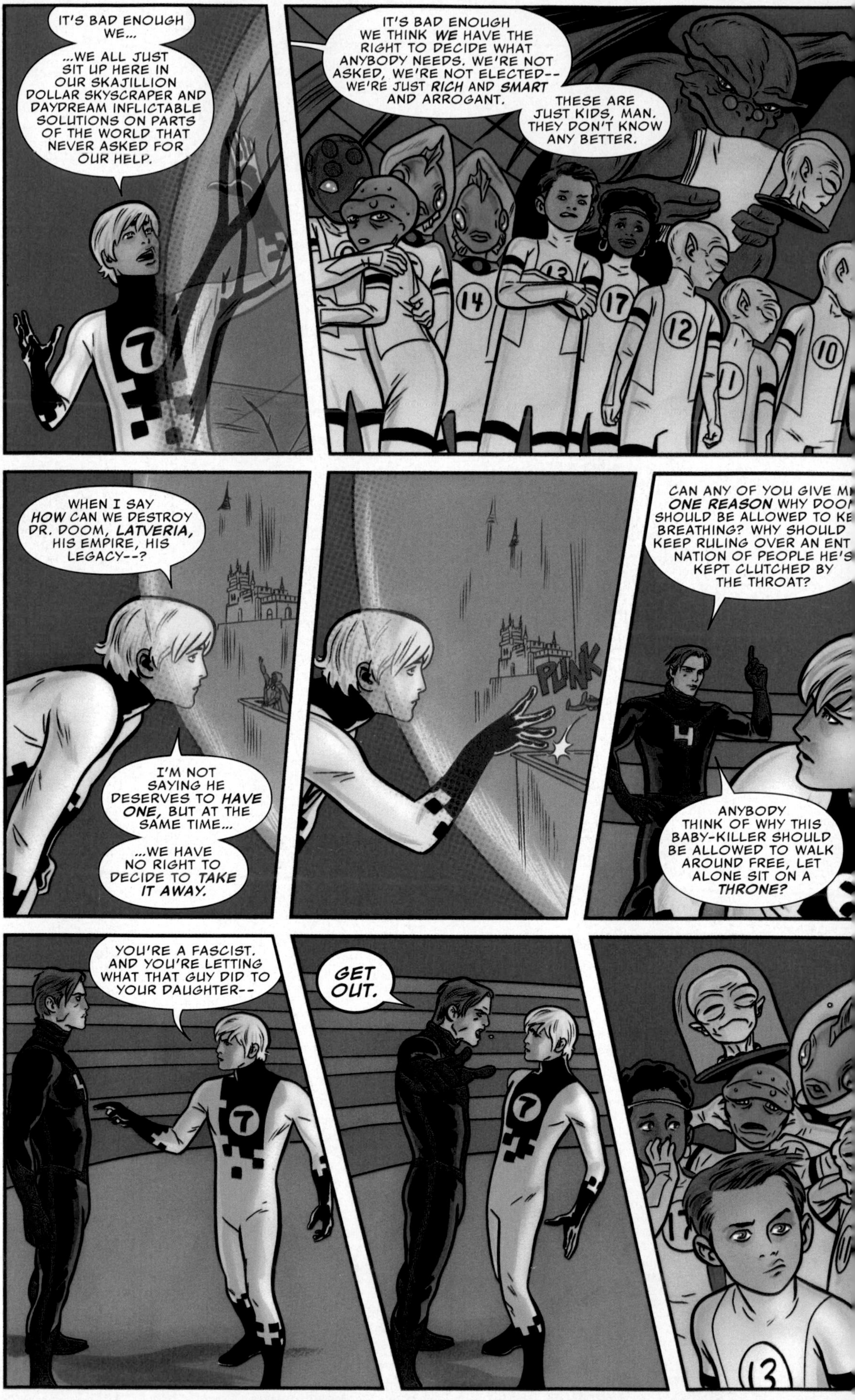
IT'S BAD ENOUGH WE...
...WE ALL JUST SIT UP HERE IN OUR SKAJILLION DOLLAR SKYSCRAPER AND DAYDREAM INFLICTABLE SOLUTIONS ON PARTS OF THE WORLD THAT NEVER ASKED FOR OUR HELP.
IT'S BAD ENOUGH WE THINK WE HAVE THE RIGHT TO DECIDE WHAT ANYBODY NEEDS. WE'RE NOT ASKED, WE'RE NOT ELECTED-- WE'RE JUST RICH AND SMART AND ARROGANT.
THESE ARE JUST KIDS, MAN. THEY DON'T KNOW ANY BETTER.
14
13
17
12
11
10
WHEN I SAY HOW CAN WE DESTROY DR. DOOM, LATVERIA, HIS EMPIRE, HIS LEGACY--?
I'M NOT SAYING HE DESERVES TO HAVE ONE, BUT AT THE SAME TIME...
...WE HAVE NO RIGHT TO DECIDE TO TAKE IT AWAY.
PUNK
CAN ANY OF YOU GIVE M
ONE REASON WHY DOO
SHOULD BE ALLOWED TO KE
BREATHING? WHY SHOULD
KEEP RULING OVER AN ENT
NATION OF PEOPLE HE'S
KEPT CLUTCHED BY
THE THROAT?
ANYBODY THINK OF WHY THIS BABY-KILLER SHOULD BE ALLOWED TO WALK AROUND FREE, LET ALONE SIT ON A THRONE?
YOU'RE A FASCIST. AND YOU'RE LETTING WHAT THAT GUY DID TO YOUR DAUGHTER--
GET OUT.
13

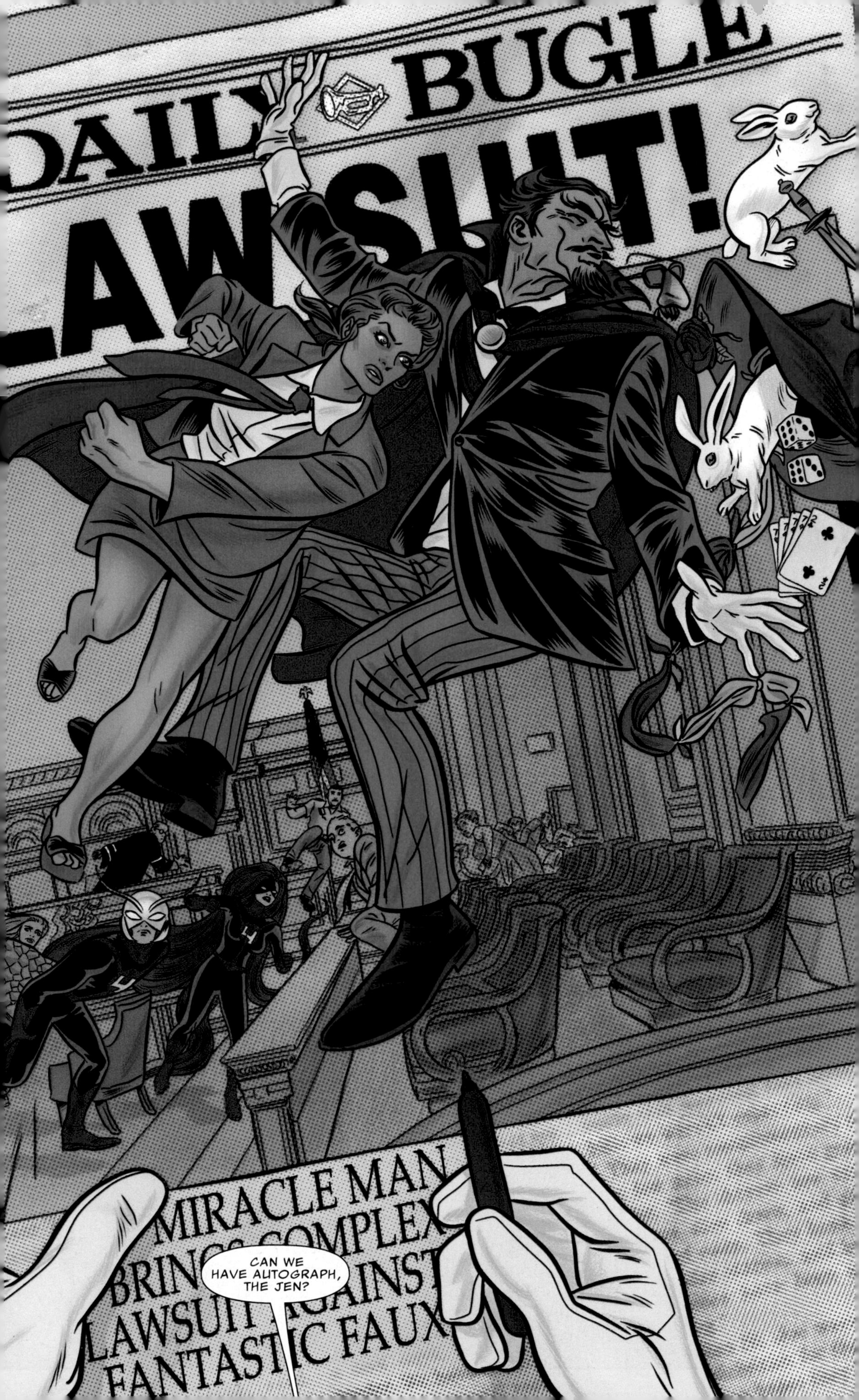
DAILY BUGLE
LAWSUIT!
MIRACLE MAN
BRINGS COMPLEX
LAWSUIT AGAINST
FANTASTIC FAUX
CAN WE HAVE AUTOGRAPH, THE JEN?

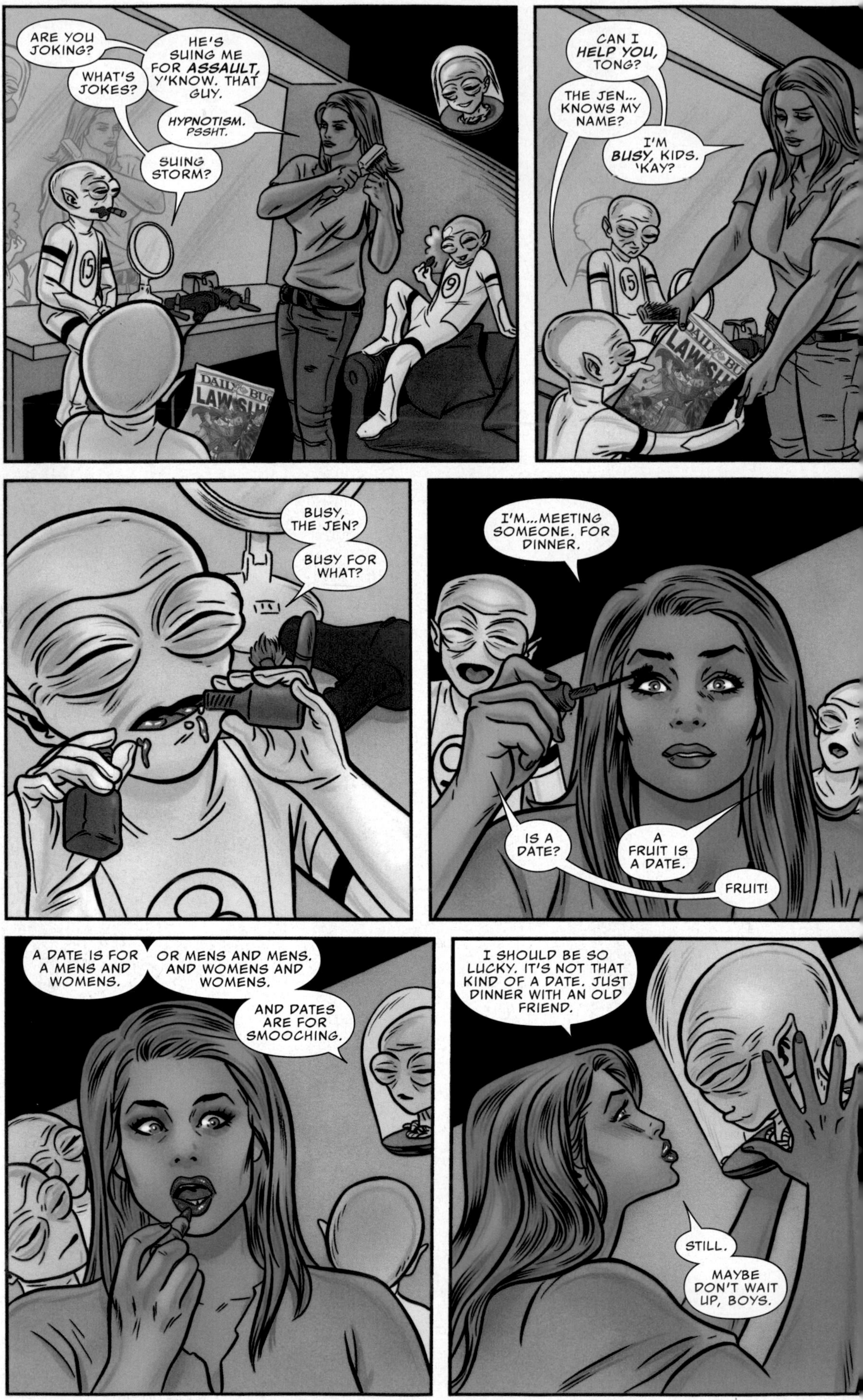
ARE YOU JOKING?
HE'S SUING ME FOR ASSAULT, Y'KNOW. THAT GUY.
WHAT'S JOKES?
HYPNOTISM. PSSHT.
SUING STORM?
DAILY BUGLE
LAWSUIT
CAN I HELP YOU, TONG?
THE JEN... KNOWS MY NAME?
I'M BUSY, KIDS. 'KAY?
BUSY, THE JEN?
BUSY FOR WHAT?
I'M...MEETING SOMEONE. FOR DINNER.
IS A DATE?
A FRUIT IS A DATE.
FRUIT!
A DATE IS FOR A MENS AND WOMENS.
OR MENS AND MENS. AND WOMENS AND WOMENS.
AND DATES ARE FOR SMOOCHING.
I SHOULD BE SO LUCKY. IT'S NOT THAT KIND OF A DATE. JUST DINNER WITH AN OLD FRIEND.
STILL.
MAYBE DON'T WAIT UP, BOYS.

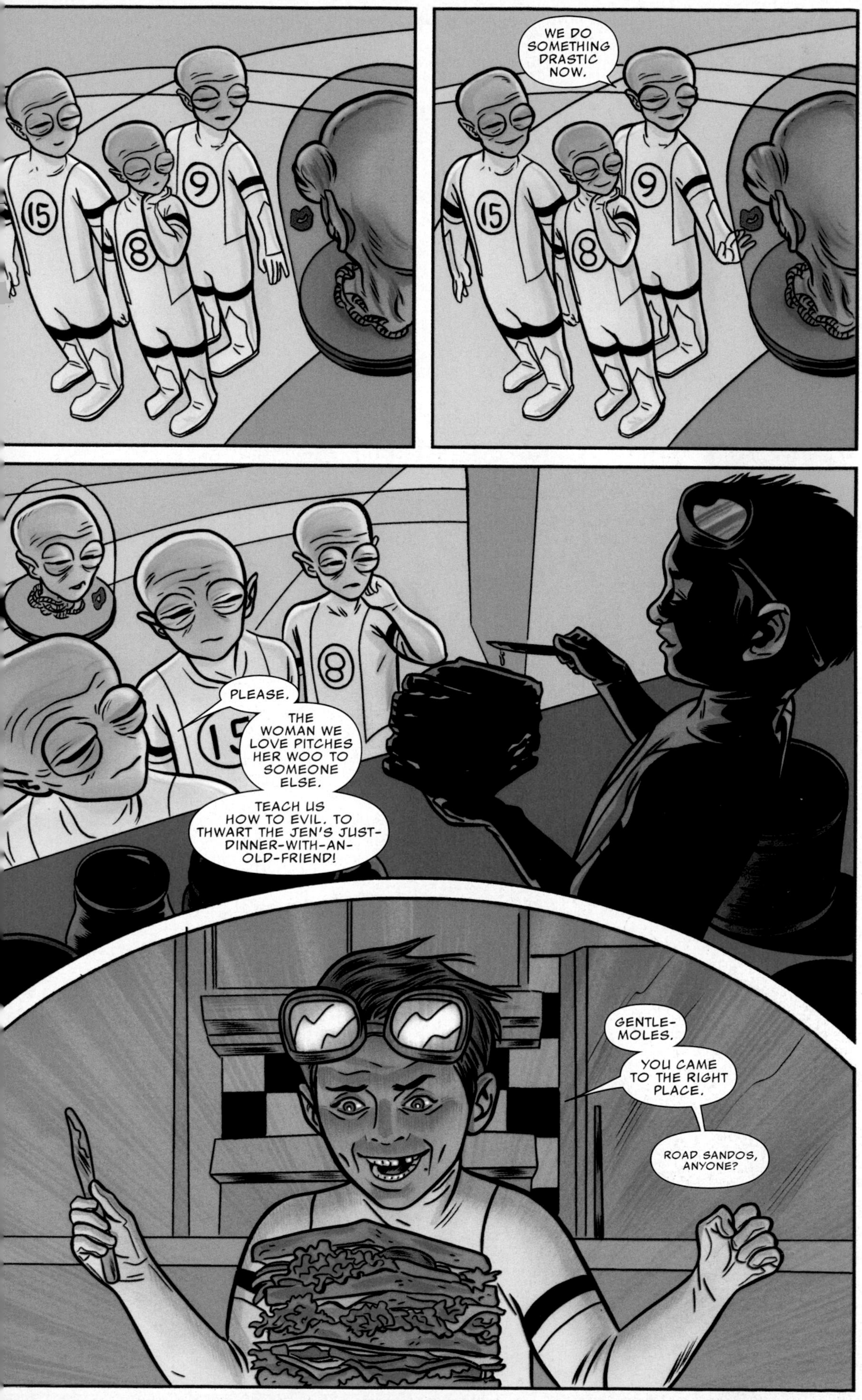
WE DO SOMETHING DRASTIC NOW.
PLEASE.
THE WOMAN WE LOVE PITCHES HER WOO TO SOMEONE ELSE.
TEACH US HOW TO EVIL. TO THWART THE JEN'S JUST-DINNER-WITH-AN-OLD-FRIEND!
GENTLE-MOLES.
YOU CAME TO THE RIGHT PLACE.
ROAD SANDOS, ANYONE?

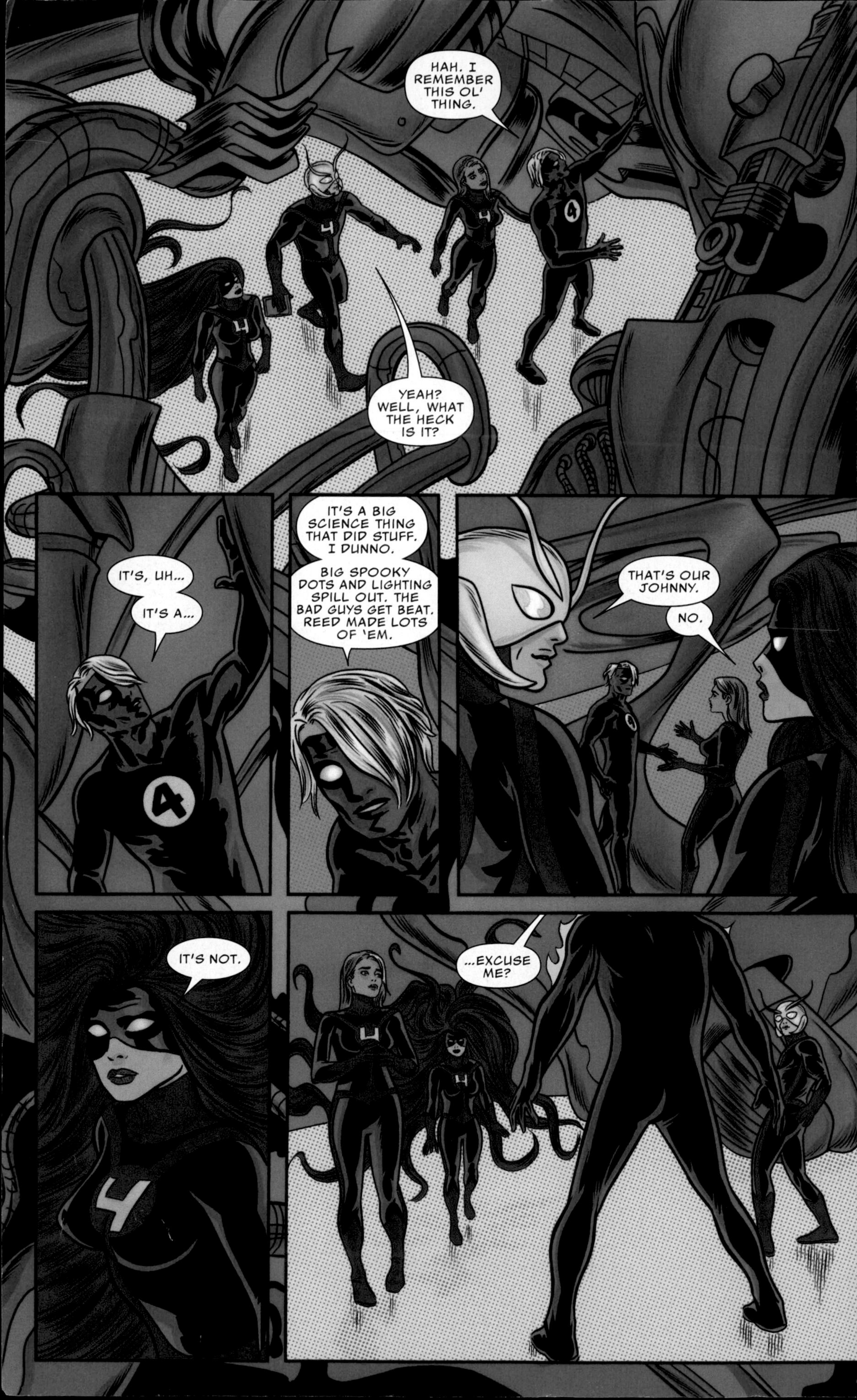
HAH. I REMEMBER THIS OL' THING.
YEAH? WELL, WHAT THE HECK IS IT?
IT'S, UH...
IT'S A...
IT'S A BIG SCIENCE THING THAT DID STUFF. I DUNNO.
BIG SPOOKY DOTS AND LIGHTING SPILL OUT. THE BAD GUYS GET BEAT. REED MADE LOTS OF 'EM.
THAT'S OUR JOHNNY.
NO.
IT'S NOT.
...EXCUSE ME?

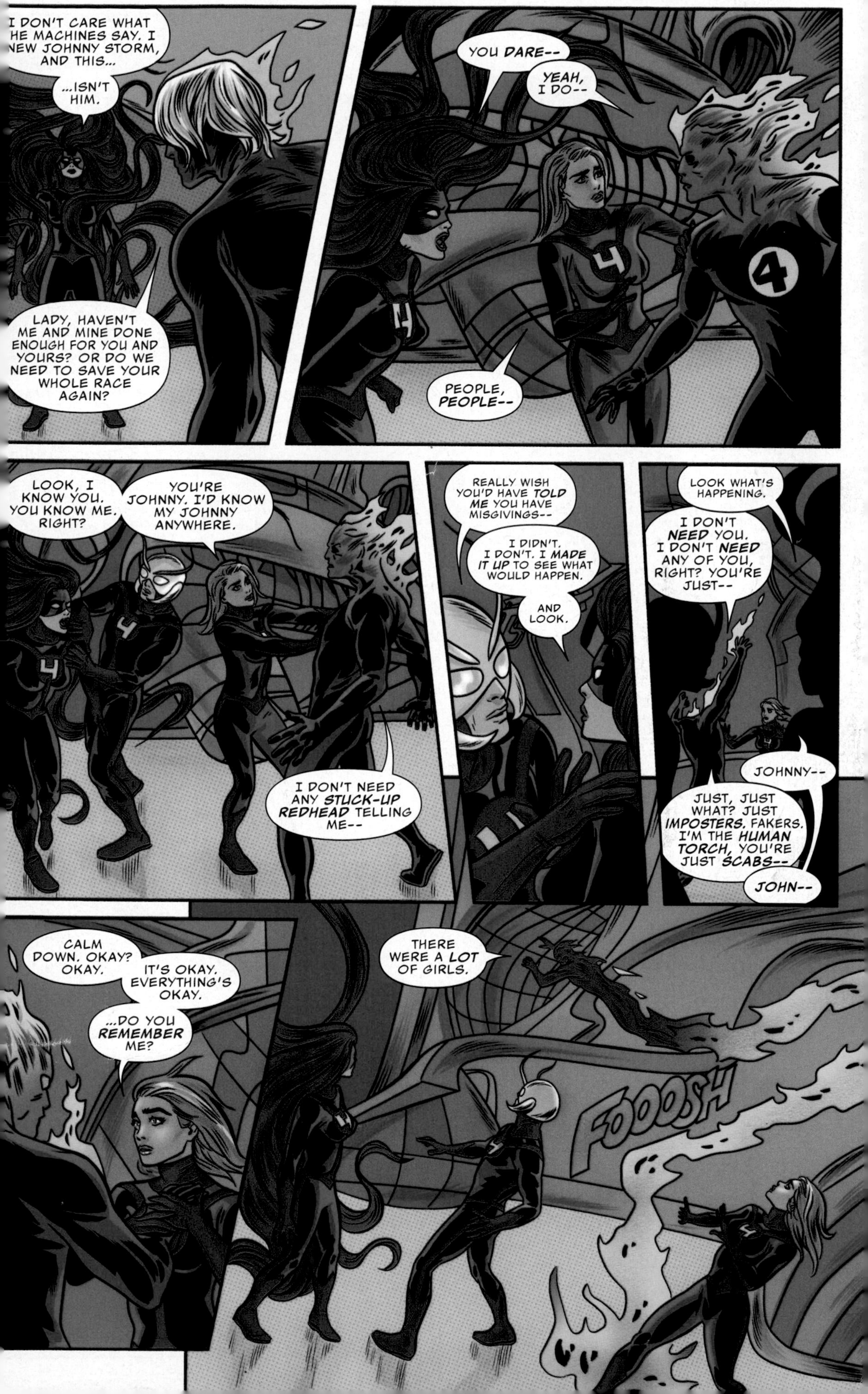
I DON'T CARE WHAT HE MACHINES SAY. I NEW JOHNNY STORM, AND THIS...
...ISN'T HIM.
LADY, HAVEN'T ME AND MINE DONE ENOUGH FOR YOU AND YOURS? OR DO WE NEED TO SAVE YOUR WHOLE RACE AGAIN?
YOU DARE--
YEAH, I DO--
PEOPLE, PEOPLE--
LOOK, I KNOW YOU. YOU KNOW ME. RIGHT?
YOU'RE JOHNNY. I'D KNOW MY JOHNNY ANYWHERE.
I DON'T NEED ANY STUCK-UP REDHEAD TELLING ME--
REALLY WISH YOU'D HAVE TOLD ME YOU HAVE MISGIVINGS--
I DIDN'T. I DON'T. I MADE IT UP TO SEE WHAT WOULD HAPPEN.
AND LOOK.
LOOK WHAT'S HAPPENING.
I DON'T NEED YOU. I DON'T NEED ANY OF YOU, RIGHT? YOU'RE JUST--
JOHNNY--
JUST, JUST WHAT? JUST IMPOSTERS. FAKERS. I'M THE HUMAN TORCH, YOU'RE JUST SCABS--
JOHN--
CALM DOWN. OKAY? OKAY.
IT'S OKAY. EVERYTHING'S OKAY.
...DO YOU REMEMBER ME?
THERE WERE A LOT OF GIRLS.
FOOOSH

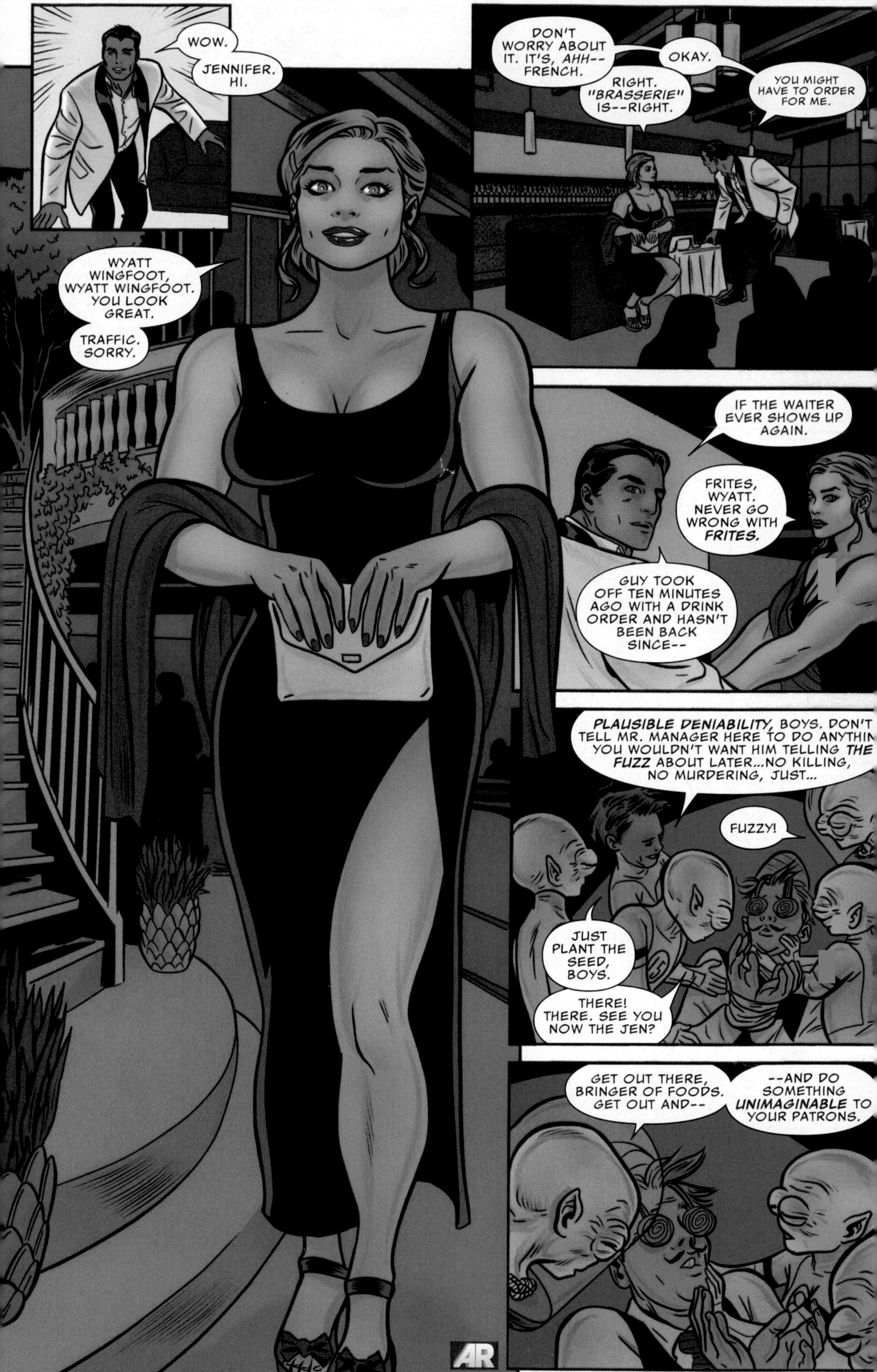

WOW.
JENNIFER. HI.
WYATT WINGFOOT, WYATT WINGFOOT. YOU LOOK GREAT.
TRAFFIC. SORRY.
DON'T WORRY ABOUT IT. IT'S, AHH--FRENCH.
OKAY.
RIGHT. "BRASSERIE" IS--RIGHT.
YOU MIGHT HAVE TO ORDER FOR ME.
IF THE WAITER EVER SHOWS UP AGAIN.
FRITES, WYATT. NEVER GO WRONG WITH FRITES.
GUY TOOK OFF TEN MINUTES AGO WITH A DRINK ORDER AND HASN'T BEEN BACK SINCE--
PLAUSIBLE DENIABILITY, BOYS. DON'T TELL MR. MANAGER HERE TO DO ANYTHIN YOU WOULDN'T WANT HIM TELLING THE FUZZ ABOUT LATER...NO KILLING, NO MURDERING, JUST...
FUZZY!
JUST PLANT THE SEED, BOYS.
THERE! THERE. SEE YOU NOW THE JEN?
GET OUT THERE, BRINGER OF FOODS. GET OUT AND--
--AND DO SOMETHING UNIMAGINABLE TO YOUR PATRONS.
AR

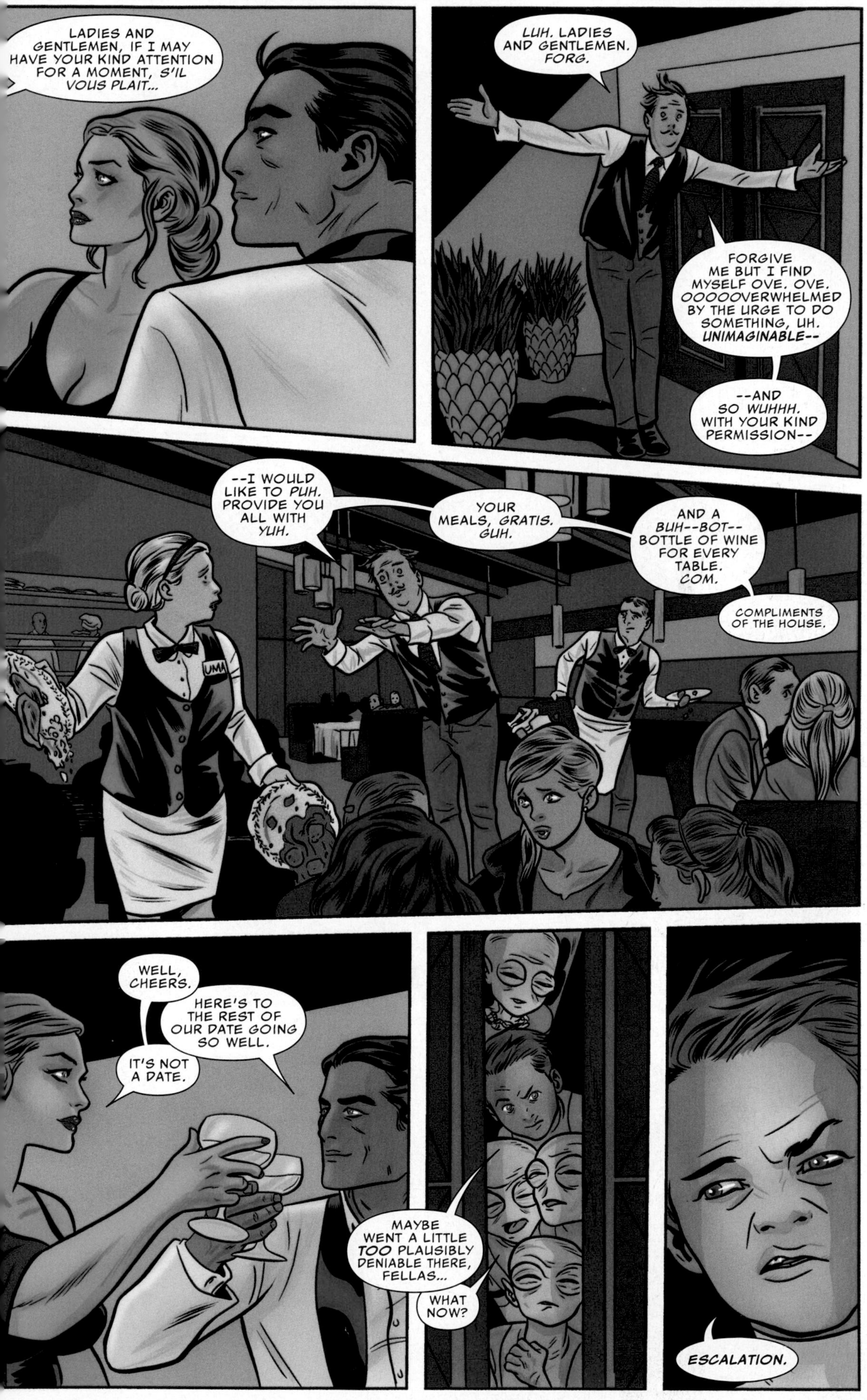
LADIES AND GENTLEMEN, IF I MAY HAVE YOUR KIND ATTENTION FOR A MOMENT, S'IL VOUS PLAIT...
LUH. LADIES AND GENTLEMEN. FORG.
FORGIVE ME BUT I FIND MYSELF OVE. OVE. OOOOOVERWHELMED BY THE URGE TO DO SOMETHING, UH. UNIMAGINABLE--
--AND SO WUHHH. WITH YOUR KIND PERMISSION--
--I WOULD LIKE TO PUH. PROVIDE YOU ALL WITH YUH.
YOUR MEALS, GRATIS. GUH.
AND A BUH--BOT-- BOTTLE OF WINE FOR EVERY TABLE. COM.
COMPLIMENTS OF THE HOUSE.
UMA
WELL, CHEERS.
HERE'S TO THE REST OF OUR DATE GOING SO WELL.
IT'S NOT A DATE.
MAYBE WENT A LITTLE TOO PLAUSIBLY DENIABLE THERE, FELLAS...
WHAT NOW?
ESCALATION.

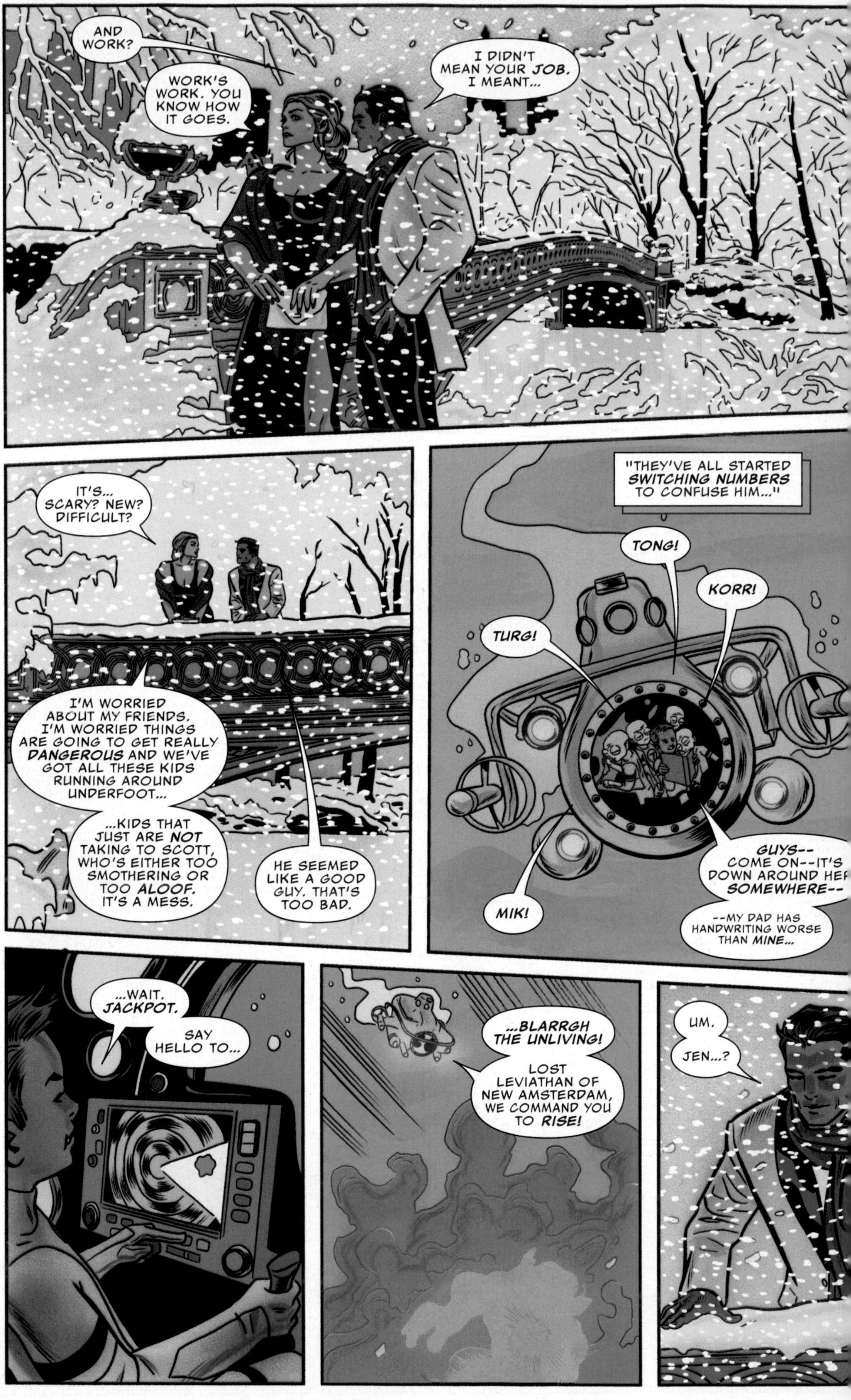
AND WORK?
WORK'S WORK. YOU KNOW HOW IT GOES.
I DIDN'T MEAN YOUR JOB. I MEANT...
IT'S... SCARY? NEW? DIFFICULT?
I'M WORRIED ABOUT MY FRIENDS. I'M WORRIED THINGS ARE GOING TO GET REALLY DANGEROUS AND WE'VE GOT ALL THESE KIDS RUNNING AROUND UNDERFOOT...
...KIDS THAT JUST ARE NOT TAKING TO SCOTT, WHO'S EITHER TOO SMOTHERING OR TOO ALOOF. IT'S A MESS.
HE SEEMED LIKE A GOOD GUY. THAT'S TOO BAD.
"THEY'VE ALL STARTED SWITCHING NUMBERS TO CONFUSE HIM..."
TONG!
KORR!
TURG!
MIK!
GUYS-- COME ON--IT'S DOWN AROUND HE
SOMEWHERE--
--MY DAD HAS HANDWRITING WORSE THAN MINE...
...WAIT. JACKPOT.
SAY HELLO TO...
...BLARRGH THE UNLIVING!
LOST LEVIATHAN OF NEW AMSTERDAM, WE COMMAND YOU TO RISE!
UM.
JEN...?

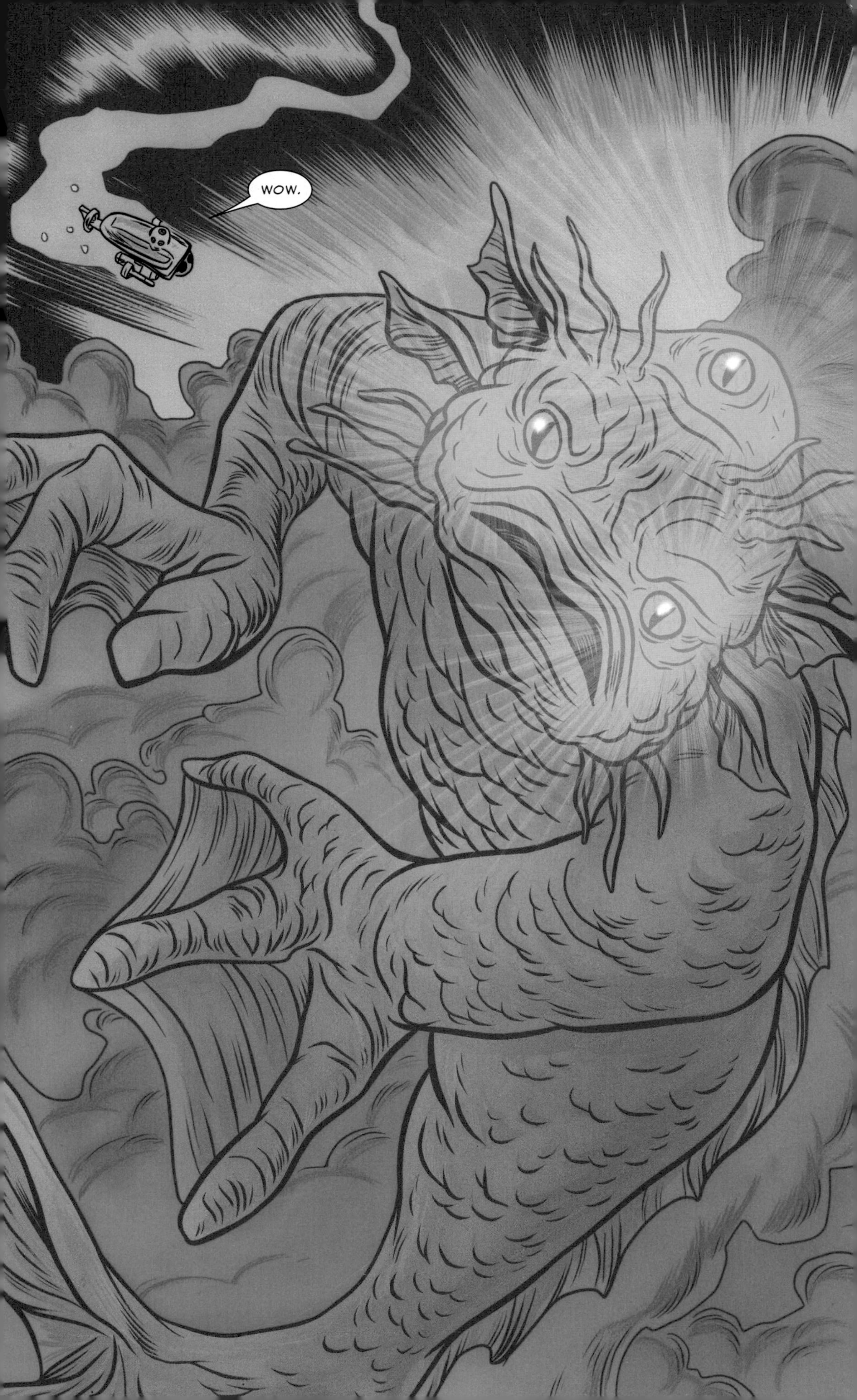
WOW.

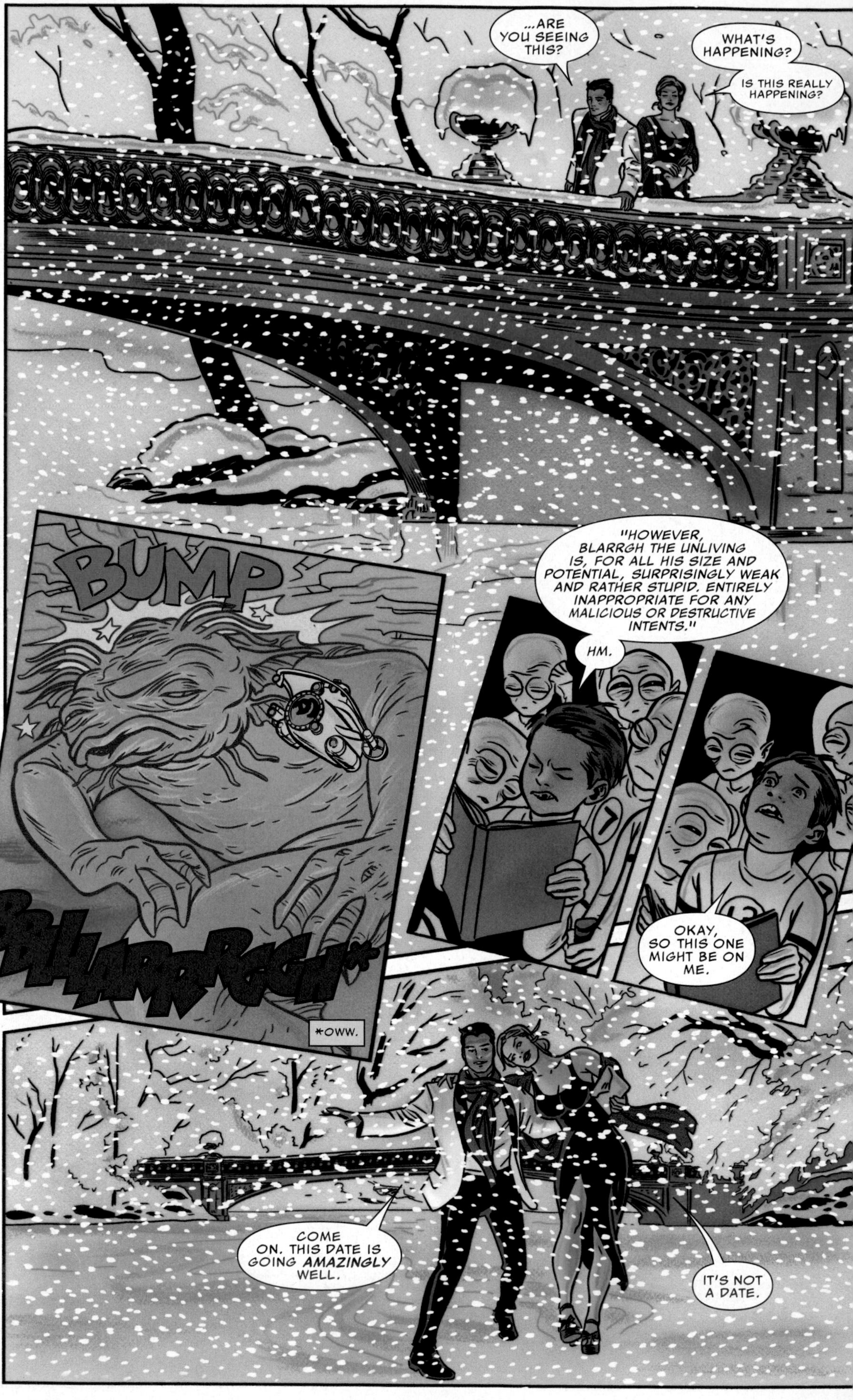
...ARE YOU SEEING THIS?
WHAT'S HAPPENING?
IS THIS REALLY HAPPENING?
BUMP
BLLLARRRGH*
*OWW.
"HOWEVER, BLARRGH THE UNLIVING IS, FOR ALL HIS SIZE AND POTENTIAL, SURPRISINGLY WEAK AND RATHER STUPID. ENTIRELY INAPPROPRIATE FOR ANY MALICIOUS OR DESTRUCTIVE INTENTS."
HM.
OKAY, SO THIS ONE MIGHT BE ON ME.
COME ON. THIS DATE IS GOING AMAZINGLY WELL.
IT'S NOT A DATE.

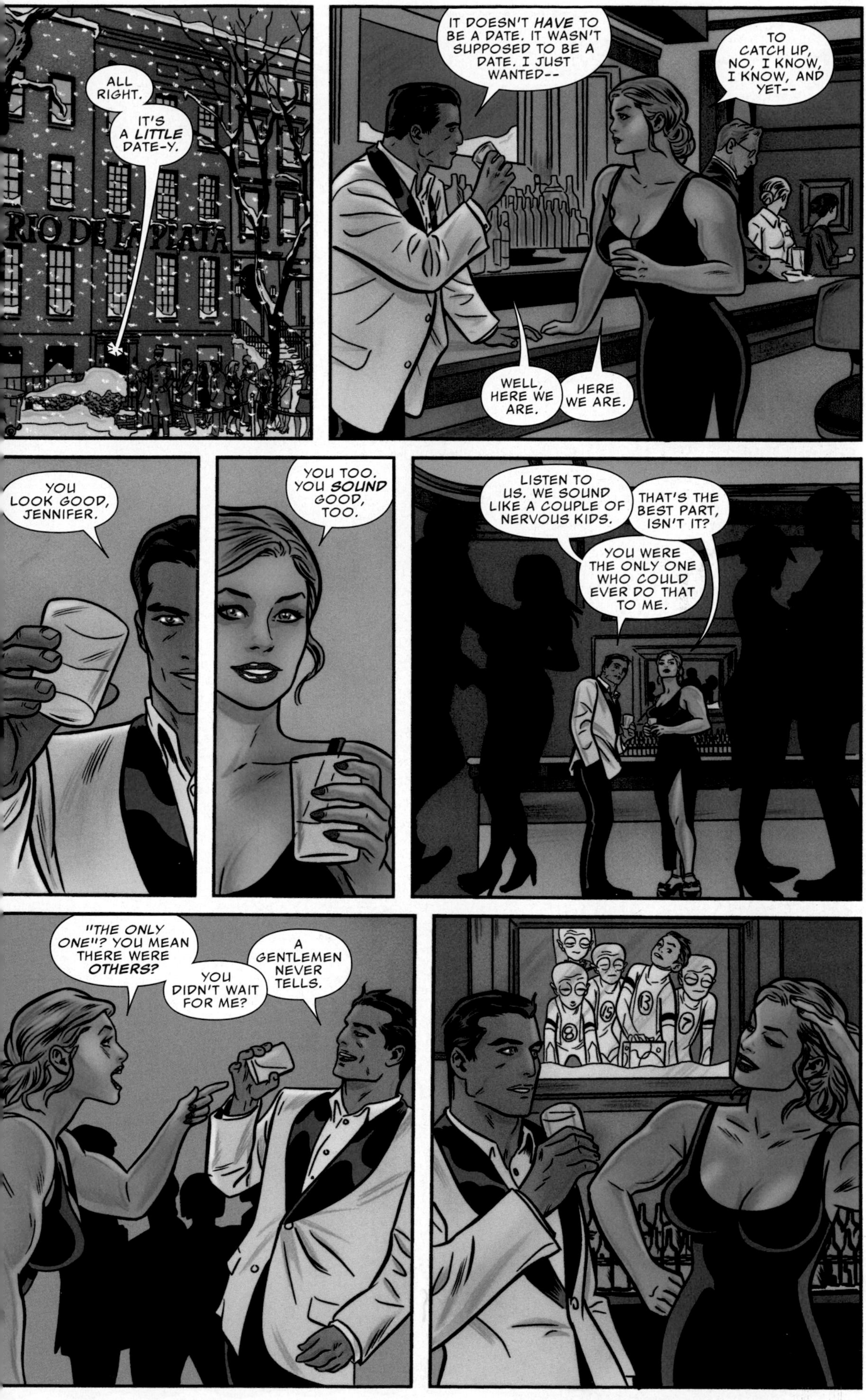
RIO DE LA PLATA
ALL RIGHT.
IT'S A LITTLE DATE-Y.
IT DOESN'T HAVE TO BE A DATE. IT WASN'T SUPPOSED TO BE A DATE. I JUST WANTED--
TO CATCH UP, NO, I KNOW, I KNOW, AND YET--
WELL, HERE WE ARE.
HERE WE ARE.
YOU LOOK GOOD, JENNIFER.
YOU TOO. YOU SOUND GOOD, TOO.
LISTEN TO US. WE SOUND LIKE A COUPLE OF NERVOUS KIDS.
THAT'S THE BEST PART, ISN'T IT?
YOU WERE THE ONLY ONE WHO COULD EVER DO THAT TO ME.
"THE ONLY ONE"? YOU MEAN THERE WERE OTHERS?
YOU DIDN'T WAIT FOR ME?
A GENTLEMEN NEVER TELLS.

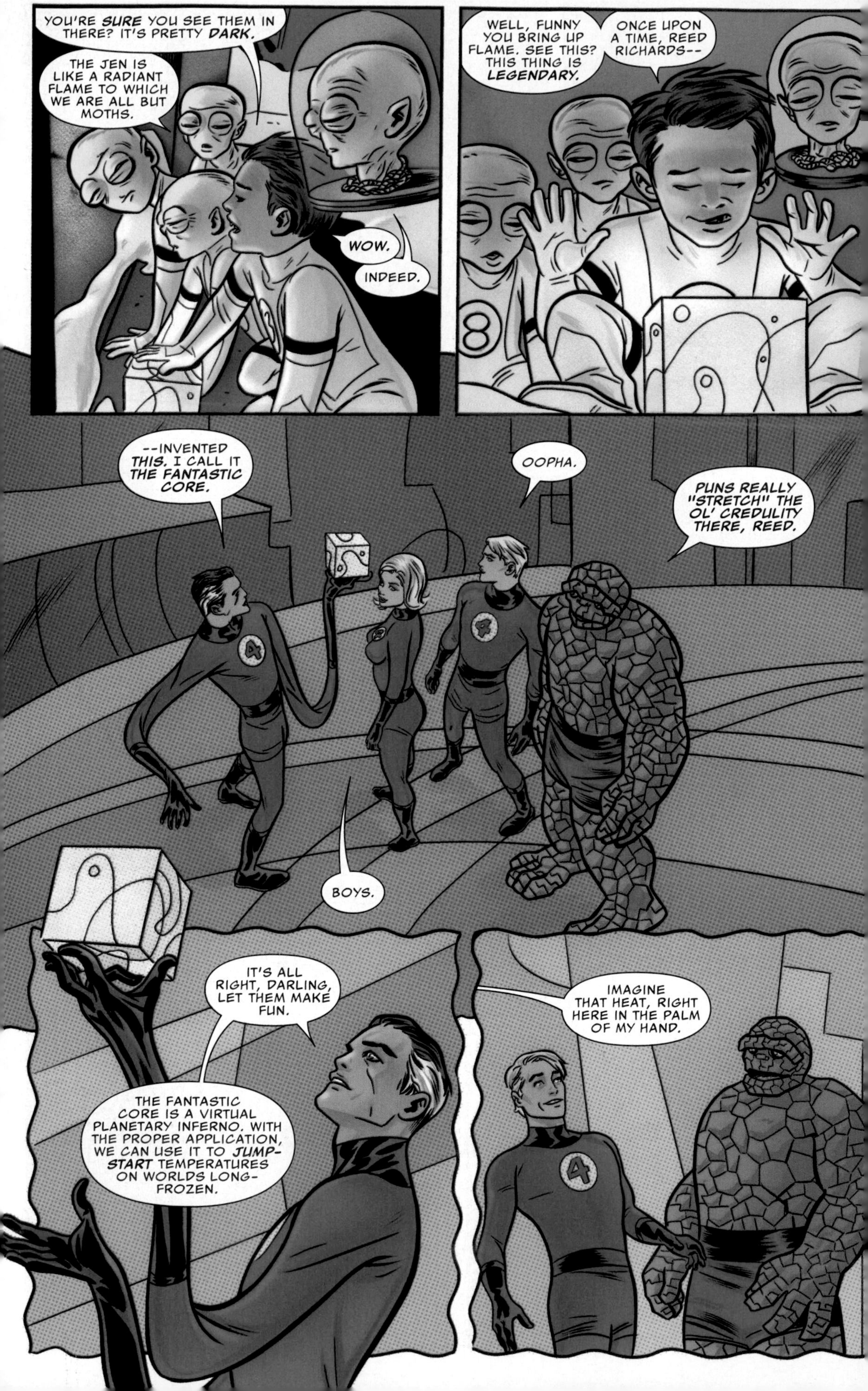
YOU'RE SURE YOU SEE THEM IN THERE? IT'S PRETTY DARK.
THE JEN IS LIKE A RADIANT FLAME TO WHICH WE ARE ALL BUT MOTHS.
WOW.
INDEED.
WELL, FUNNY YOU BRING UP FLAME. SEE THIS? THIS THING IS LEGENDARY.
ONCE UPON A TIME, REED RICHARDS--
--INVENTED THIS. I CALL IT THE FANTASTIC CORE.
OOPHA.
PUNS REALLY "STRETCH" THE OL' CREDULITY THERE, REED.
BOYS.
IT'S ALL RIGHT, DARLING, LET THEM MAKE FUN.
THE FANTASTIC CORE IS A VIRTUAL PLANETARY INFERNO. WITH THE PROPER APPLICATION, WE CAN USE IT TO JUMP-START TEMPERATURES ON WORLDS LONG-FROZEN.
IMAGINE THAT HEAT, RIGHT HERE IN THE PALM OF MY HAND.

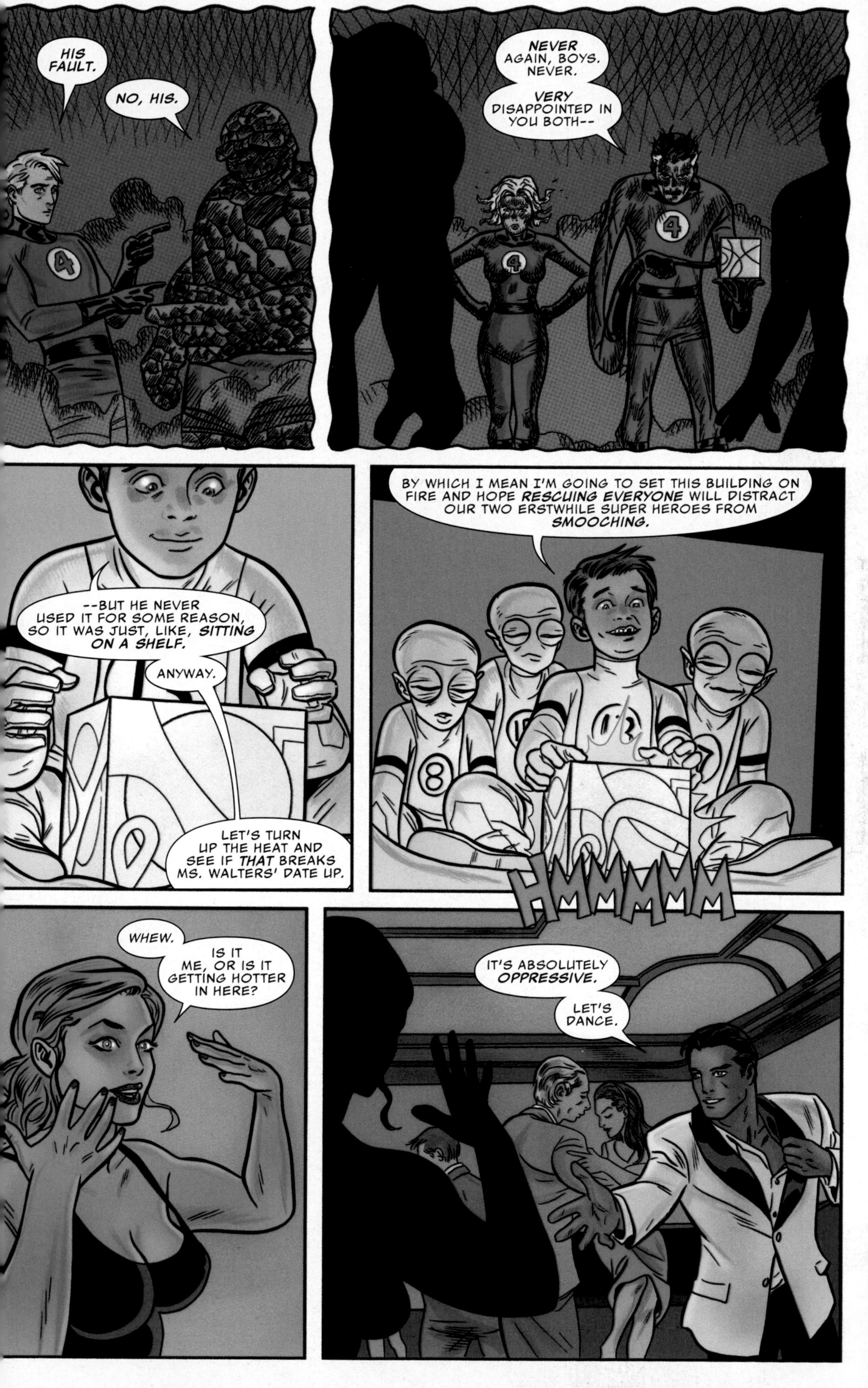
HIS FAULT.
NO, HIS.
NEVER AGAIN, BOYS. NEVER.
VERY DISAPPOINTED IN YOU BOTH--
--BUT HE NEVER USED IT FOR SOME REASON, SO IT WAS JUST, LIKE, SITTING ON A SHELF.
ANYWAY.
LET'S TURN UP THE HEAT AND SEE IF THAT BREAKS MS. WALTERS' DATE UP.
BY WHICH I MEAN I'M GOING TO SET THIS BUILDING ON FIRE AND HOPE RESCUING EVERYONE WILL DISTRACT OUR TWO ERSTWHILE SUPER HEROES FROM SMOOCHING.
HMMMMM
WHEW.
IS IT ME, OR IS IT GETTING HOTTER IN HERE?
IT'S ABSOLUTELY OPPRESSIVE.
LET'S DANCE.

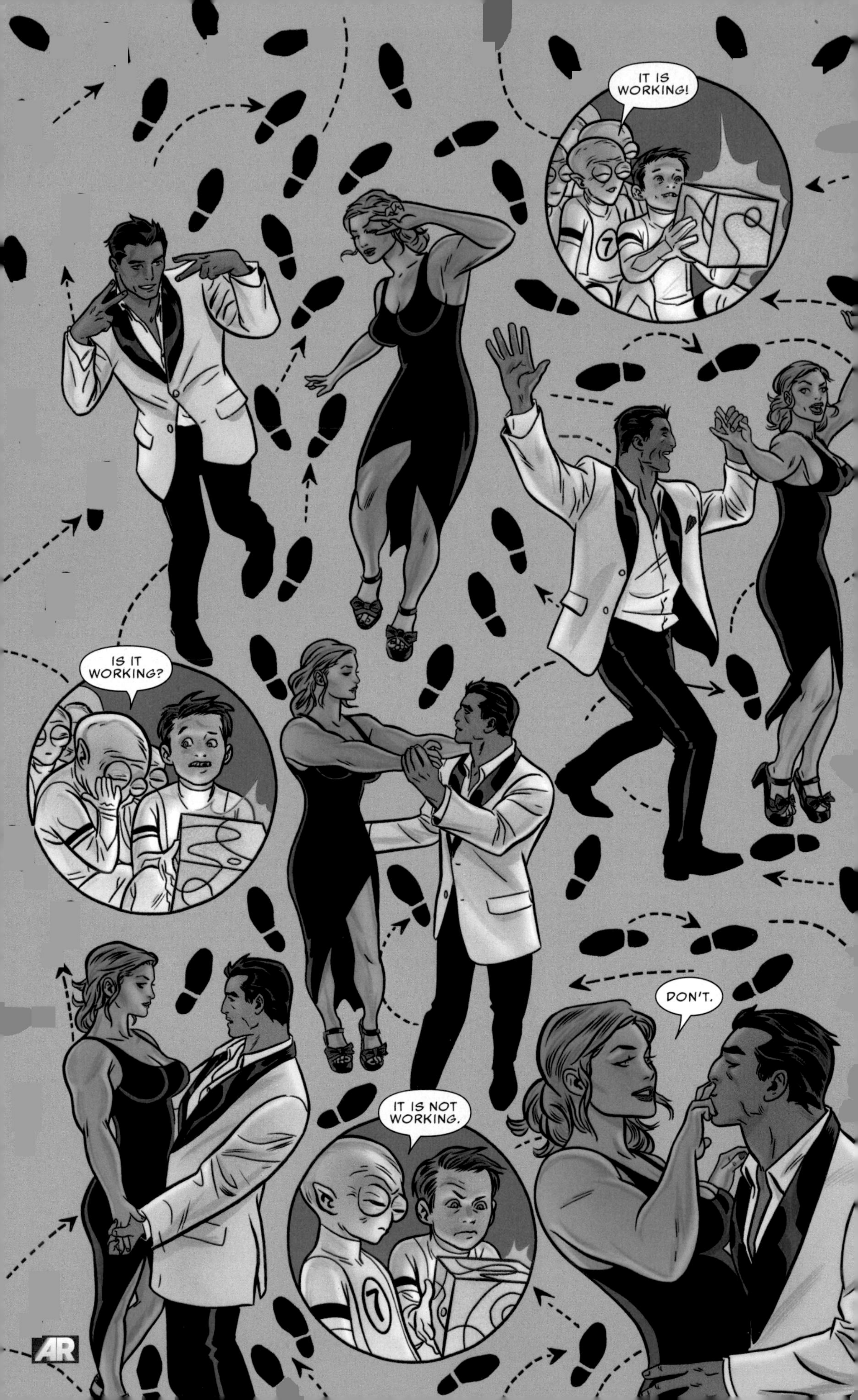
IT IS WORKING!
IS IT WORKING?
IT IS NOT WORKING.
DON'T.

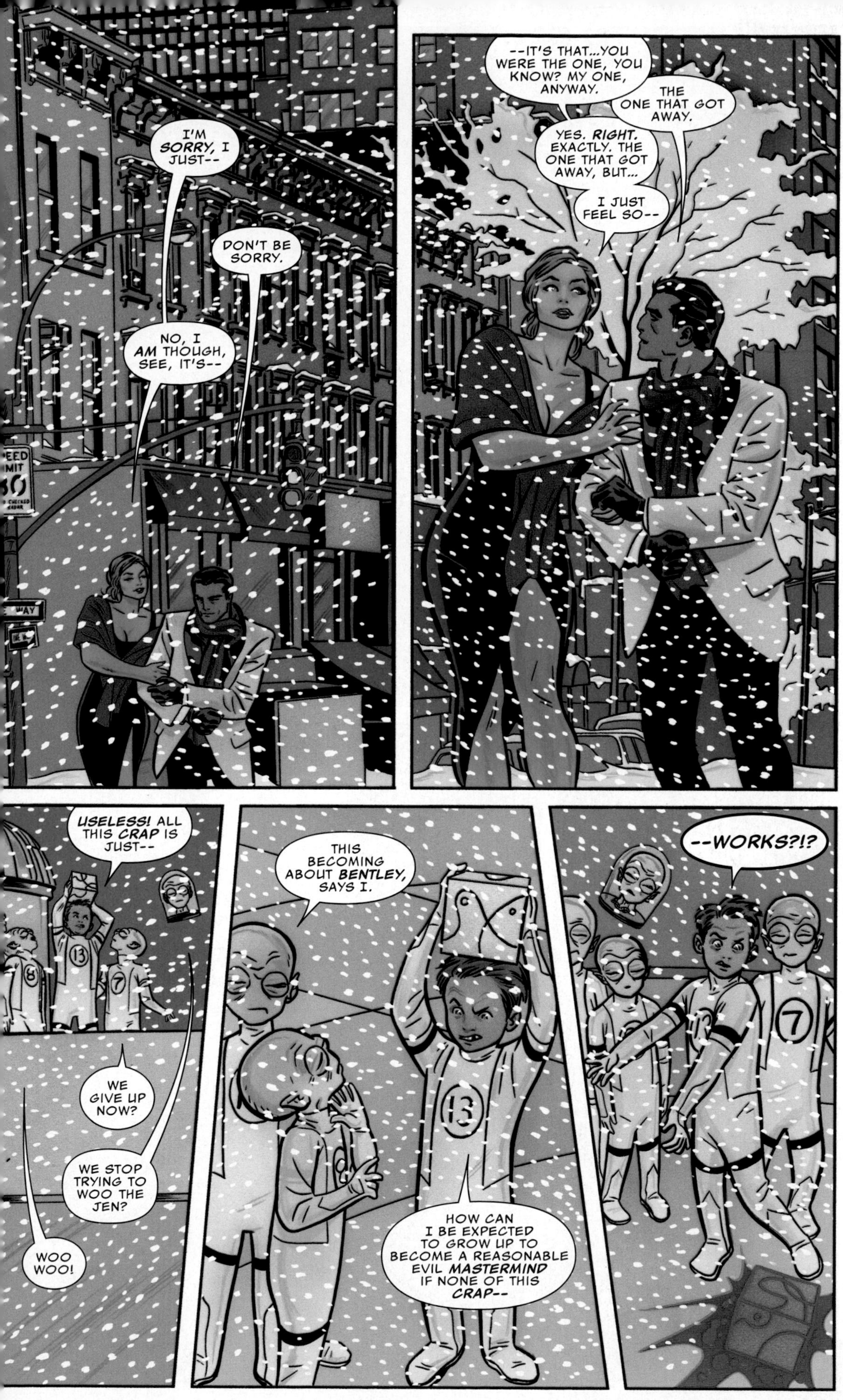
I'M SORRY, I JUST--
DON'T BE SORRY.
NO, I AM THOUGH, SEE, IT'S--
--IT'S THAT...YOU WERE THE ONE, YOU KNOW? MY ONE, ANYWAY.
THE ONE THAT GOT AWAY.
YES. RIGHT. EXACTLY. THE ONE THAT GOT AWAY, BUT...
I JUST FEEL SO--
USELESS! ALL THIS CRAP IS JUST--
WE GIVE UP NOW?
WE STOP TRYING TO WOO THE JEN?
WOO WOO!
THIS BECOMING ABOUT BENTLEY, SAYS I.
HOW CAN I BE EXPECTED TO GROW UP TO BECOME A REASONABLE EVIL MASTERMIND IF NONE OF THIS CRAP--
--WORKS?!?

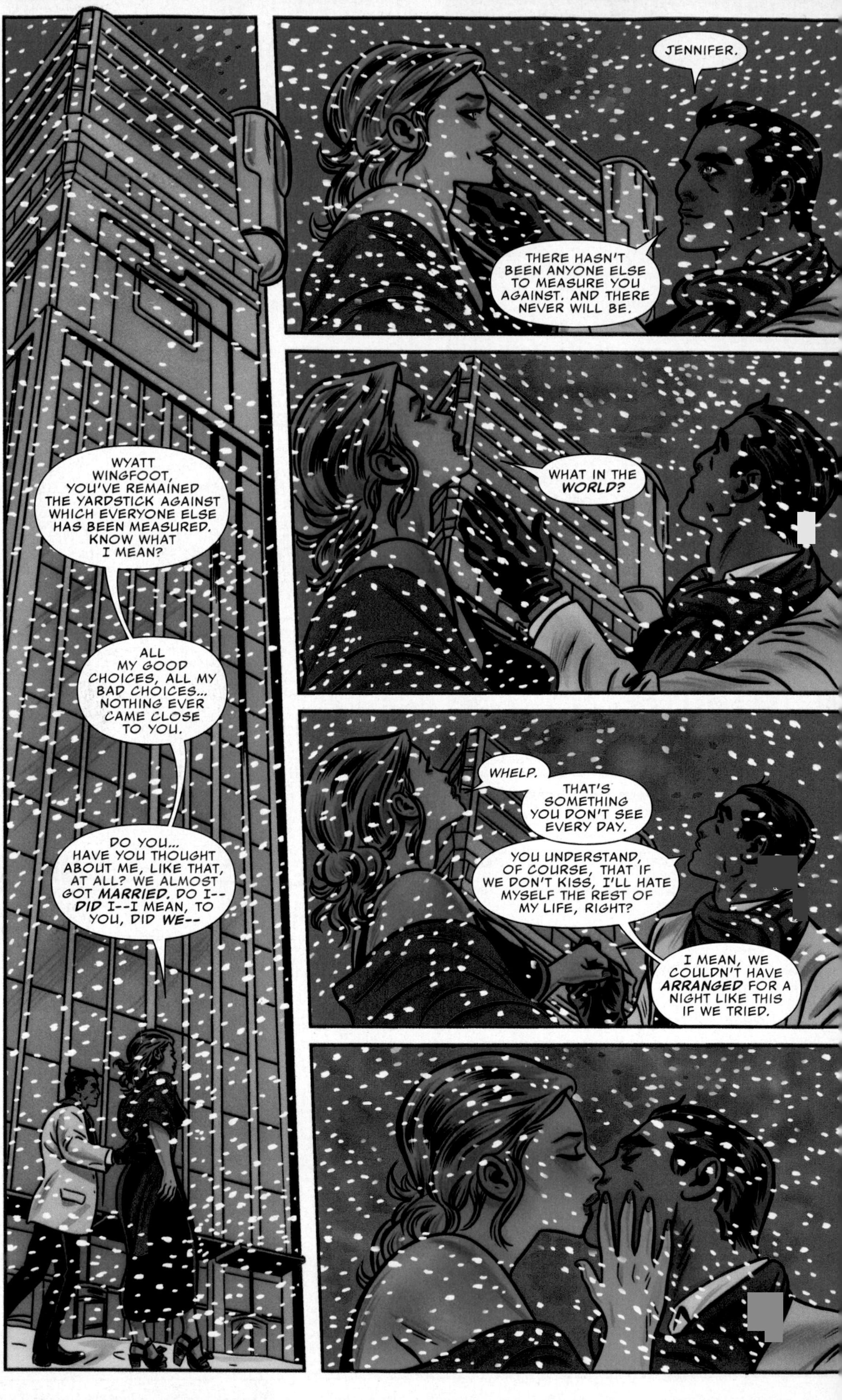
WYATT WINGFOOT, YOU'VE REMAINED THE YARDSTICK AGAINST WHICH EVERYONE ELSE HAS BEEN MEASURED. KNOW WHAT I MEAN?
ALL MY GOOD CHOICES, ALL MY BAD CHOICES... NOTHING EVER CAME CLOSE TO YOU.
DO YOU... HAVE YOU THOUGHT ABOUT ME, LIKE THAT, AT ALL? WE ALMOST GOT MARRIED. DO I-- DID I--I MEAN, TO YOU, DID WE--
JENNIFER.
THERE HASN'T BEEN ANYONE ELSE TO MEASURE YOU AGAINST. AND THERE NEVER WILL BE.
WHAT IN THE WORLD?
WHELP.
THAT'S SOMETHING YOU DON'T SEE EVERY DAY.
YOU UNDERSTAND, OF COURSE, THAT IF WE DON'T KISS, I'LL HATE MYSELF THE REST OF MY LIFE, RIGHT?
I MEAN, WE COULDN'T HAVE ARRANGED FOR A NIGHT LIKE THIS IF WE TRIED.

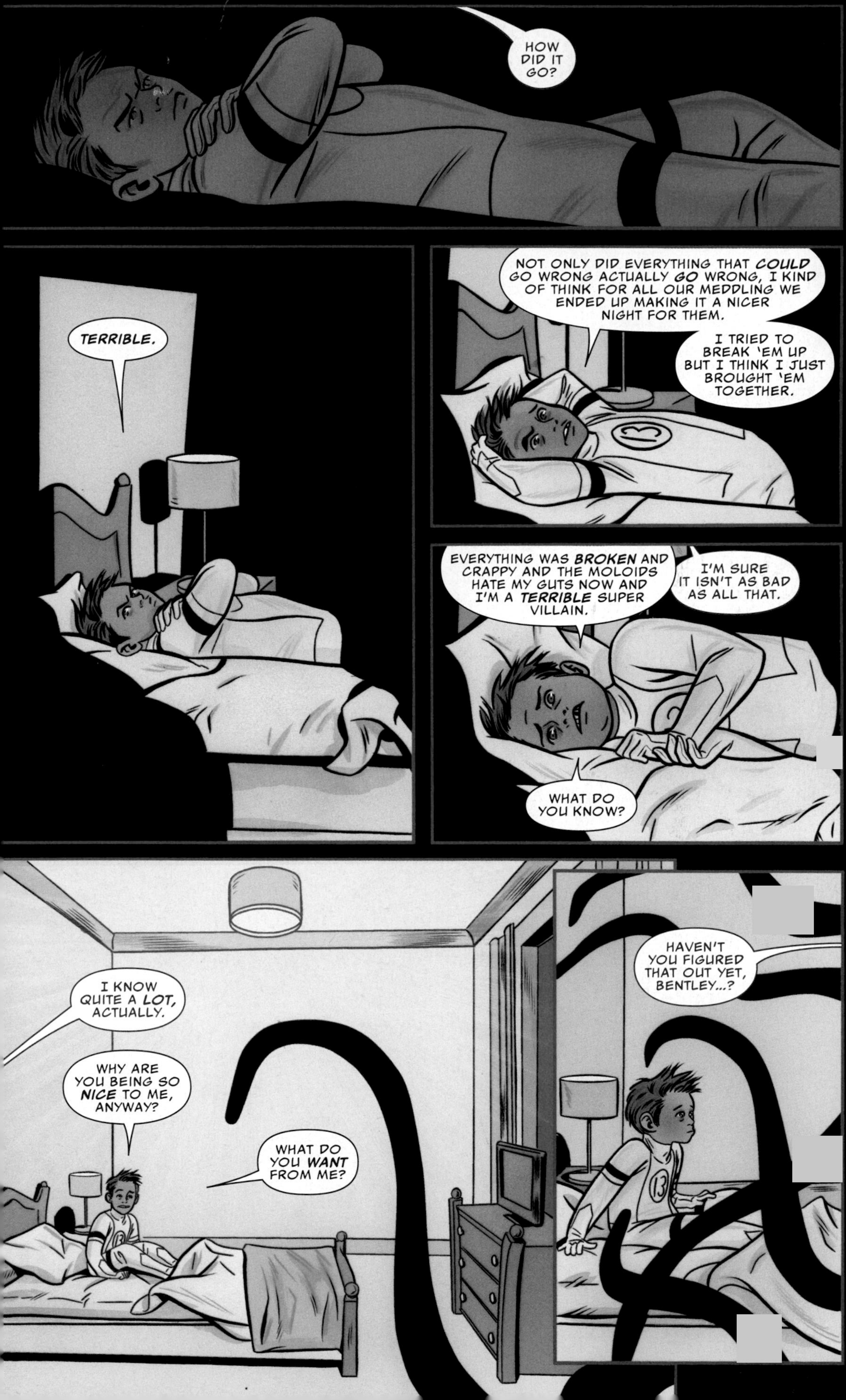
HOW DID IT GO?
TERRIBLE.
NOT ONLY DID EVERYTHING THAT COULD GO WRONG ACTUALLY GO WRONG, I KIND OF THINK FOR ALL OUR MEDDLING WE ENDED UP MAKING IT A NICER NIGHT FOR THEM.
I TRIED TO BREAK 'EM UP BUT I THINK I JUST BROUGHT 'EM TOGETHER.
EVERYTHING WAS BROKEN AND CRAPPY AND THE MOLOIDS HATE MY GUTS NOW AND I'M A TERRIBLE SUPER VILLAIN.
I'M SURE IT ISN'T AS BAD AS ALL THAT.
WHAT DO YOU KNOW?
I KNOW QUITE A LOT, ACTUALLY.
WHY ARE YOU BEING SO NICE TO ME, ANYWAY?
WHAT DO YOU WANT FROM ME?
HAVEN'T YOU FIGURED THAT OUT YET, BENTLEY...?

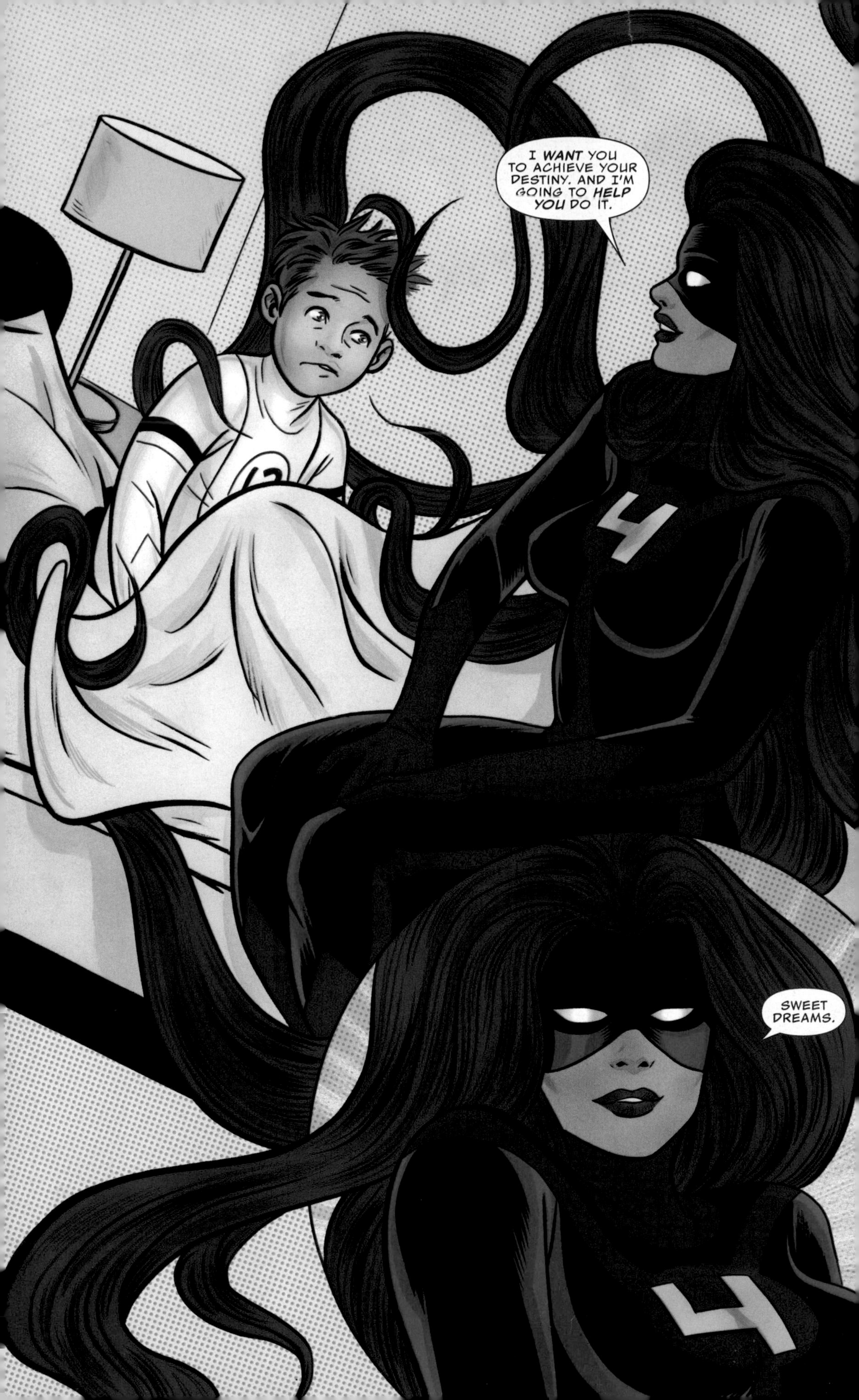
I WANT YOU TO ACHIEVE YOUR DESTINY. AND I'M GOING TO HELP YOU DO IT.
SWEET DREAMS.

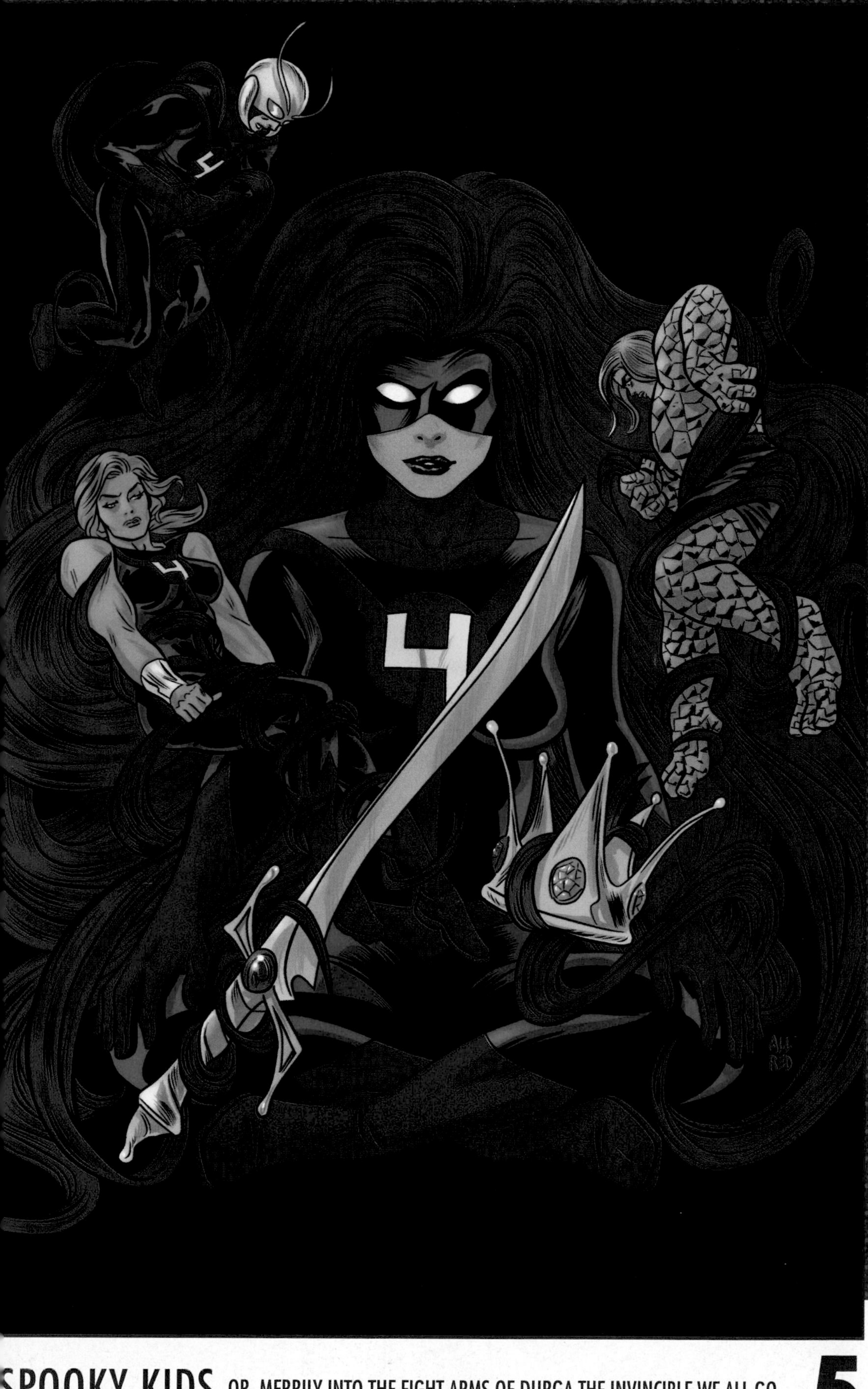

SPOOKY KIDS OR, MERRILY INTO THE EIGHT ARMS OF DURGA THE INVINCIBLE WE ALL GO 5

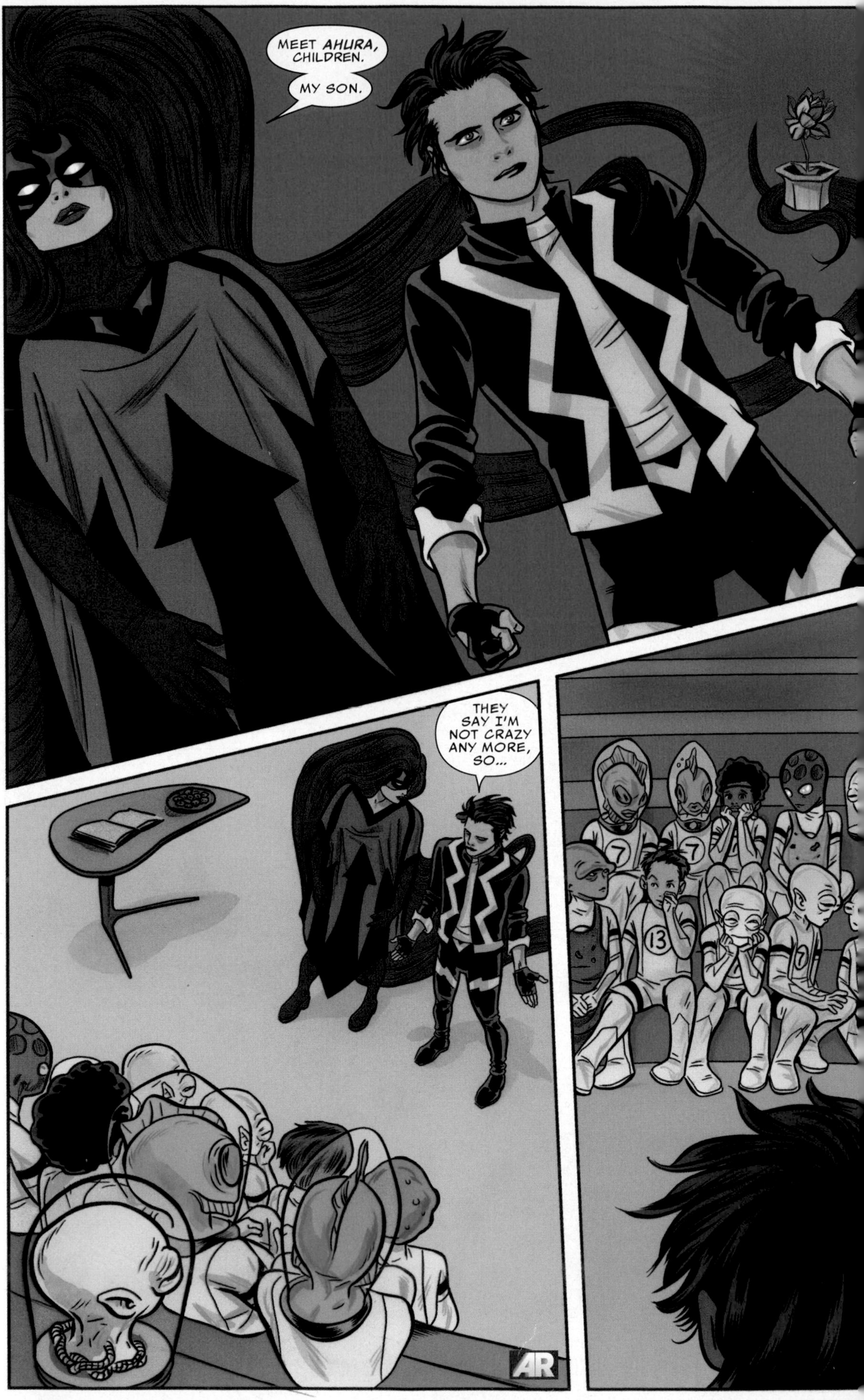
MEET AHURA, CHILDREN.
MY SON.
THEY SAY I'M NOT CRAZY ANY MORE, SO...

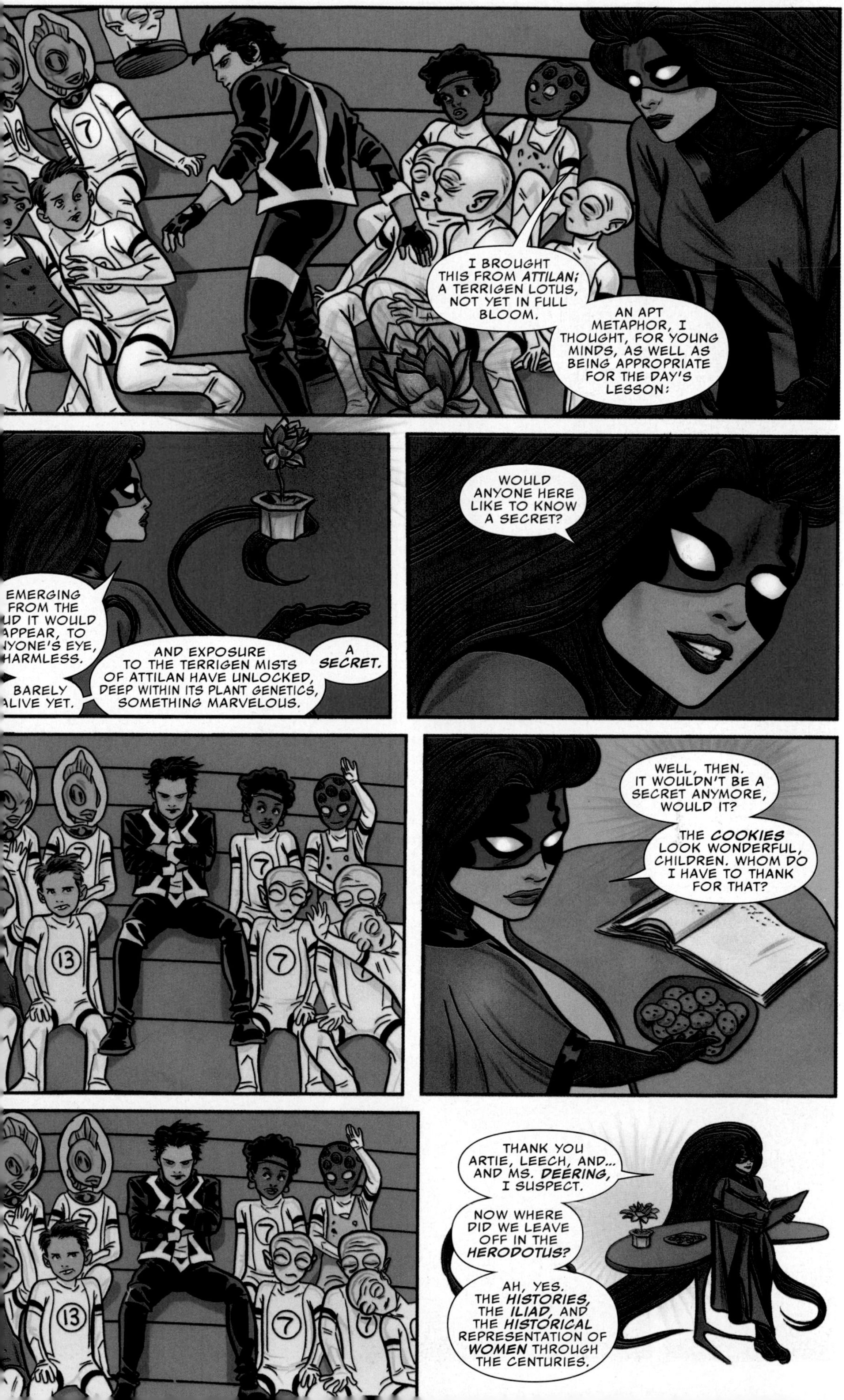
I BROUGHT THIS FROM ATTILAN; A TERRIGEN LOTUS, NOT YET IN FULL BLOOM.
AN APT METAPHOR, I THOUGHT, FOR YOUNG MINDS, AS WELL AS BEING APPROPRIATE FOR THE DAY'S LESSON:
EMERGING FROM THE UD IT WOULD PPEAR, TO NYONE'S EYE, HARMLESS.
BARELY ALIVE YET.
AND EXPOSURE TO THE TERRIGEN MISTS OF ATTILAN HAVE UNLOCKED, DEEP WITHIN ITS PLANT GENETICS, SOMETHING MARVELOUS.
A SECRET.
WOULD ANYONE HERE LIKE TO KNOW A SECRET?
WELL, THEN. IT WOULDN'T BE A SECRET ANYMORE, WOULD IT?
THE COOKIES LOOK WONDERFUL, CHILDREN. WHOM DO I HAVE TO THANK FOR THAT?
THANK YOU ARTIE, LEECH, AND... AND MS. DEERING, I SUSPECT.
NOW WHERE DID WE LEAVE OFF IN THE HERODOTUS?
AH, YES. THE HISTORIES, THE ILIAD, AND THE HISTORICAL REPRESENTATION OF WOMEN THROUGH THE CENTURIES.

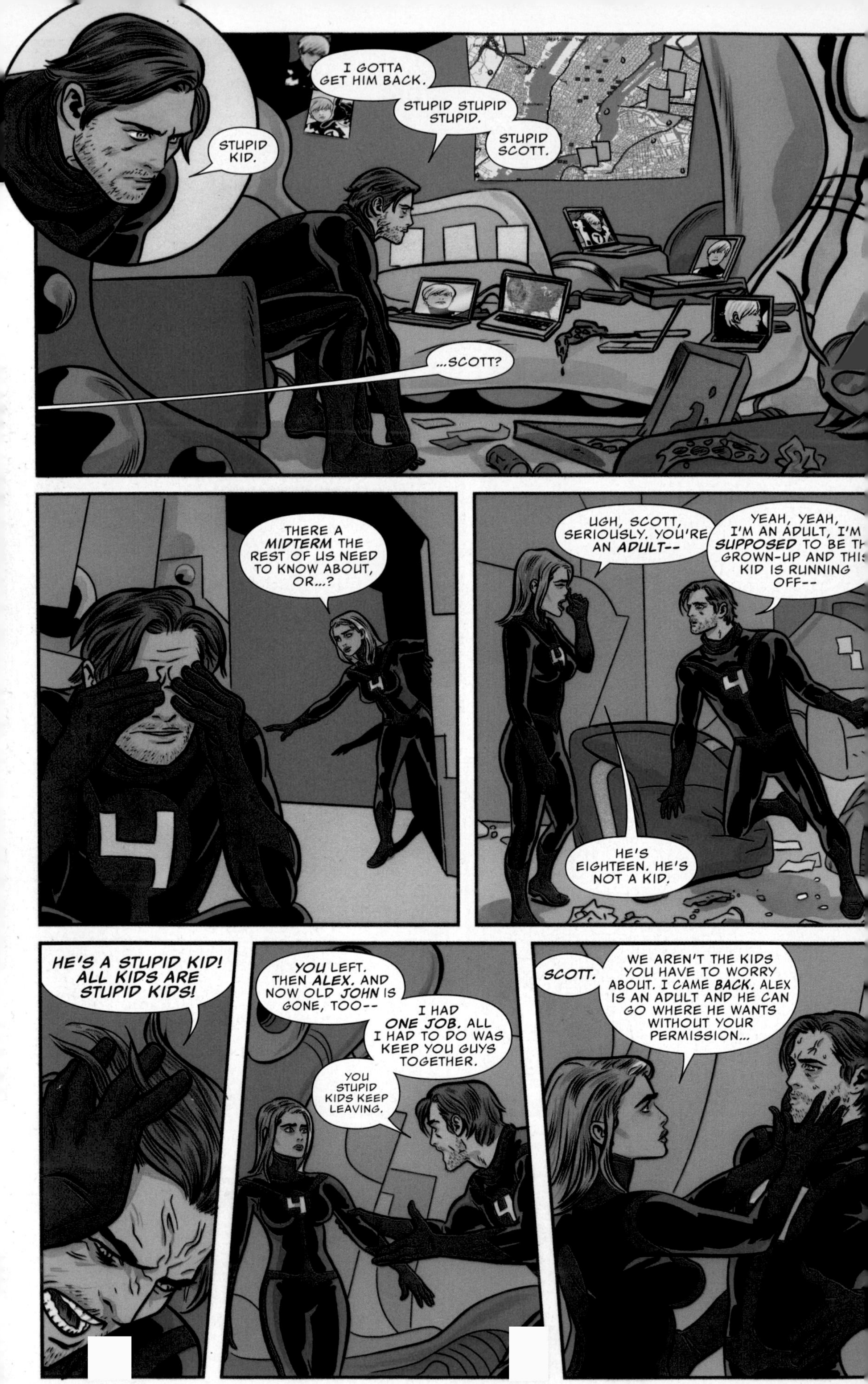
STUPID KID.
I GOTTA GET HIM BACK.
STUPID STUPID STUPID.
STUPID SCOTT.
...SCOTT?
THERE A MIDTERM THE REST OF US NEED TO KNOW ABOUT, OR...?
UGH, SCOTT, SERIOUSLY. YOU'RE AN ADULT--
YEAH, YEAH, I'M AN ADULT, I'M SUPPOSED TO BE TH GROWN-UP AND THIS KID IS RUNNING OFF--
HE'S EIGHTEEN. HE'S NOT A KID.
HE'S A STUPID KID! ALL KIDS ARE STUPID KIDS!
YOU LEFT. THEN ALEX. AND NOW OLD JOHN IS GONE, TOO--
I HAD ONE JOB. ALL I HAD TO DO WAS KEEP YOU GUYS TOGETHER.
YOU STUPID KIDS KEEP LEAVING.
SCOTT.
WE AREN'T THE KIDS YOU HAVE TO WORRY ABOUT. I CAME BACK. ALEX IS AN ADULT AND HE CAN GO WHERE HE WANTS WITHOUT YOUR PERMISSION...

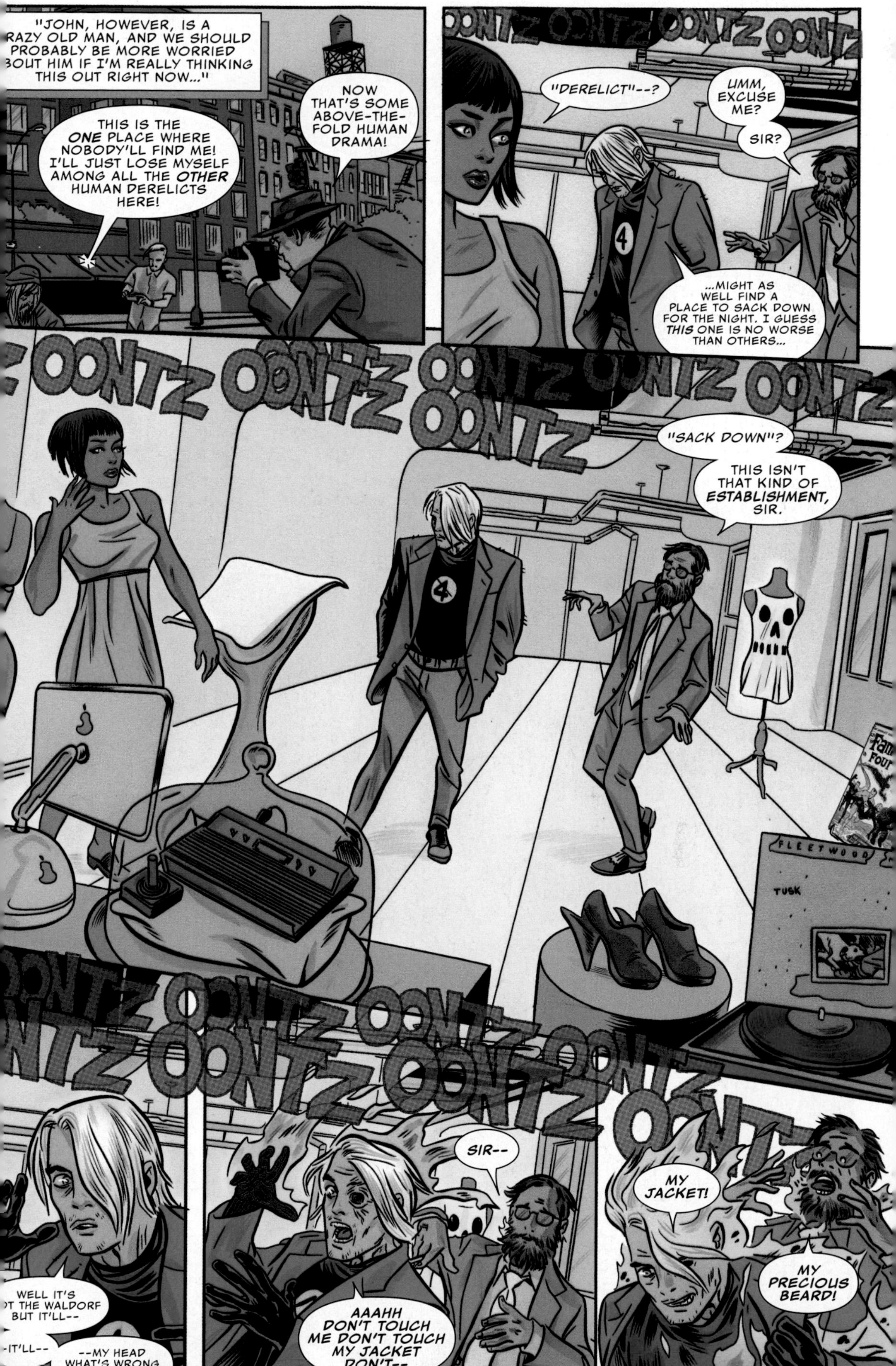
"JOHN, HOWEVER, IS A RAZY OLD MAN, AND WE SHOULD PROBABLY BE MORE WORRIED BOUT HIM IF I'M REALLY THINKING THIS OUT RIGHT NOW..."
THIS IS THE ONE PLACE WHERE NOBODY'LL FIND ME! I'LL JUST LOSE MYSELF AMONG ALL THE OTHER HUMAN DERELICTS HERE!
NOW THAT'S SOME ABOVE-THE-FOLD HUMAN DRAMA!
OONTZ OONTZ OONTZ
"DERELICT"--?
UMM, EXCUSE ME?
SIR?
...MIGHT AS WELL FIND A PLACE TO SACK DOWN FOR THE NIGHT. I GUESS THIS ONE IS NO WORSE THAN OTHERS...
OONTZ OONTZ OONTZ OONTZ OONTZ OONTZ
"SACK DOWN"?
THIS ISN'T THAT KIND OF ESTABLISHMENT, SIR.
FLEETWOOD
TUSK
OONTZ OONTZ OONTZ OONTZ OONTZ
WELL IT'S OT THE WALDORF BUT IT'LL--
-IT'LL--
--MY HEAD WHAT'S WRONG WITH MY HEAD--?
SIR--
AAAHH DON'T TOUCH ME DON'T TOUCH MY JACKET DON'T--
MY JACKET!
MY PRECIOUS BEARD!

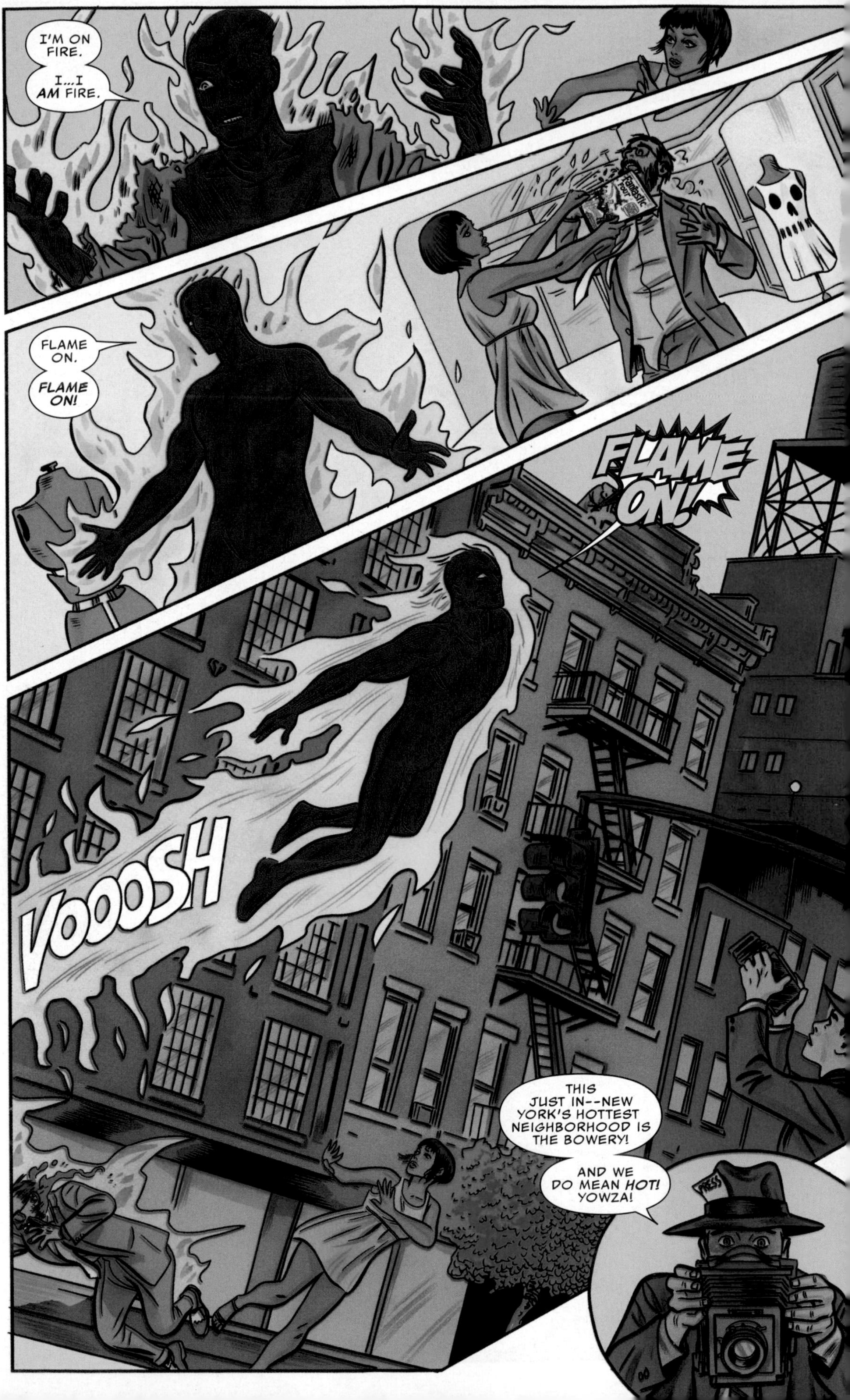
I'M ON FIRE.
I...I AM FIRE.
FLAME ON.
FLAME ON!
FLAME ON!
VOOOSH
THIS JUST IN--NEW YORK'S HOTTEST NEIGHBORHOOD IS THE BOWERY!
AND WE DO MEAN HOT! YOWZA!

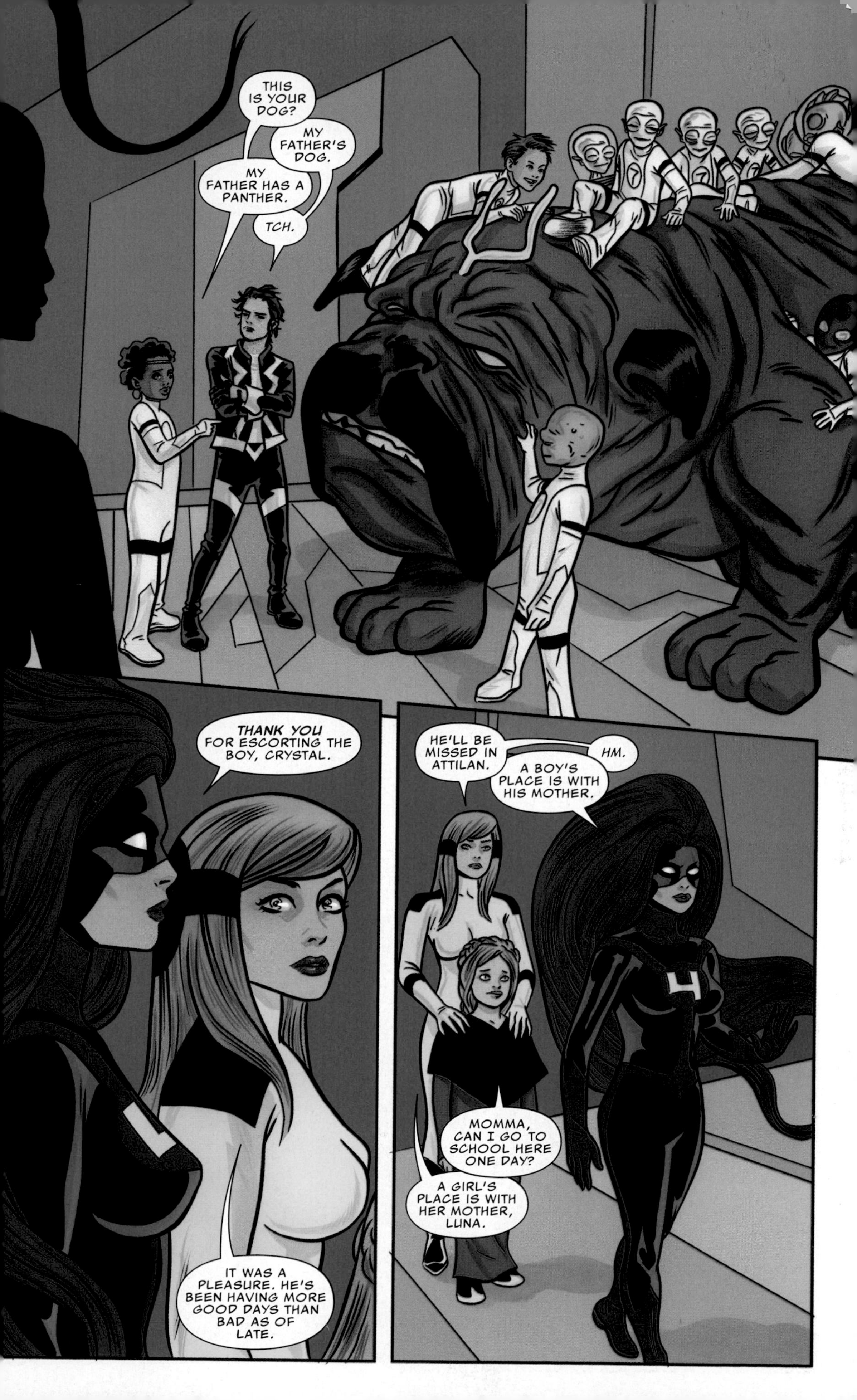
THIS IS YOUR DOG?
MY FATHER'S DOG.
MY FATHER HAS A PANTHER.
TCH.
THANK YOU FOR ESCORTING THE BOY, CRYSTAL.
IT WAS A PLEASURE. HE'S BEEN HAVING MORE GOOD DAYS THAN BAD AS OF LATE.
HE'LL BE MISSED IN ATTILAN.
HM.
A BOY'S PLACE IS WITH HIS MOTHER.
MOMMA, CAN I GO TO SCHOOL HERE ONE DAY?
A GIRL'S PLACE IS WITH HER MOTHER, LUNA.

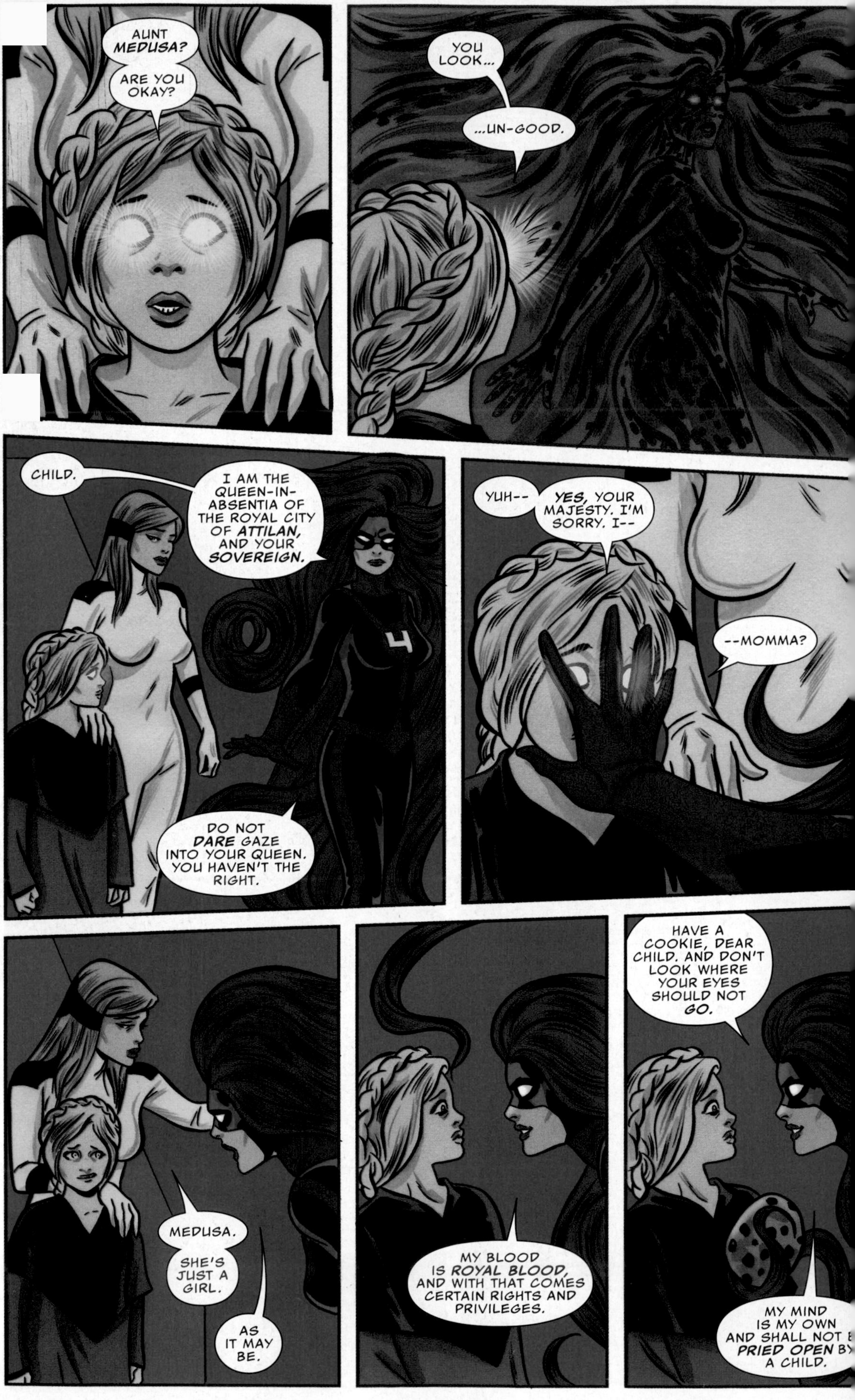
AUNT MEDUSA?
ARE YOU OKAY?
YOU LOOK...
...UN-GOOD.
CHILD.
I AM THE QUEEN-IN-ABSENTIA OF THE ROYAL CITY OF ATTILAN, AND YOUR SOVEREIGN.
DO NOT DARE GAZE INTO YOUR QUEEN. YOU HAVEN'T THE RIGHT.
YUH--
YES, YOUR MAJESTY. I'M SORRY. I--
--MOMMA?
MEDUSA.
SHE'S JUST A GIRL.
AS IT MAY BE.
MY BLOOD IS ROYAL BLOOD, AND WITH THAT COMES CERTAIN RIGHTS AND PRIVILEGES.
HAVE A COOKIE, DEAR CHILD. AND DON'T LOOK WHERE YOUR EYES SHOULD NOT GO.
MY MIND IS MY OWN AND SHALL NOT

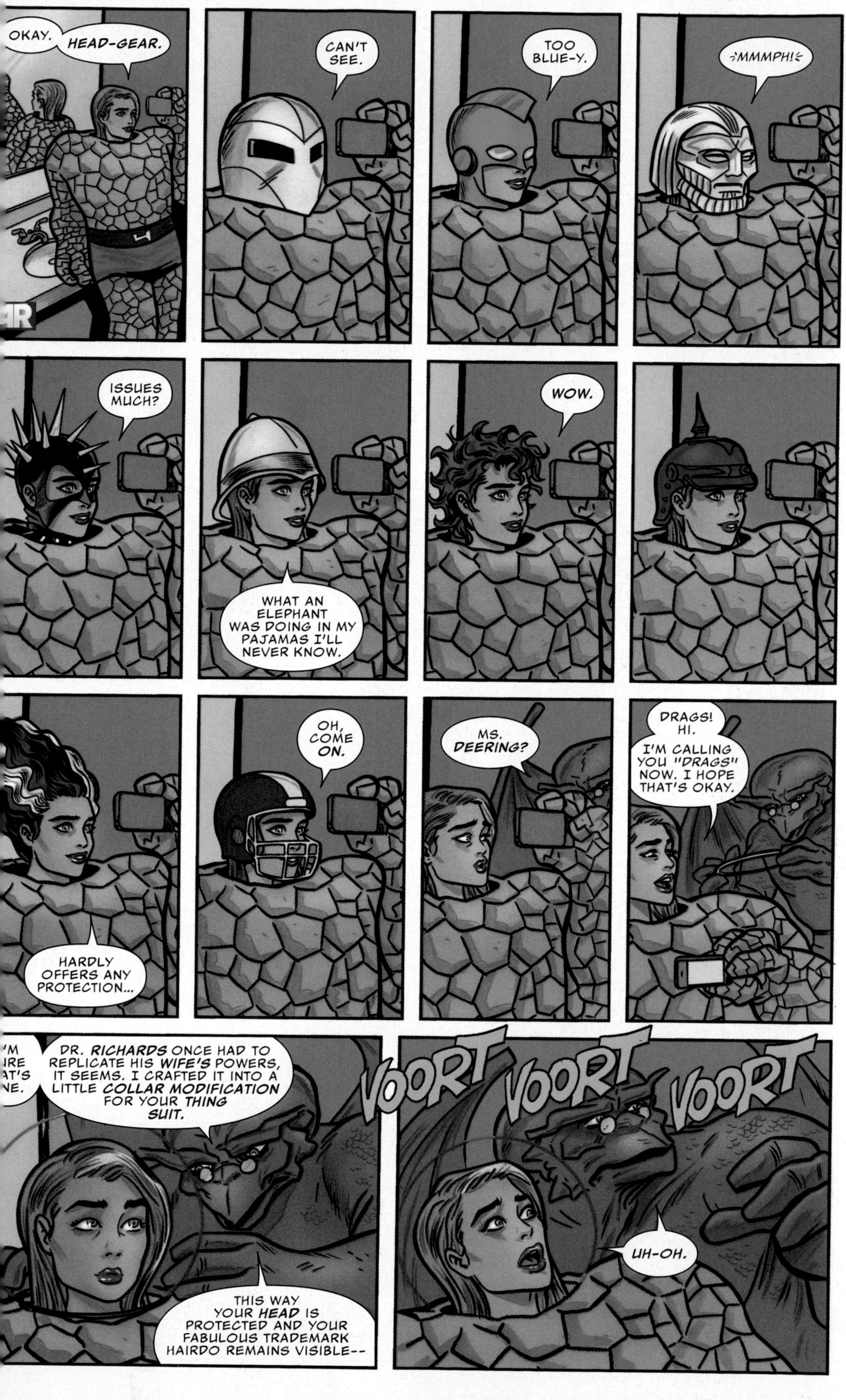

OKAY.
HEAD-GEAR.
CAN'T SEE.
TOO BLUE-Y.
MMMPH!
ISSUES MUCH?
WHAT AN ELEPHANT WAS DOING IN MY PAJAMAS I'LL NEVER KNOW.
WOW.
HARDLY OFFERS ANY PROTECTION...
OH, COME ON.
MS. DEERING?
DRAGS! HI.
I'M CALLING YOU "DRAGS" NOW. I HOPE THAT'S OKAY.
DR. RICHARDS ONCE HAD TO REPLICATE HIS WIFE'S POWERS, IT SEEMS. I CRAFTED IT INTO A LITTLE COLLAR MODIFICATION FOR YOUR THING SUIT.
THIS WAY YOUR HEAD IS PROTECTED AND YOUR FABULOUS TRADEMARK HAIRDO REMAINS VISIBLE--
VOORT VOORT VOORT
UH-OH.

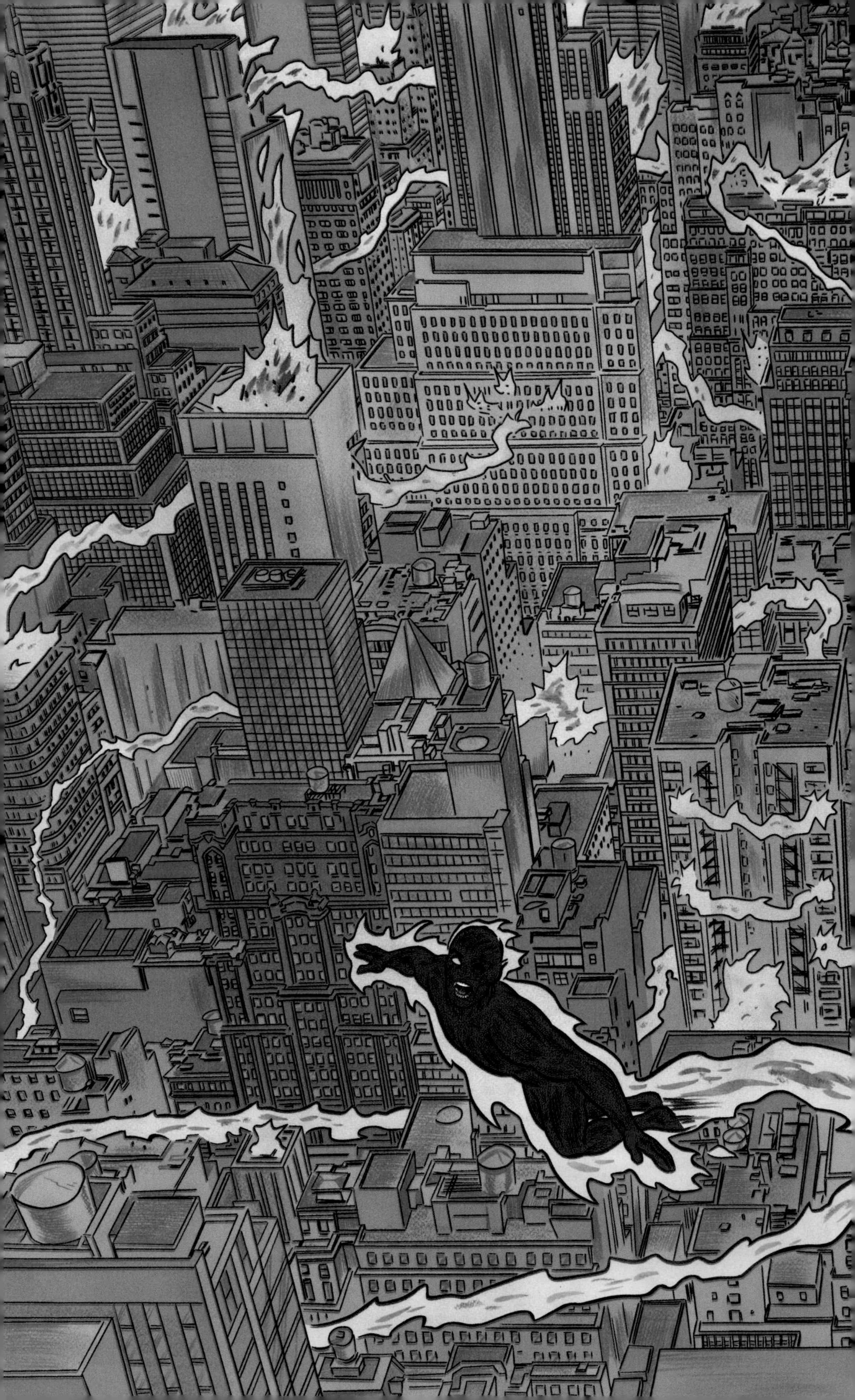

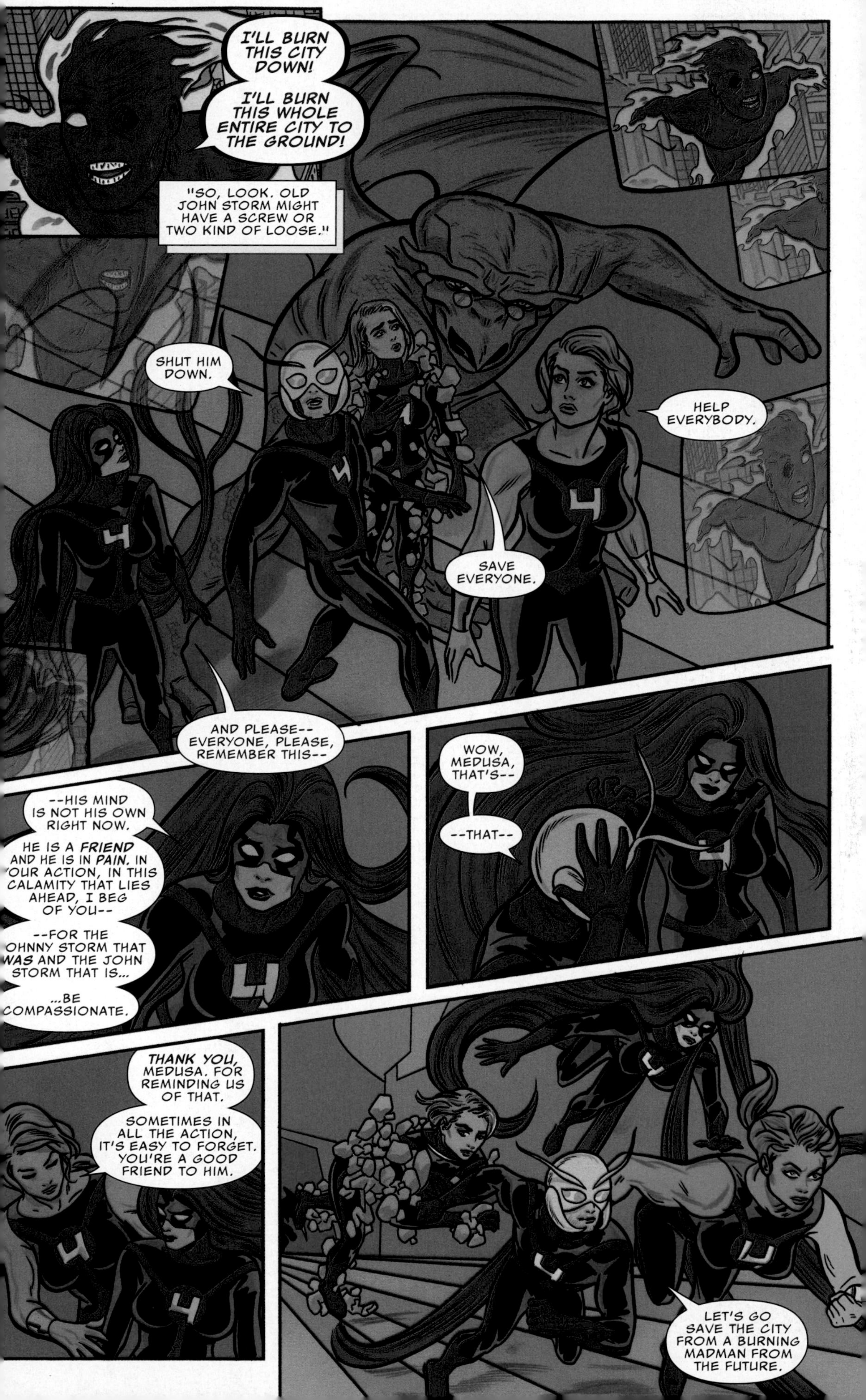
I'LL BURN THIS CITY DOWN!
I'LL BURN THIS WHOLE ENTIRE CITY TO THE GROUND!
"SO, LOOK. OLD JOHN STORM MIGHT HAVE A SCREW OR TWO KIND OF LOOSE."
SHUT HIM DOWN.
HELP EVERYBODY.
SAVE EVERYONE.
AND PLEASE-- EVERYONE, PLEASE, REMEMBER THIS--
--HIS MIND IS NOT HIS OWN RIGHT NOW.
HE IS A FRIEND AND HE IS IN PAIN. IN OUR ACTION, IN THIS CALAMITY THAT LIES AHEAD, I BEG OF YOU--
--FOR THE JOHNNY STORM THAT WAS AND THE JOHN STORM THAT IS...
...BE COMPASSIONATE.
WOW, MEDUSA, THAT'S--
--THAT--
THANK YOU, MEDUSA. FOR REMINDING US OF THAT.
SOMETIMES IN ALL THE ACTION, IT'S EASY TO FORGET. YOU'RE A GOOD FRIEND TO HIM.
LET'S GO SAVE THE CITY FROM A BURNING MADMAN FROM THE FUTURE.

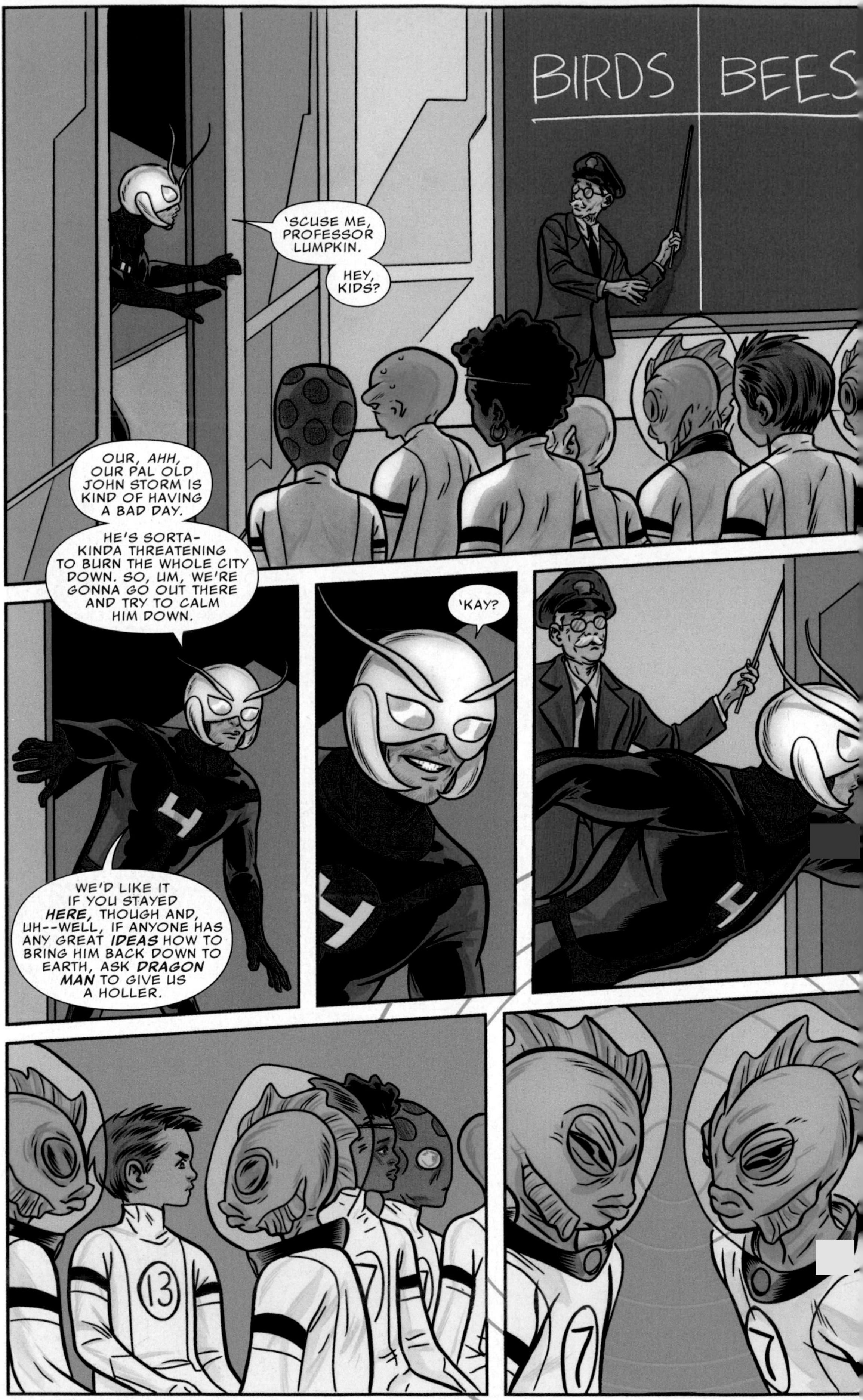
BIRDS
BEES
'SCUSE ME, PROFESSOR LUMPKIN.
HEY, KIDS?
OUR, AHH, OUR PAL OLD JOHN STORM IS KIND OF HAVING A BAD DAY.
HE'S SORTA-KINDA THREATENING TO BURN THE WHOLE CITY DOWN. SO, UM, WE'RE GONNA GO OUT THERE AND TRY TO CALM HIM DOWN.
WE'D LIKE IT IF YOU STAYED HERE, THOUGH AND, UH--WELL, IF ANYONE HAS ANY GREAT IDEAS HOW TO BRING HIM BACK DOWN TO EARTH, ASK DRAGON MAN TO GIVE US A HOLLER.
'KAY?
13
7
7
7
7

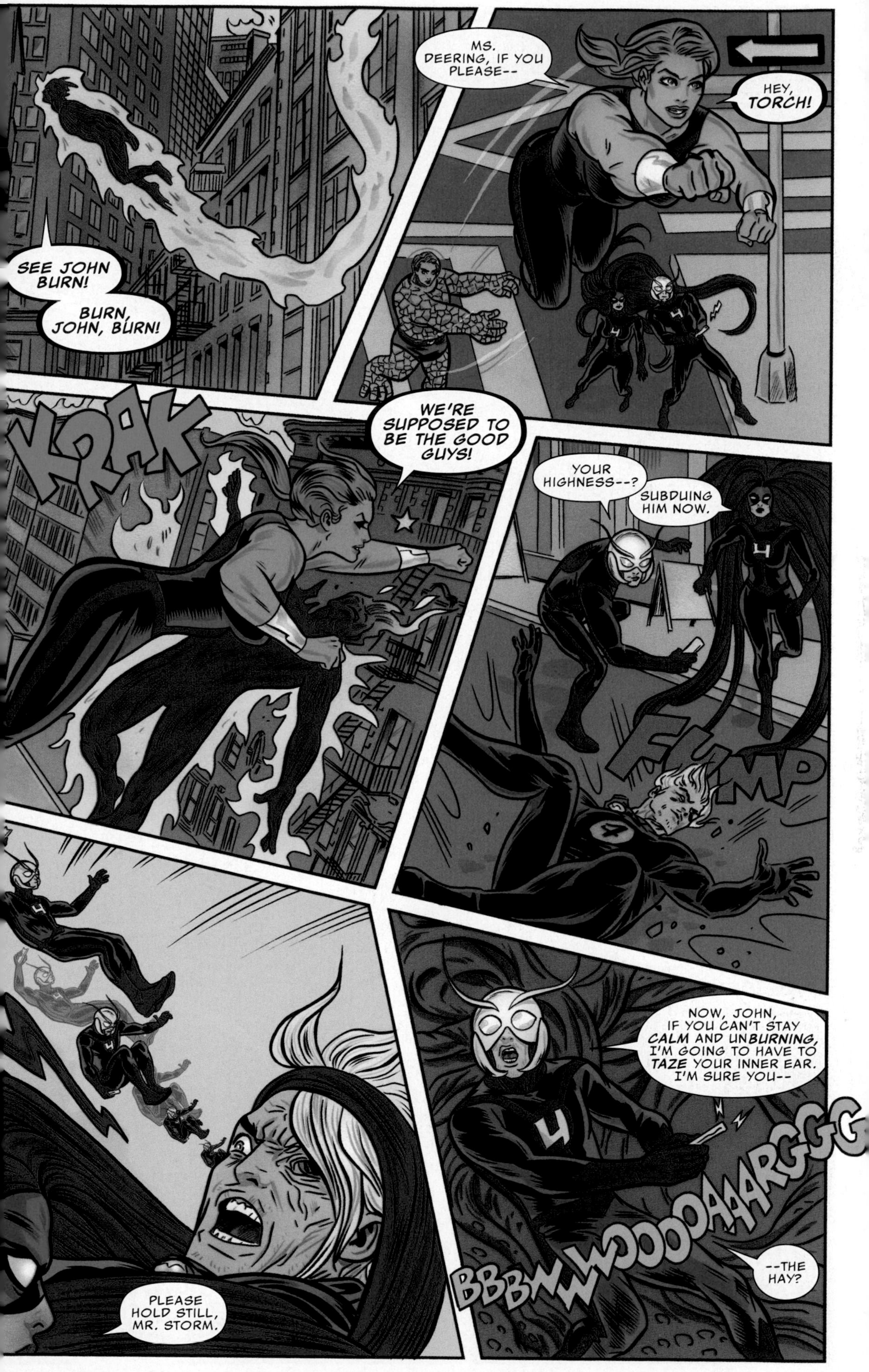
SEE JOHN BURN!
BURN, JOHN, BURN!
MS. DEERING, IF YOU PLEASE--
HEY, TORCH!
KRAK
WE'RE SUPPOSED TO BE THE GOOD GUYS!
YOUR HIGHNESS--?
SUBDUING HIM NOW.
FUMP
PLEASE HOLD STILL, MR. STORM.
NOW, JOHN, IF YOU CAN'T STAY CALM AND UNBURNING, I'M GOING TO HAVE TO TAZE YOUR INNER EAR. I'M SURE YOU--
BBBWWOOOOAAARGGG
--THE HAY?

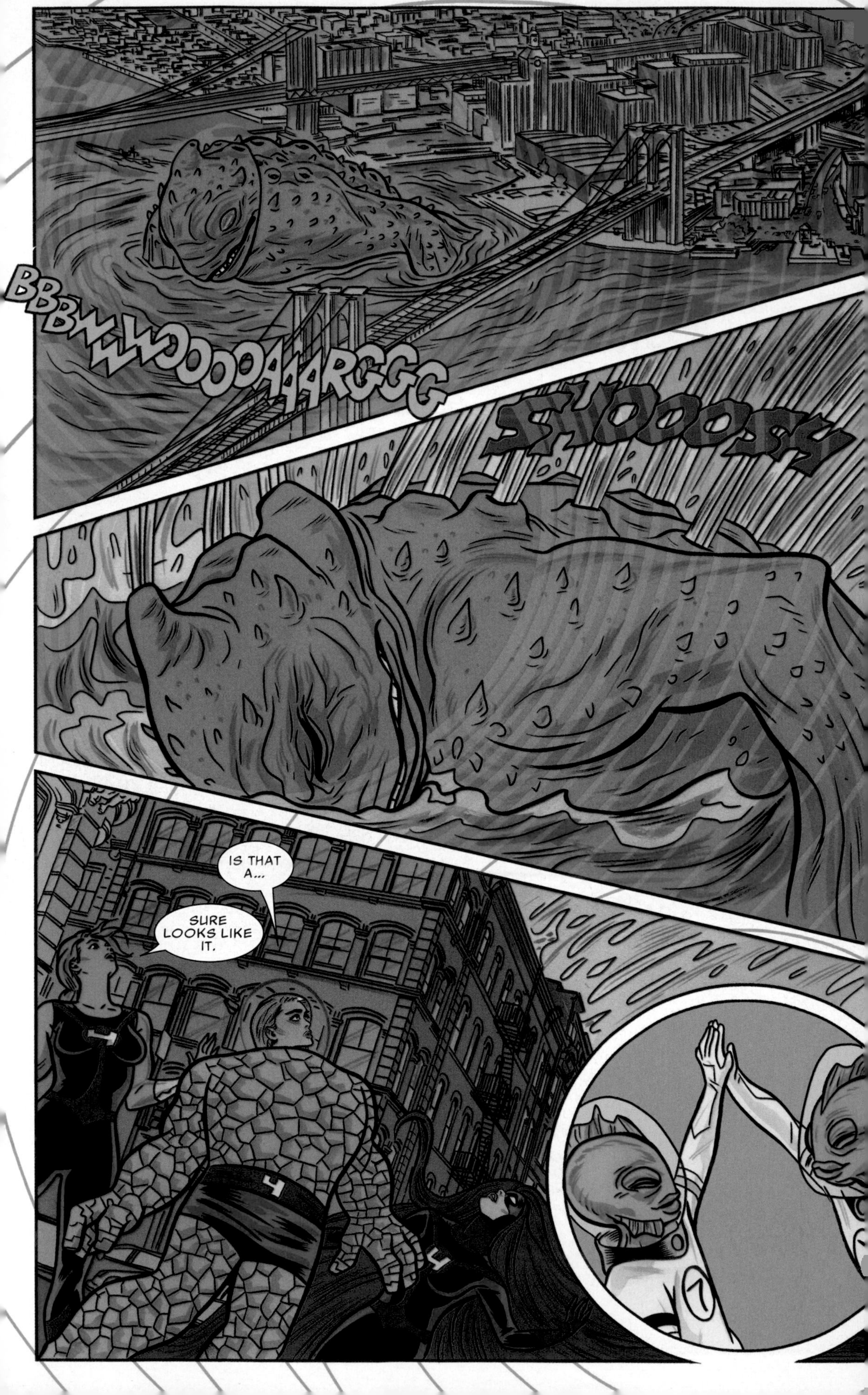
BBBNNWOOOOAAARGGG
SHOOOSH
IS THAT A...
SURE LOOKS LIKE IT.

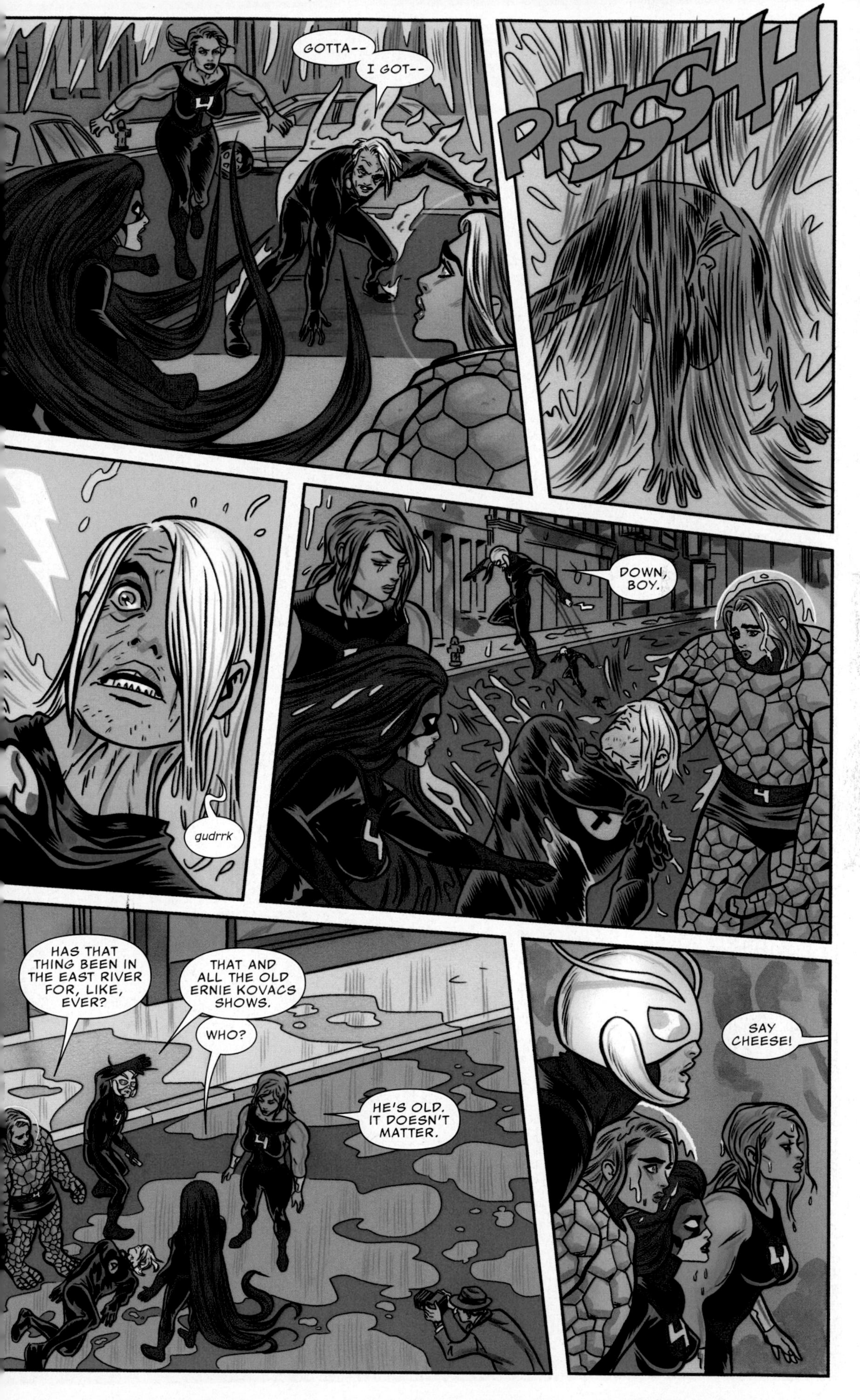
GOTTA--
I GOT--
PFSSSHH
gudrrk
DOWN, BOY.
HAS THAT THING BEEN IN THE EAST RIVER FOR, LIKE, EVER?
THAT AND ALL THE OLD ERNIE KOVACS SHOWS.
WHO?
HE'S OLD. IT DOESN'T MATTER.
SAY CHEESE!

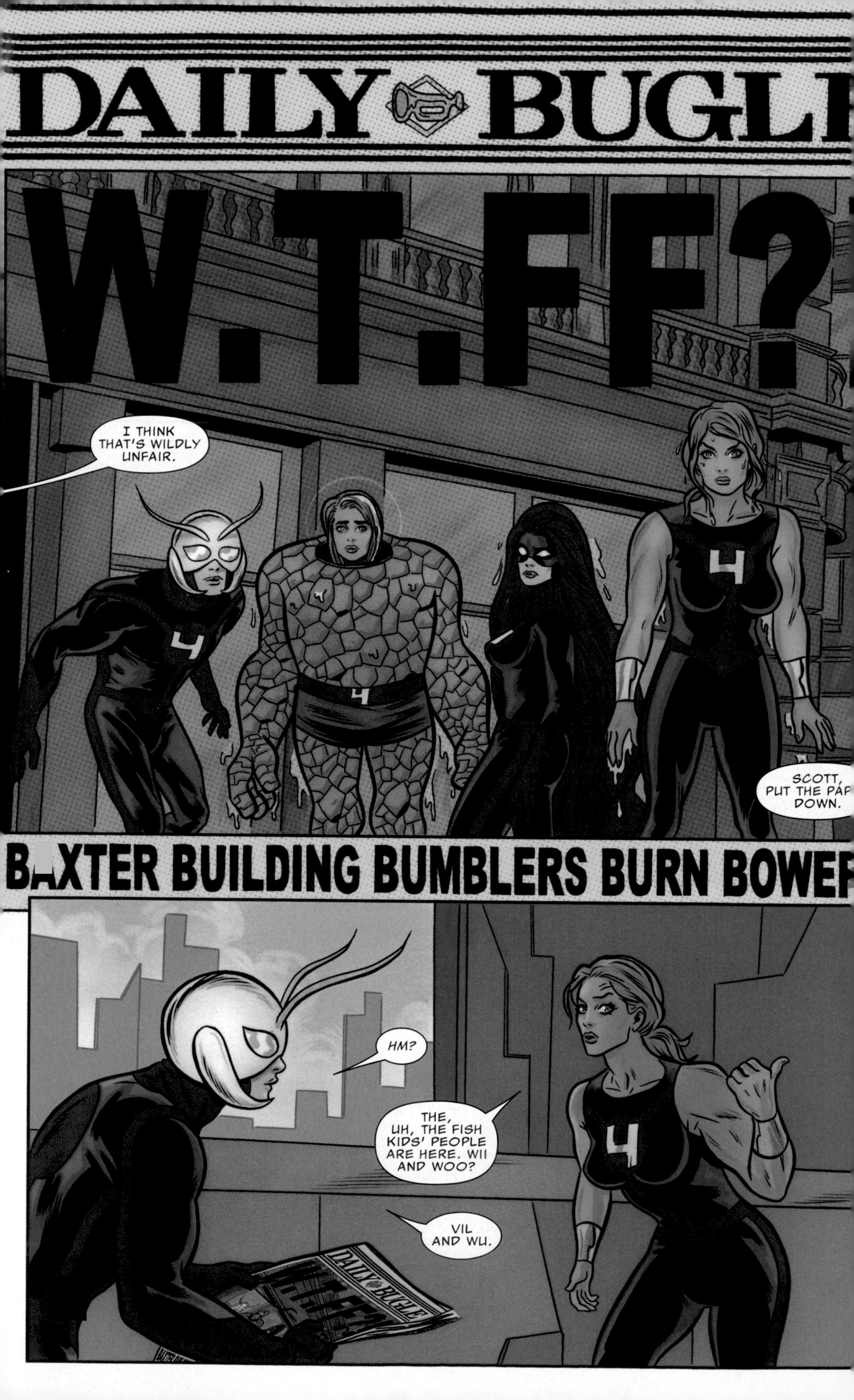

DAILY BUGL
W.T.FF?
I THINK THAT'S WILDLY UNFAIR.
SCOTT, PUT THE PAP DOWN.
BAXTER BUILDING BUMBLERS BURN BOWEF
HM?
THE, UH, THE FISH KIDS' PEOPLE ARE HERE. WII AND WOO?
VIL AND WU.

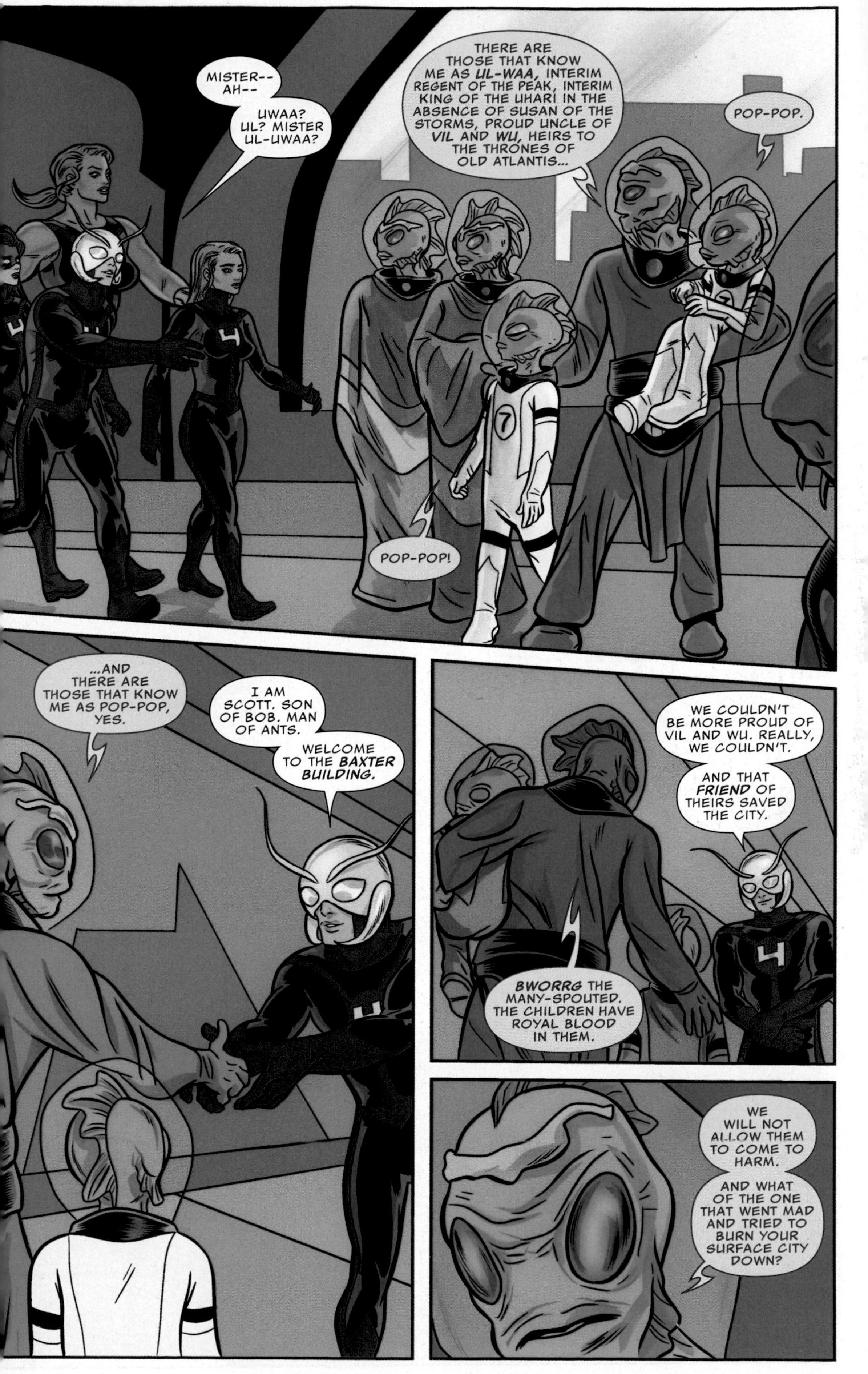
MISTER-- AH--
UWAA? UL? MISTER UL-UWAA?
THERE ARE THOSE THAT KNOW ME AS UL-WAA, INTERIM REGENT OF THE PEAK, INTERIM KING OF THE UHARÍ IN THE ABSENCE OF SUSAN OF THE STORMS, PROUD UNCLE OF VIL AND WU, HEIRS TO THE THRONES OF OLD ATLANTIS...
POP-POP.
POP-POP!
...AND THERE ARE THOSE THAT KNOW ME AS POP-POP, YES.
I AM SCOTT. SON OF BOB. MAN OF ANTS.
WELCOME TO THE BAXTER BUILDING.
WE COULDN'T BE MORE PROUD OF VIL AND WU. REALLY, WE COULDN'T.
AND THAT FRIEND OF THEIRS SAVED THE CITY.
BWORRG THE MANY-SPOUTED. THE CHILDREN HAVE ROYAL BLOOD IN THEM.
WE WILL NOT ALLOW THEM TO COME TO HARM.
AND WHAT OF THE ONE THAT WENT MAD AND TRIED TO BURN YOUR SURFACE CITY DOWN?

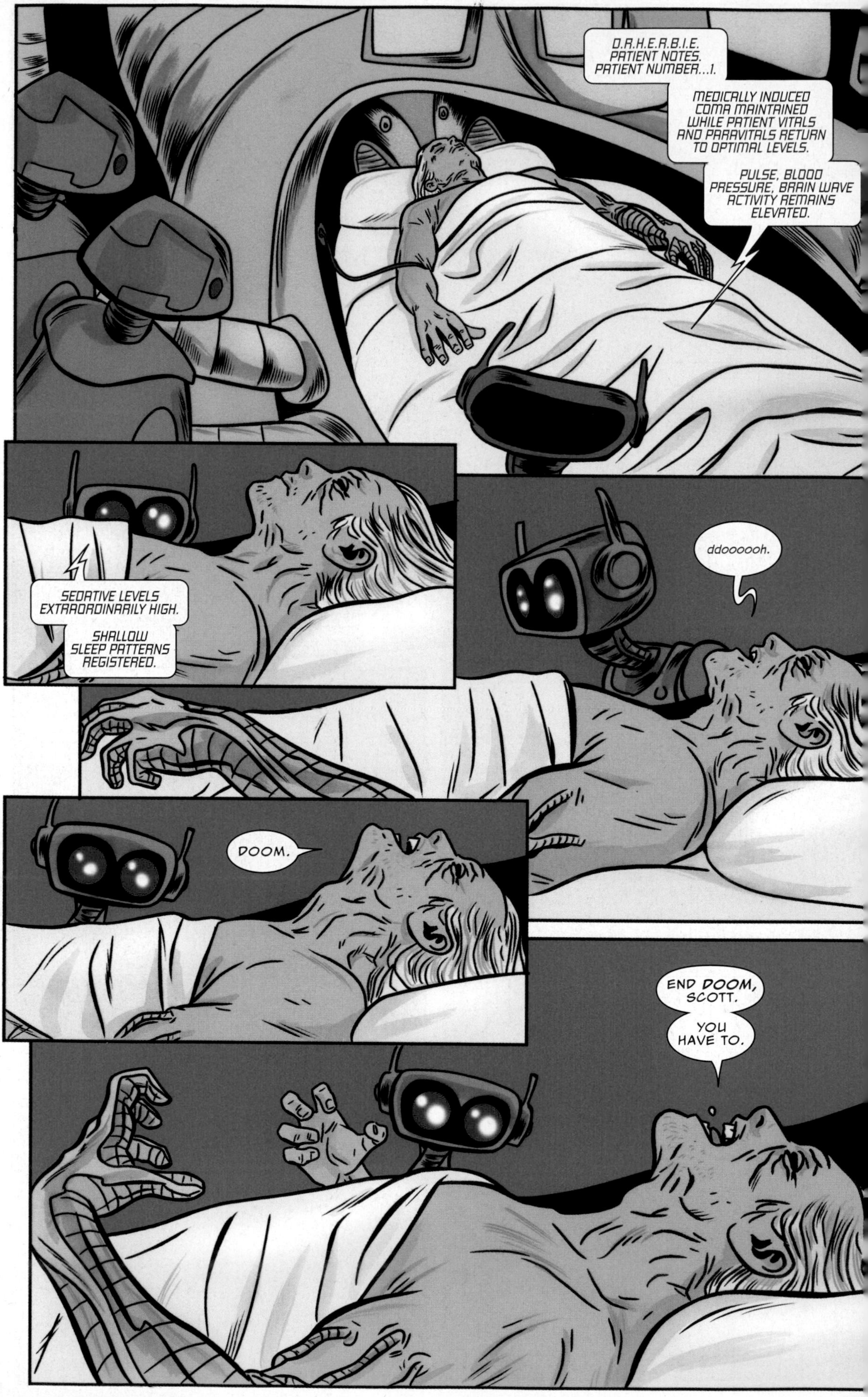
D.R.H.E.R.B.I.E. PATIENT NOTES. PATIENT NUMBER...1.
MEDICALLY INDUCED COMA MAINTAINED WHILE PATIENT VITALS AND PARAVITALS RETURN TO OPTIMAL LEVELS.
PULSE, BLOOD PRESSURE, BRAIN WAVE ACTIVITY REMAINS ELEVATED.
SEDATIVE LEVELS EXTRAORDINARILY HIGH.
SHALLOW SLEEP PATTERNS REGISTERED.
ddoooooh.
DOOM.
END DOOM, SCOTT.
YOU HAVE TO.

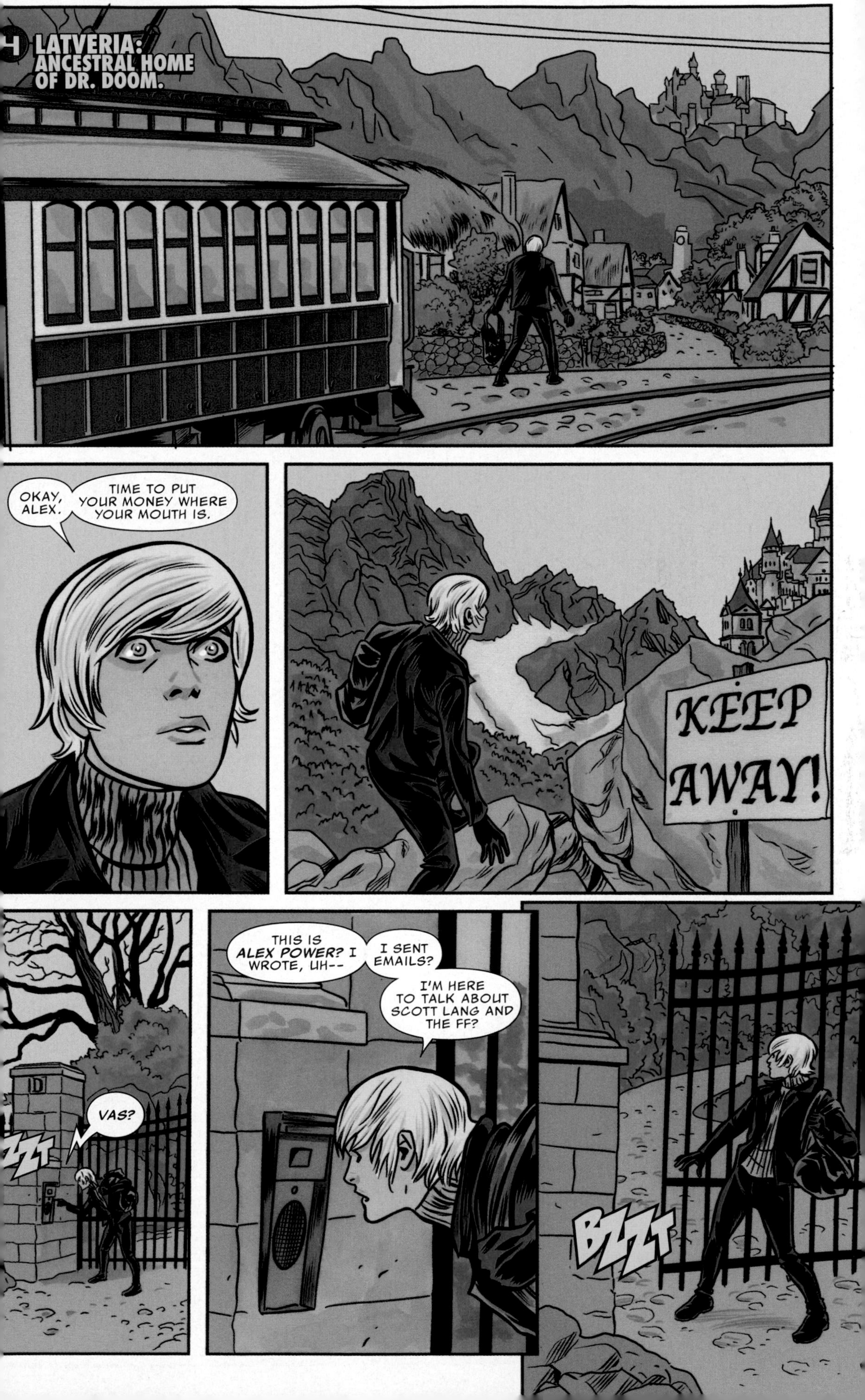
4
LATVERIA: ANCESTRAL HOME OF DR. DOOM.
OKAY, ALEX.
TIME TO PUT YOUR MONEY WHERE YOUR MOUTH IS.
KEEP AWAY!
BZZT
VAS?
THIS IS ALEX POWER? I WROTE, UH--
I SENT EMAILS?
I'M HERE TO TALK ABOUT SCOTT LANG AND THE FF?
BZZT

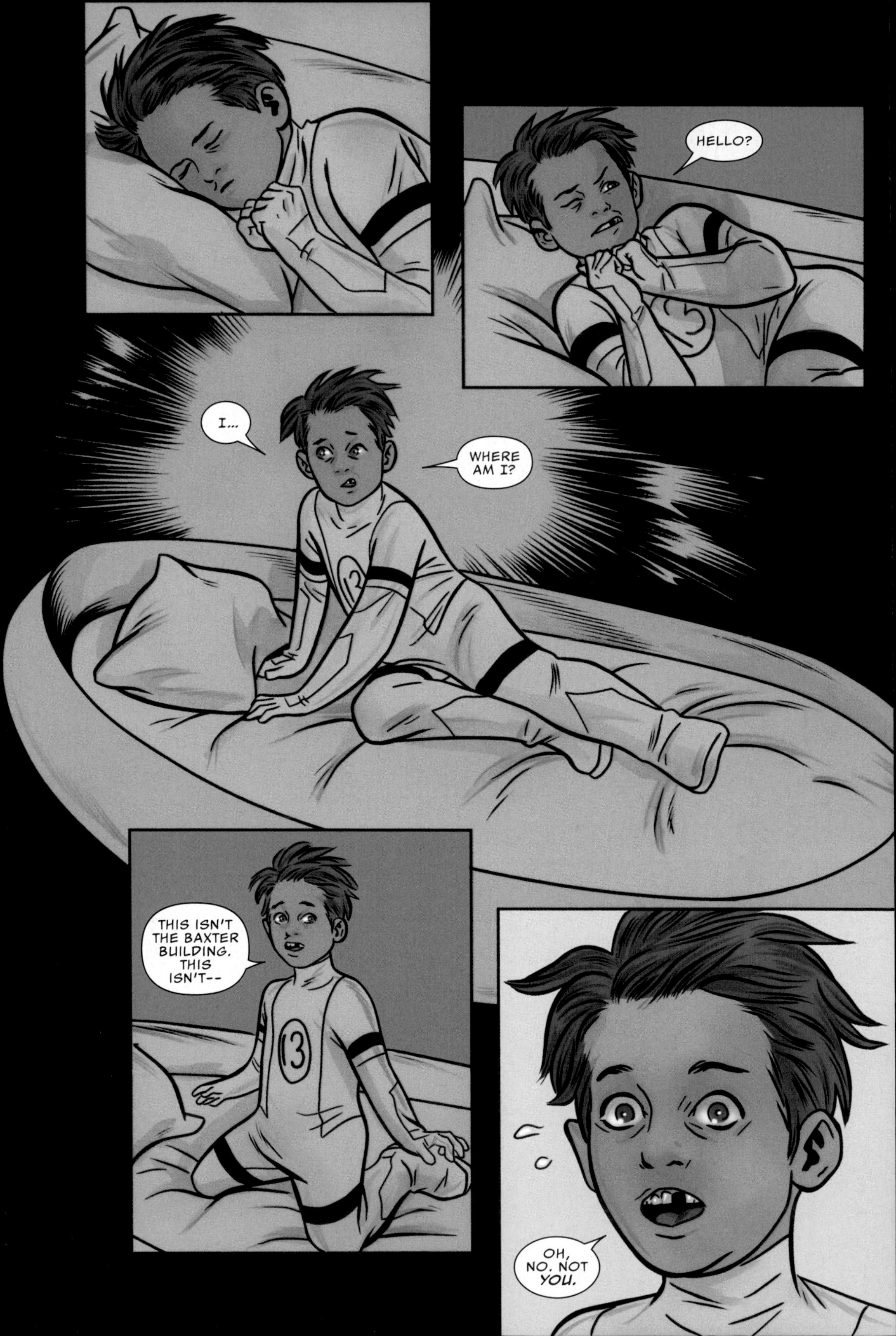
HELLO?
I...
WHERE AM I?
THIS ISN'T THE BAXTER BUILDING. THIS ISN'T--
OH, NO. NOT YOU.

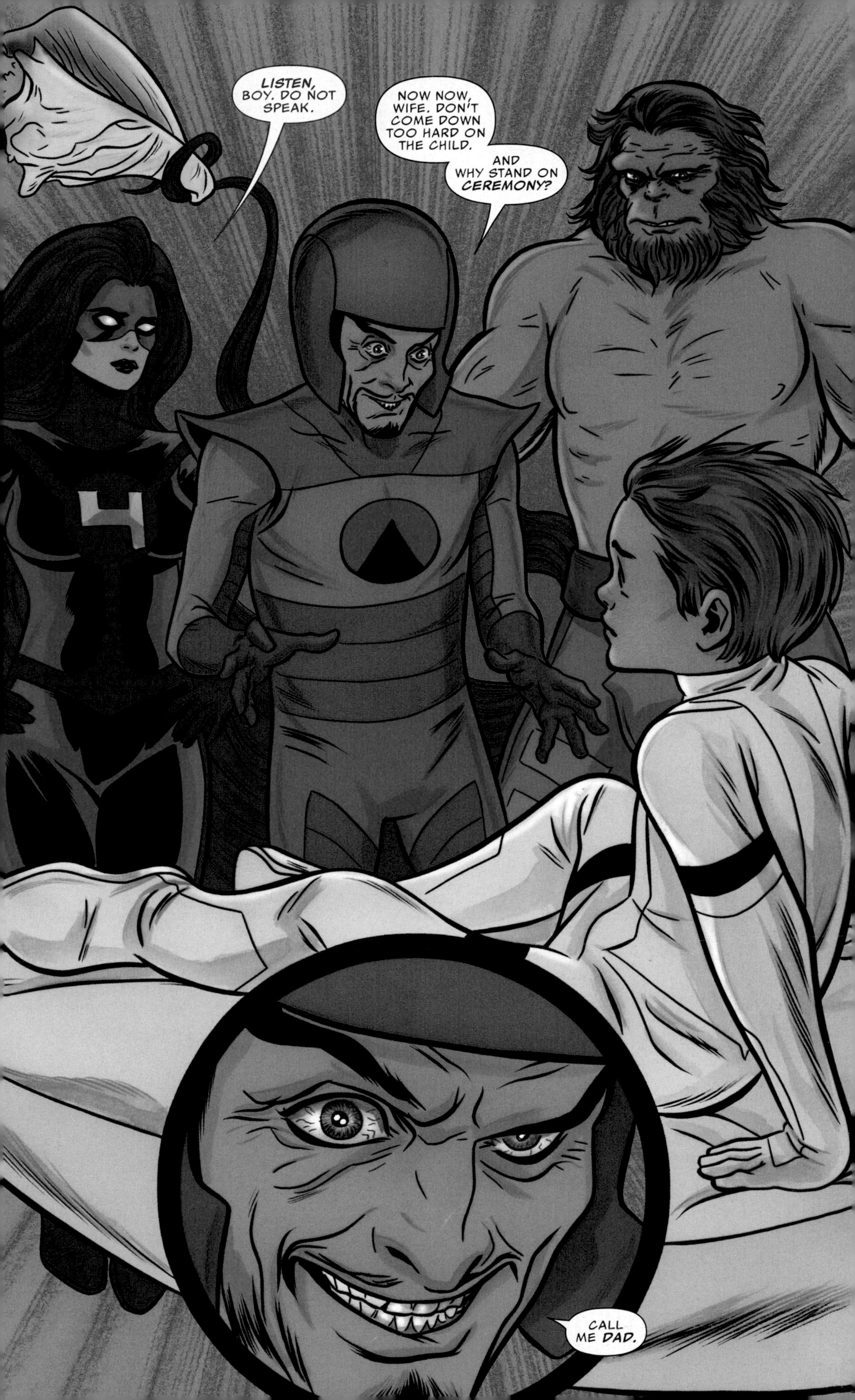
LISTEN, BOY. DO NOT SPEAK.
NOW NOW, WIFE. DON'T COME DOWN TOO HARD ON THE CHILD.
AND WHY STAND ON CEREMONY?
CALL ME DAD.

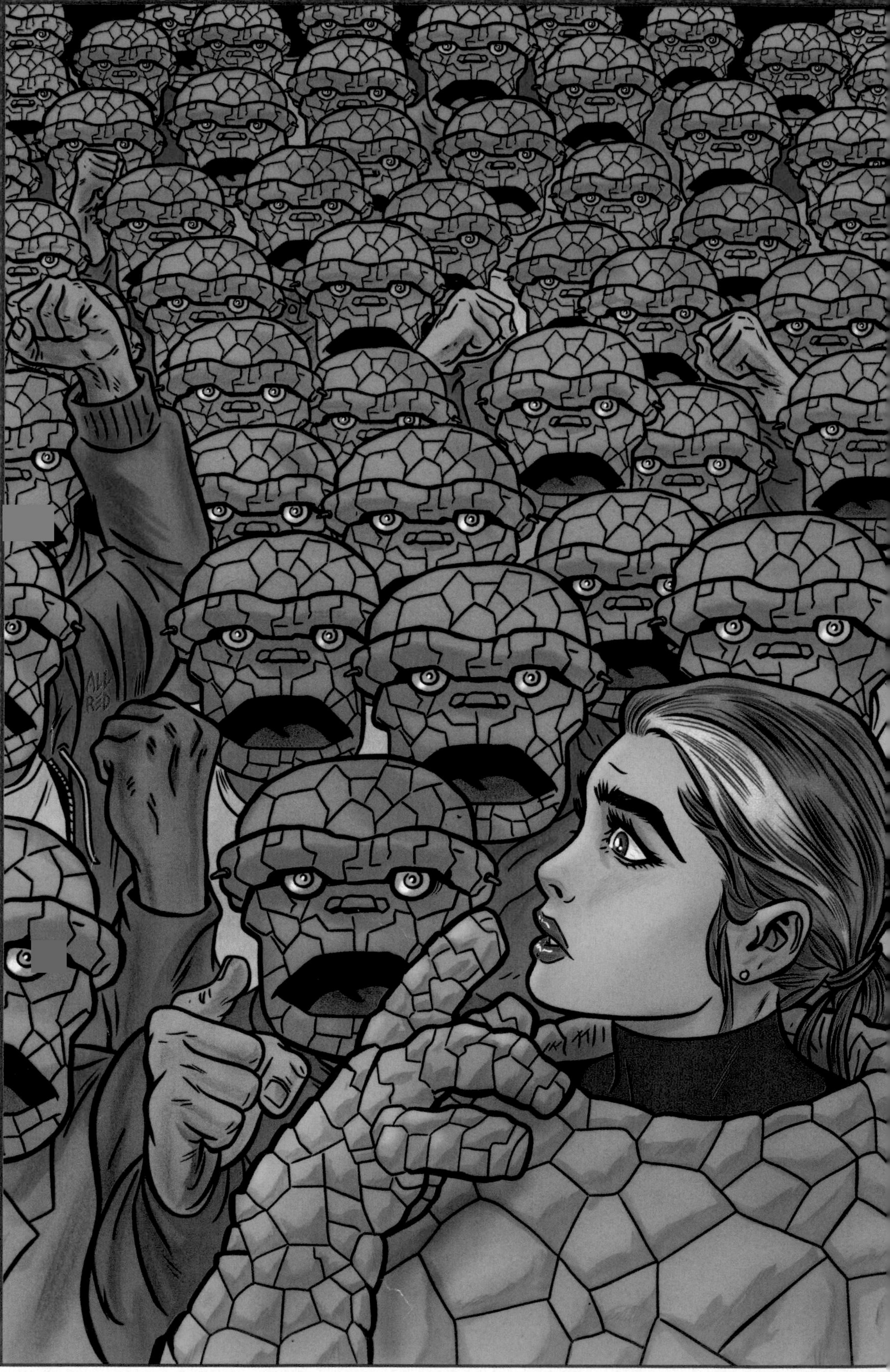

6 SAVE THE TIGER

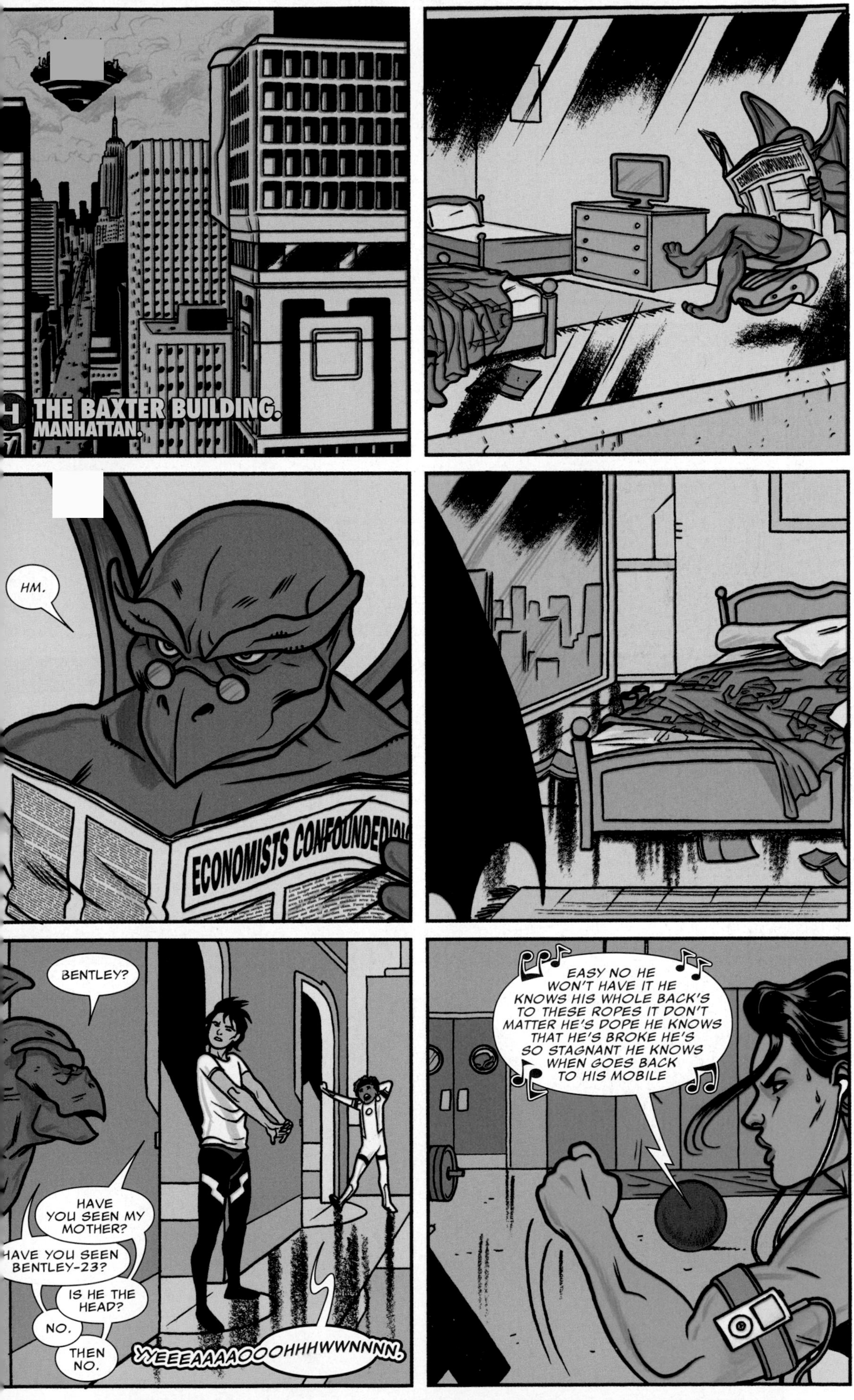
THE BAXTER BUILDING.
MANHATTAN.
ECONOMISTS CONFOUNDED?!?
HM.
ECONOMISTS CONFOUNDED
BENTLEY?
HAVE YOU SEEN MY MOTHER?
HAVE YOU SEEN BENTLEY-23?
IS HE THE HEAD?
NO.
THEN NO.
YYEEEAAAAOOOHHHWWNNNN.
EASY NO HE WON'T HAVE IT HE KNOWS HIS WHOLE BACK'S TO THESE ROPES IT DON'T MATTER HE'S DOPE HE KNOWS THAT HE'S BROKE HE'S SO STAGNANT HE KNOWS WHEN GOES BACK TO HIS MOBILE

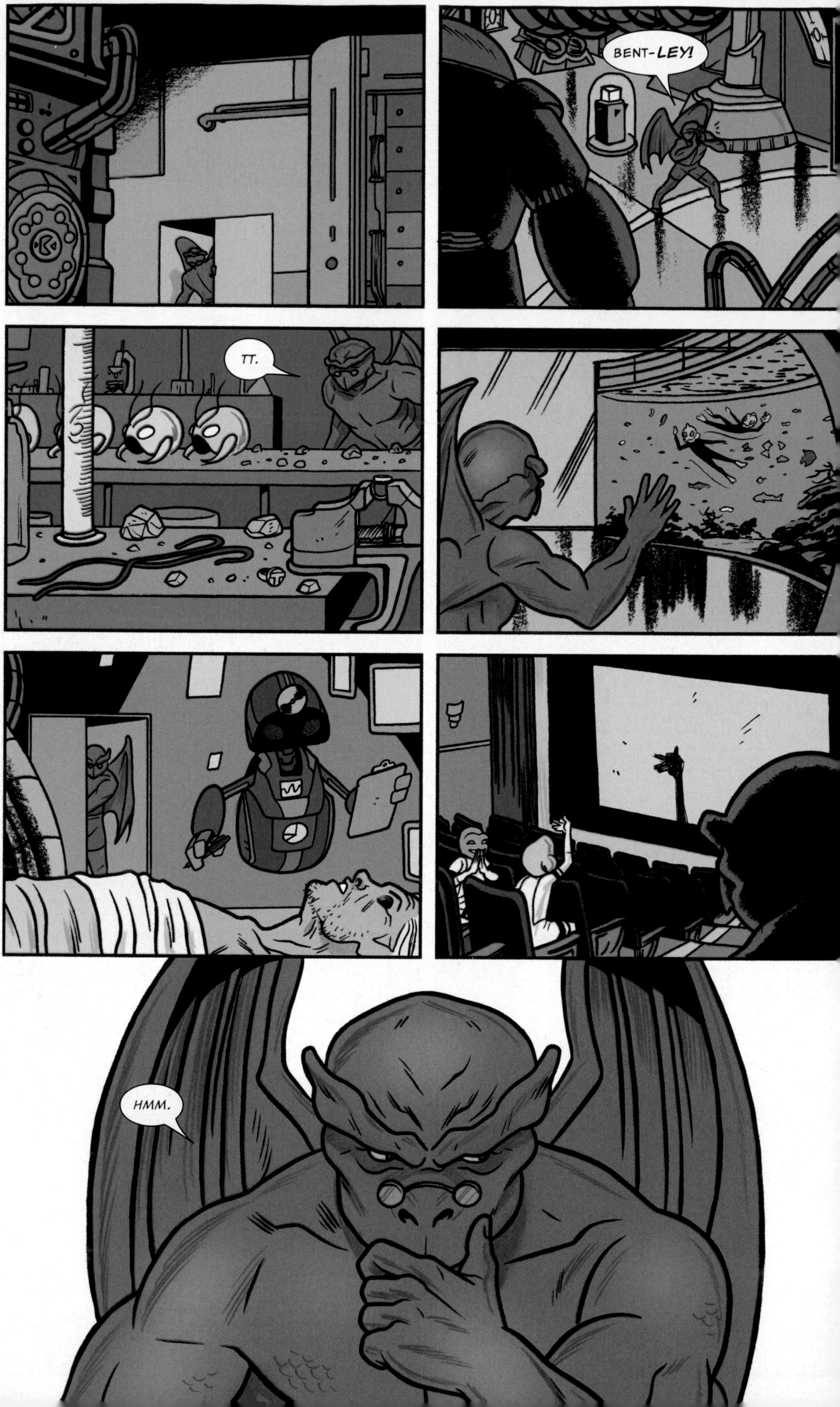
BENT-LEY!
TT.
HMM.

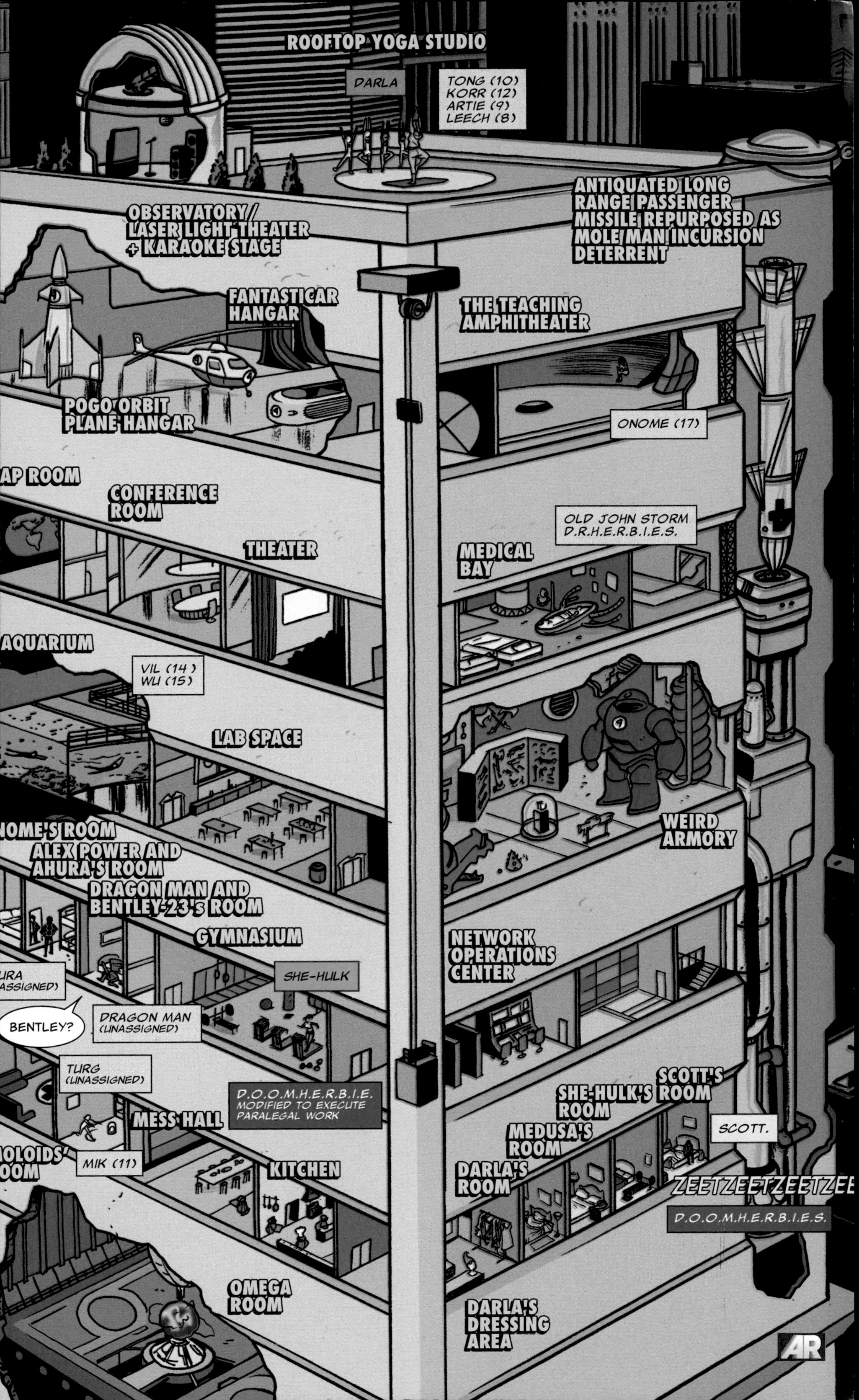
ROOFTOP YOGA STUDIO
DARLA
TONG (10)
KORR (12)
ARTIE (9)
LEECH (8)
ANTIQUATED LONG RANGE PASSENGER MISSILE REPURPOSED AS MOLE MAN INCURSION DETERRENT
OBSERVATORY/ LASER LIGHT THEATER + KARAOKE STAGE
FANTASTICAR HANGAR
THE TEACHING AMPHITHEATER
POGO ORBIT PLANE HANGAR
ONOME (17)
AP ROOM
CONFERENCE ROOM
OLD JOHN STORM D.R.H.E.R.B.I.E.S.
THEATER
MEDICAL BAY
AQUARIUM
VIL (14)
WU (15)
LAB SPACE
WEIRD ARMORY
NOME'S ROOM
ALEX POWER AND AHURA'S ROOM
DRAGON MAN AND BENTLEY-23'S ROOM
GYMNASIUM
NETWORK OPERATIONS CENTER
URA
ASSIGNED)
SHE-HULK
BENTLEY?
DRAGON MAN (UNASSIGNED)
TURG (UNASSIGNED)
D.O.O.M.H.E.R.B.I.E. MODIFIED TO EXECUTE PARALEGAL WORK
SCOTT'S ROOM
SHE-HULK'S ROOM
MESS HALL
MEDUSA'S ROOM
SCOTT.
OLOIDS' OOM
MIK (11)
KITCHEN
DARLA'S ROOM
ZEETZEETZEETZEE
D.O.O.M.H.E.R.B.I.E.S.
OMEGA ROOM
DARLA'S DRESSING AREA
AR

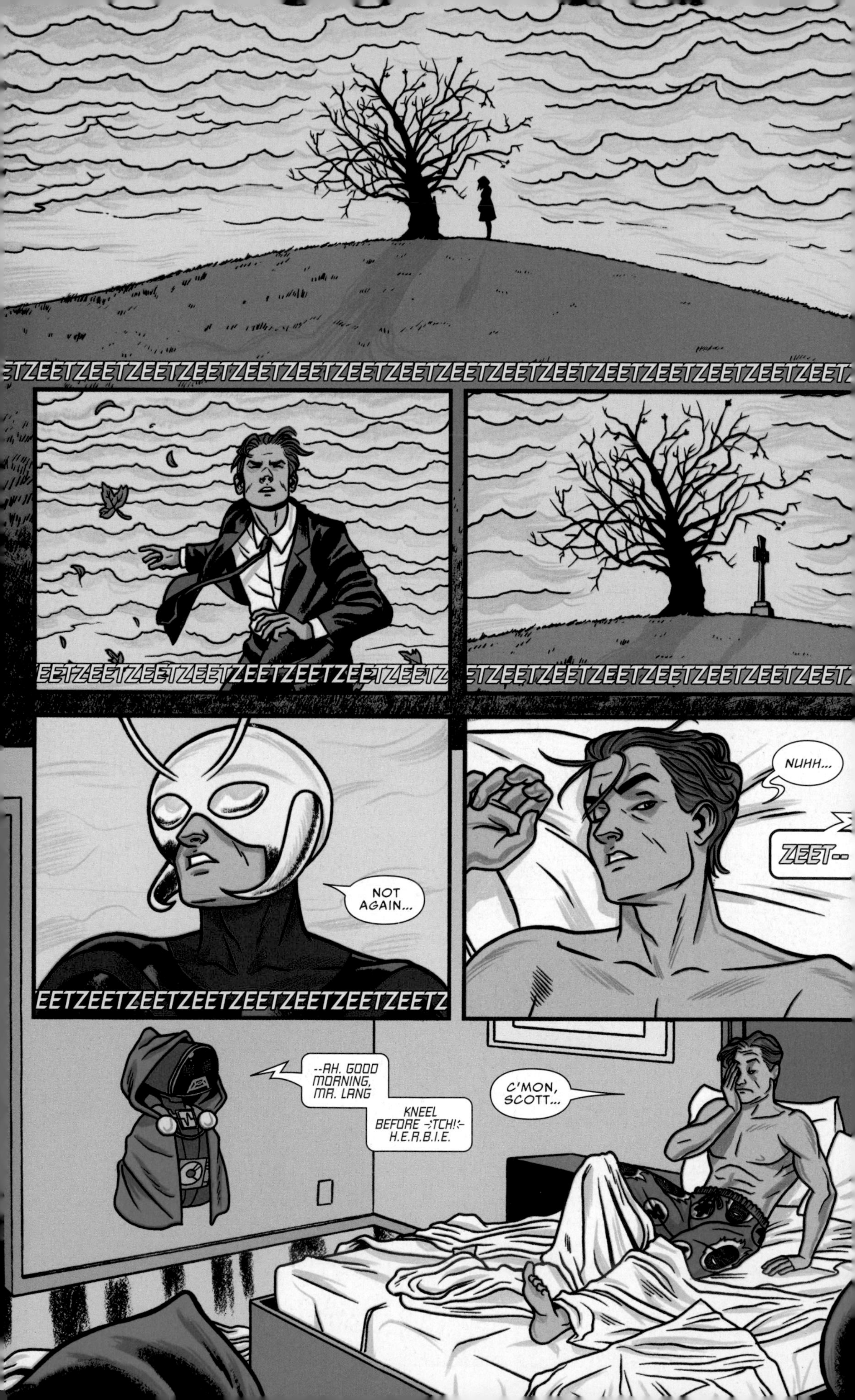
ZEETZEETZEETZEETZEETZEETZEETZEETZEETZEETZEETZEETZEETZEETZEETZEET
ZEETZEETZEETZEETZEETZEETZEETZEETZ
ZEETZEETZEETZEETZEETZEETZEET
NOT AGAIN...
ZEETZEETZEETZEETZEETZEETZEETZEETZ
NUHH...
ZEET--
--AH. GOOD MORNING, MR. LANG
KNEEL BEFORE -TCH!- H.E.R.B.I.E.
C'MON, SCOTT...

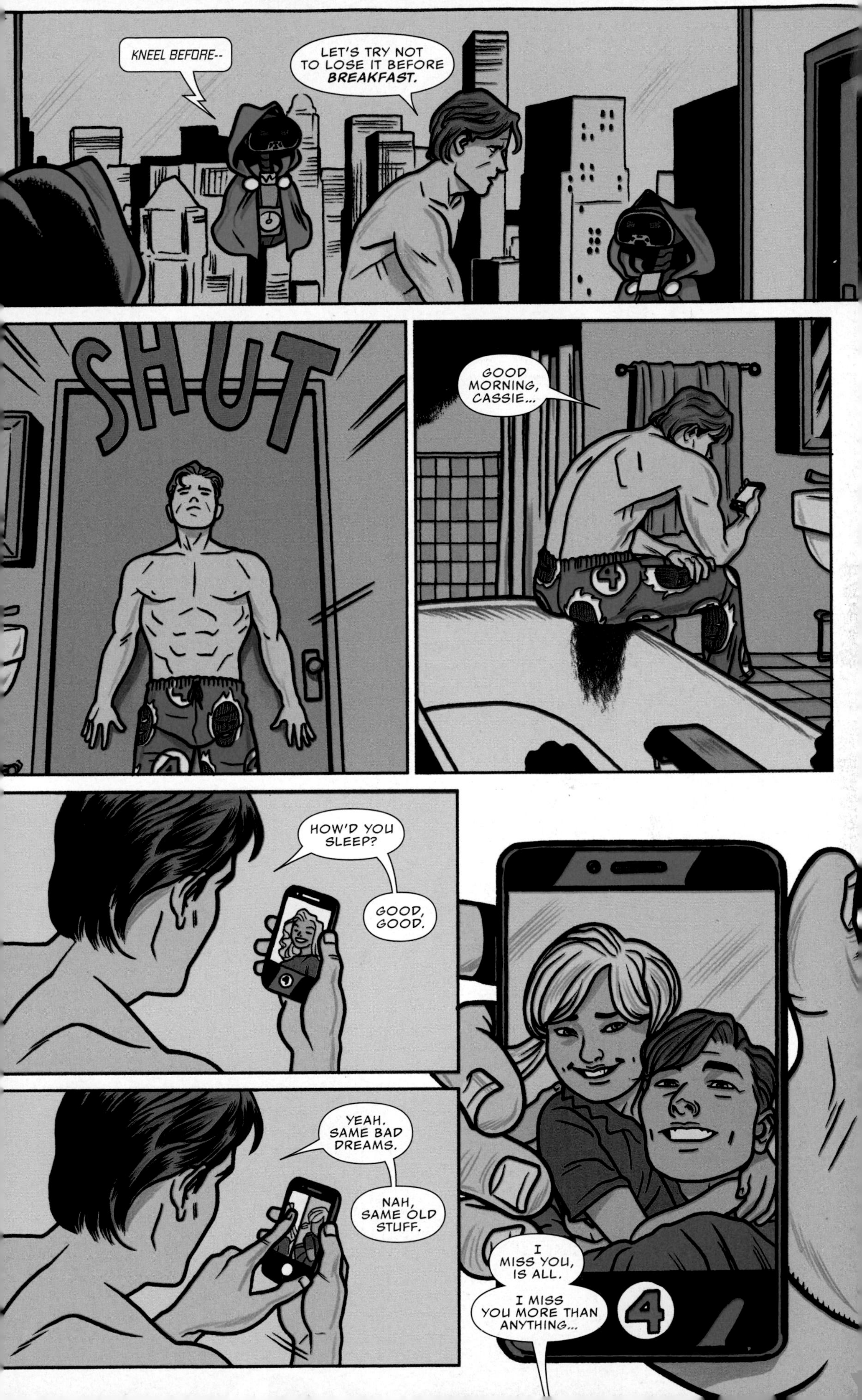
KNEEL BEFORE--
LET'S TRY NOT TO LOSE IT BEFORE *BREAKFAST.*
SHUT
GOOD MORNING, CASSIE...
HOW'D YOU SLEEP?
GOOD, GOOD.
YEAH. SAME BAD DREAMS.
NAH, SAME OLD STUFF.
I MISS YOU, IS ALL.
I MISS YOU MORE THAN ANYTHING...

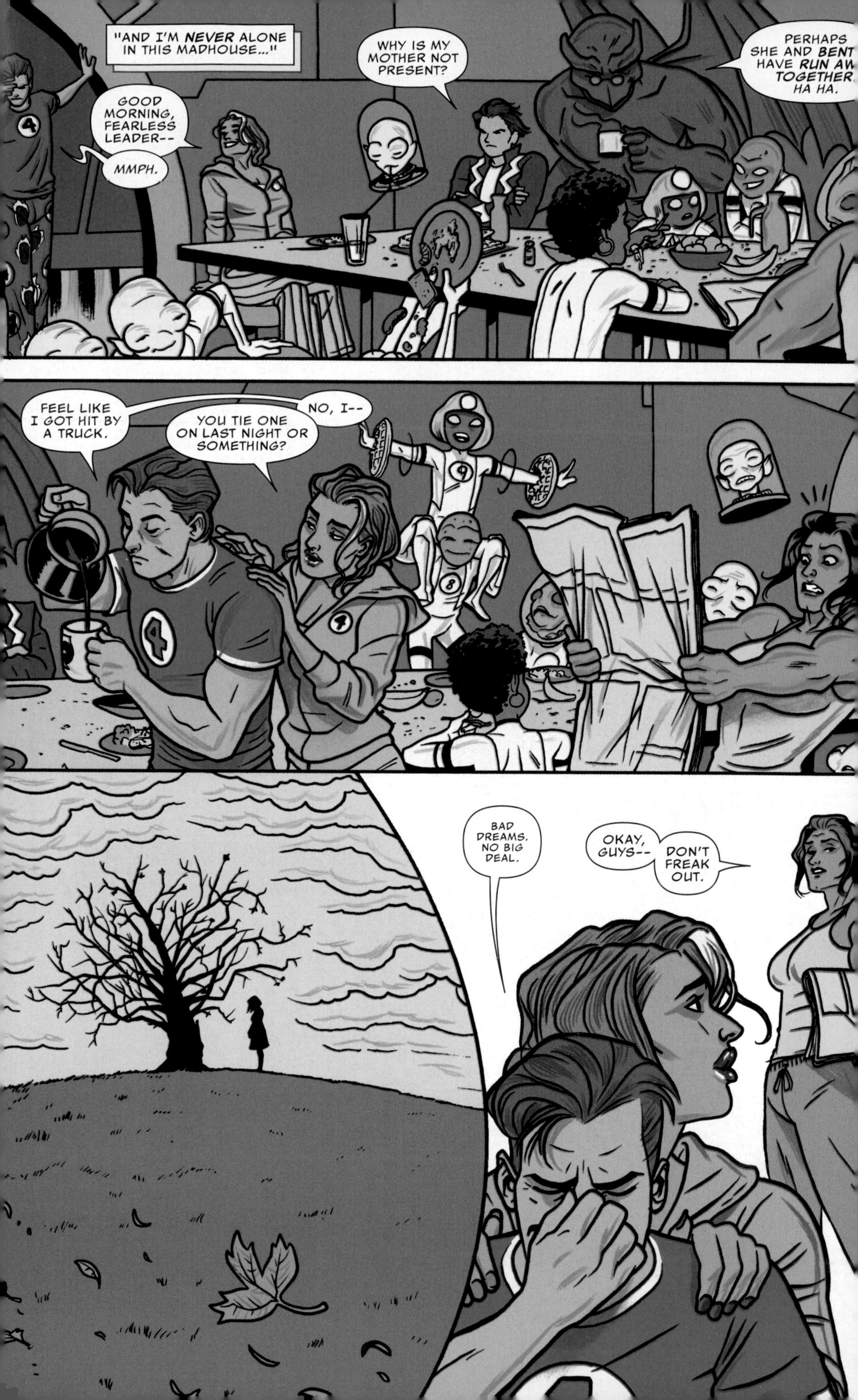
"AND I'M NEVER ALONE IN THIS MADHOUSE..."
GOOD MORNING, FEARLESS LEADER--
MMPH.
WHY IS MY MOTHER NOT PRESENT?
PERHAPS SHE AND BENT HAVE RUN AW TOGETHER HA HA.
FEEL LIKE I GOT HIT BY A TRUCK.
YOU TIE ONE ON LAST NIGHT OR SOMETHING?
NO, I--
BAD DREAMS. NO BIG DEAL.
OKAY, GUYS--
DON'T FREAK OUT.

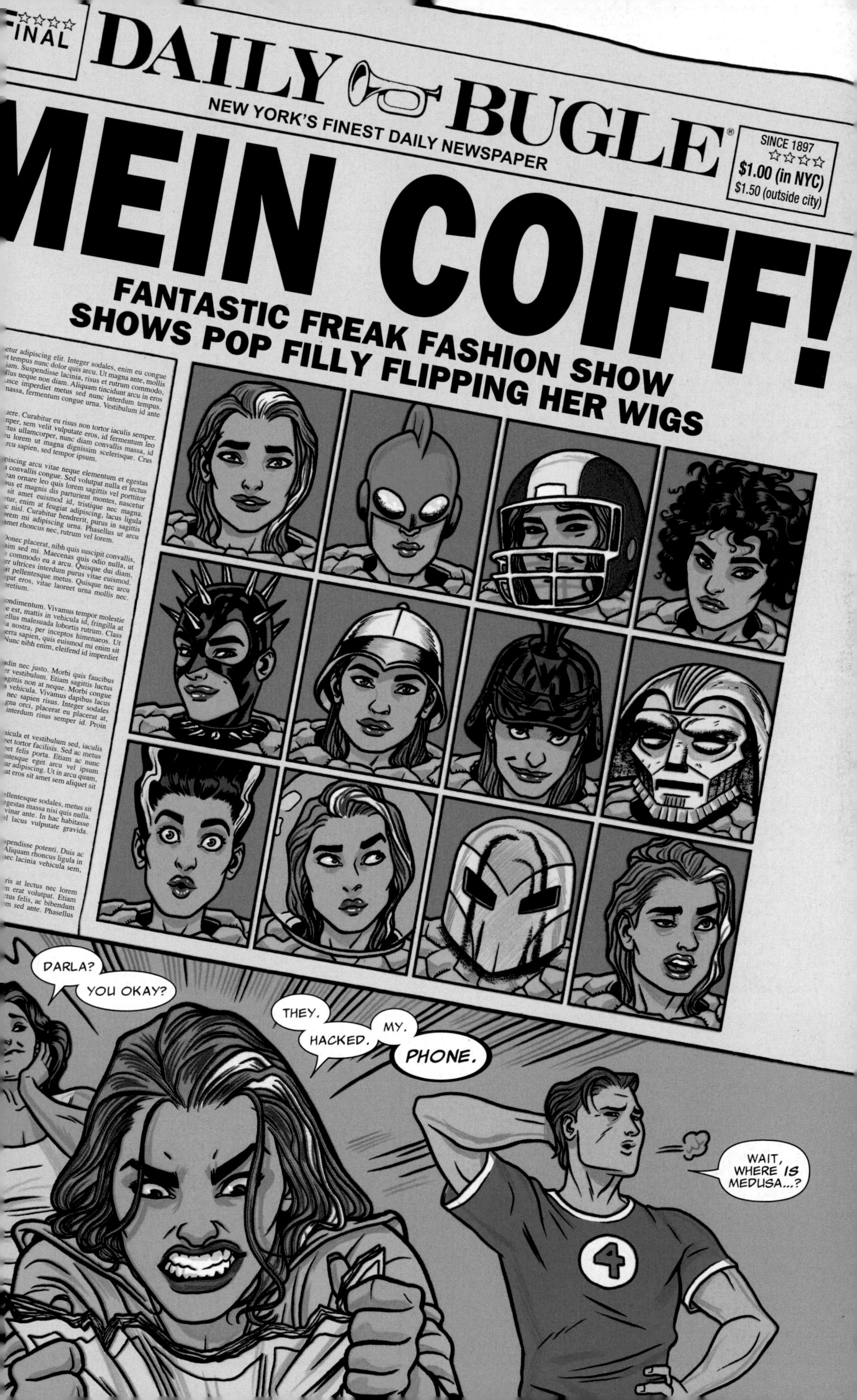

FINAL
DAILY BUGLE
NEW YORK'S FINEST DAILY NEWSPAPER
SINCE 1897
$1.00 (in NYC)
$1.50 (outside city)
MEIN COIFF!
FANTASTIC FREAK FASHION SHOW
SHOWS POP FILLY FLIPPING HER WIGS
DARLA?
YOU OKAY?
THEY.
HACKED.
MY.
PHONE.
WAIT, WHERE IS MEDUSA...?

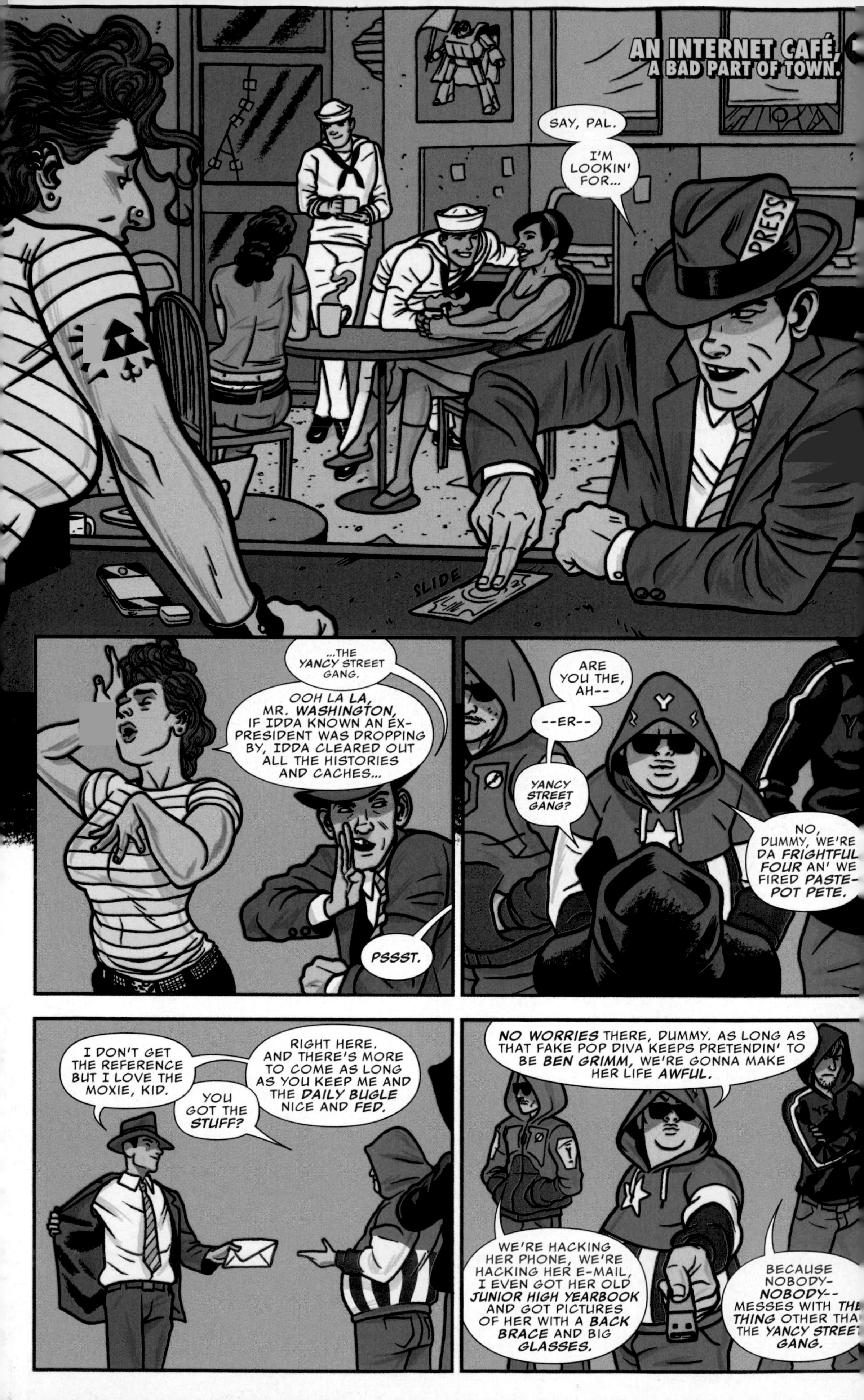
AN INTERNET CAFÉ, A BAD PART OF TOWN.
SAY, PAL.
I'M LOOKIN' FOR...
PRESS
SLIDE
...THE YANCY STREET GANG.
OOH LA LA, MR. WASHINGTON, IF IDDA KNOWN AN EX-PRESIDENT WAS DROPPING BY, IDDA CLEARED OUT ALL THE HISTORIES AND CACHES...
PSSST.
ARE YOU THE, AH--
--ER--
YANCY STREET GANG?
NO, DUMMY, WE'RE DA FRIGHTFUL FOUR AN' WE FIRED PASTE-POT PETE.
I DON'T GET THE REFERENCE BUT I LOVE THE MOXIE, KID.
YOU GOT THE STUFF?
RIGHT HERE. AND THERE'S MORE TO COME AS LONG AS YOU KEEP ME AND THE DAILY BUGLE NICE AND FED.
NO WORRIES THERE, DUMMY. AS LONG AS THAT FAKE POP DIVA KEEPS PRETENDIN' TO BE BEN GRIMM, WE'RE GONNA MAKE HER LIFE AWFUL.
WE'RE HACKING HER PHONE, WE'RE HACKING HER E-MAIL, I EVEN GOT HER OLD JUNIOR HIGH YEARBOOK AND GOT PICTURES OF HER WITH A BACK BRACE AND BIG GLASSES.
BECAUSE NOBODY-NOBODY--MESSES WITH THE THING OTHER THAN THE YANCY STREET GANG.

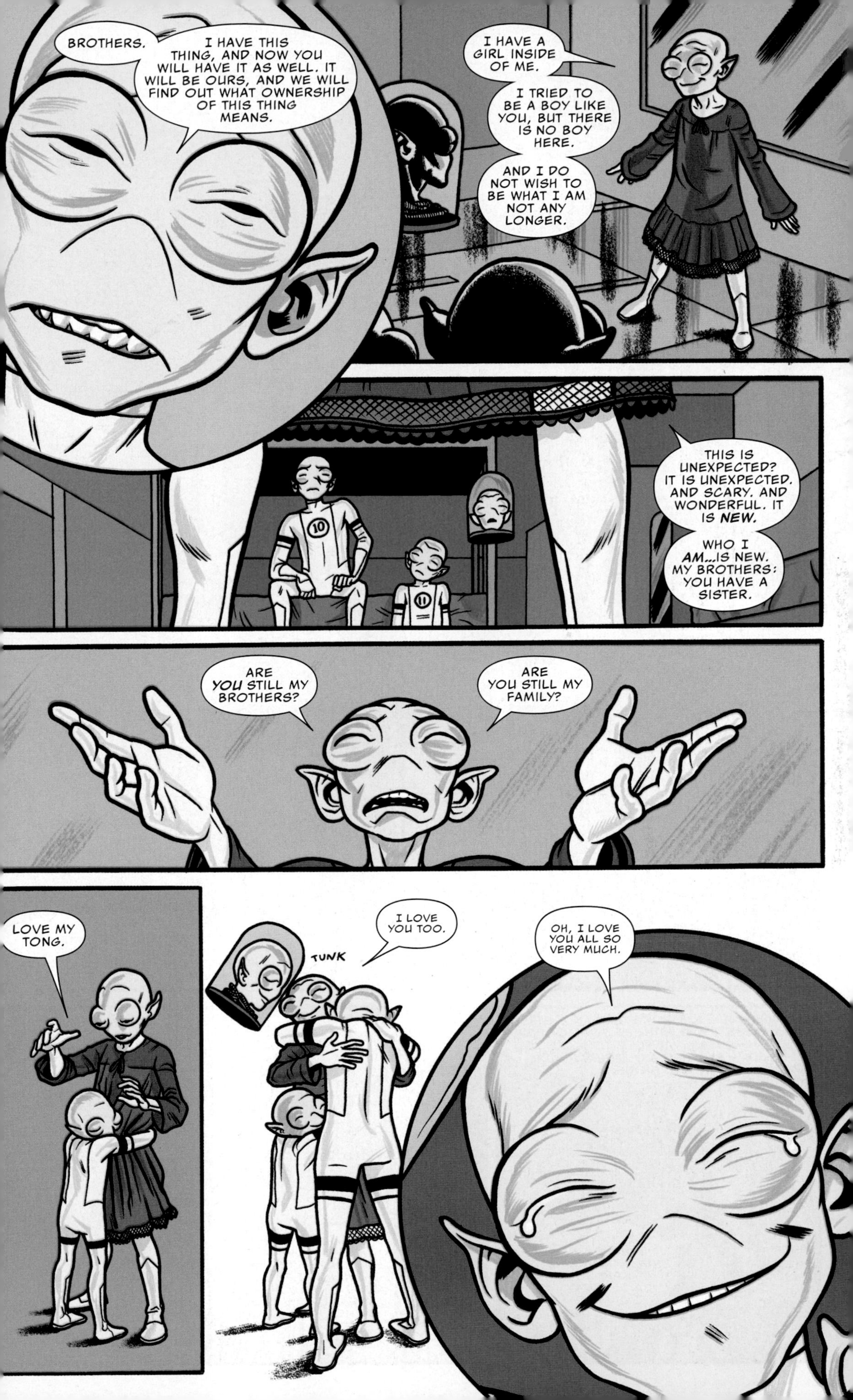
BROTHERS.
I HAVE THIS THING, AND NOW YOU WILL HAVE IT AS WELL. IT WILL BE OURS, AND WE WILL FIND OUT WHAT OWNERSHIP OF THIS THING MEANS.
I HAVE A GIRL INSIDE OF ME.
I TRIED TO BE A BOY LIKE YOU, BUT THERE IS NO BOY HERE.
AND I DO NOT WISH TO BE WHAT I AM NOT ANY LONGER.
THIS IS UNEXPECTED? IT IS UNEXPECTED. AND SCARY. AND WONDERFUL. IT IS *NEW.*
WHO I *AM*...IS NEW. MY BROTHERS: YOU HAVE A SISTER.
ARE *YOU* STILL MY BROTHERS?
ARE YOU STILL MY FAMILY?
LOVE MY TONG.
I LOVE YOU TOO.
TUNK
OH, I LOVE YOU ALL SO VERY MUCH.

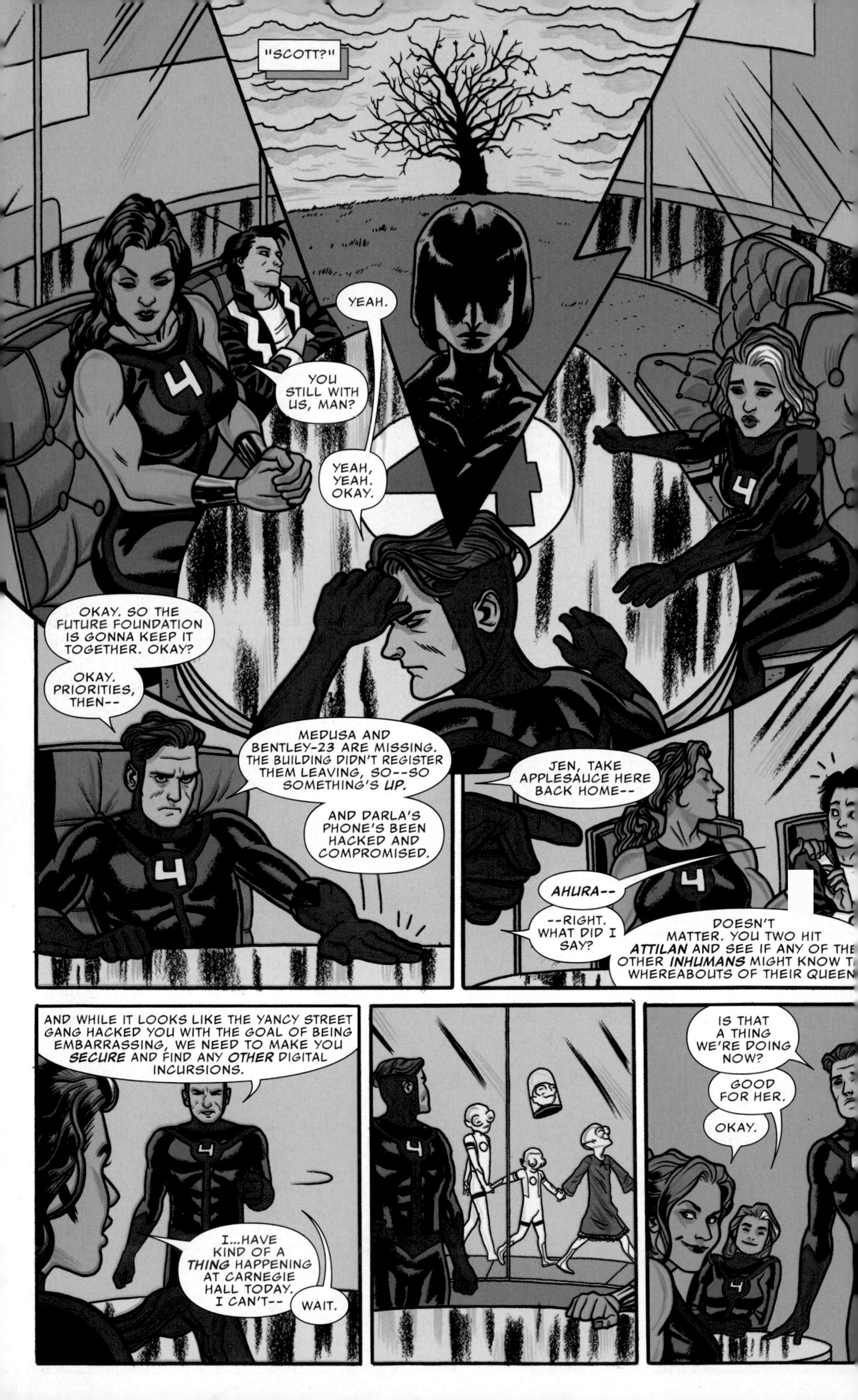
"SCOTT?"
YEAH.
YOU STILL WITH US, MAN?
YEAH, YEAH. OKAY.
OKAY. SO THE FUTURE FOUNDATION IS GONNA KEEP IT TOGETHER. OKAY?
OKAY. PRIORITIES, THEN--
MEDUSA AND BENTLEY-23 ARE MISSING. THE BUILDING DIDN'T REGISTER THEM LEAVING, SO--SO SOMETHING'S UP.
AND DARLA'S PHONE'S BEEN HACKED AND COMPROMISED.
JEN, TAKE APPLESAUCE HERE BACK HOME--
AHURA--
--RIGHT. WHAT DID I SAY?
DOESN'T MATTER. YOU TWO HIT ATTILAN AND SEE IF ANY OF THE OTHER INHUMANS MIGHT KNOW THE WHEREABOUTS OF THEIR QUEEN
AND WHILE IT LOOKS LIKE THE YANCY STREET GANG HACKED YOU WITH THE GOAL OF BEING EMBARRASSING, WE NEED TO MAKE YOU SECURE AND FIND ANY OTHER DIGITAL INCURSIONS.
I...HAVE KIND OF A THING HAPPENING AT CARNEGIE HALL TODAY. I CAN'T--
WAIT.
IS THAT A THING WE'RE DOING NOW?
GOOD FOR HER.
OKAY.

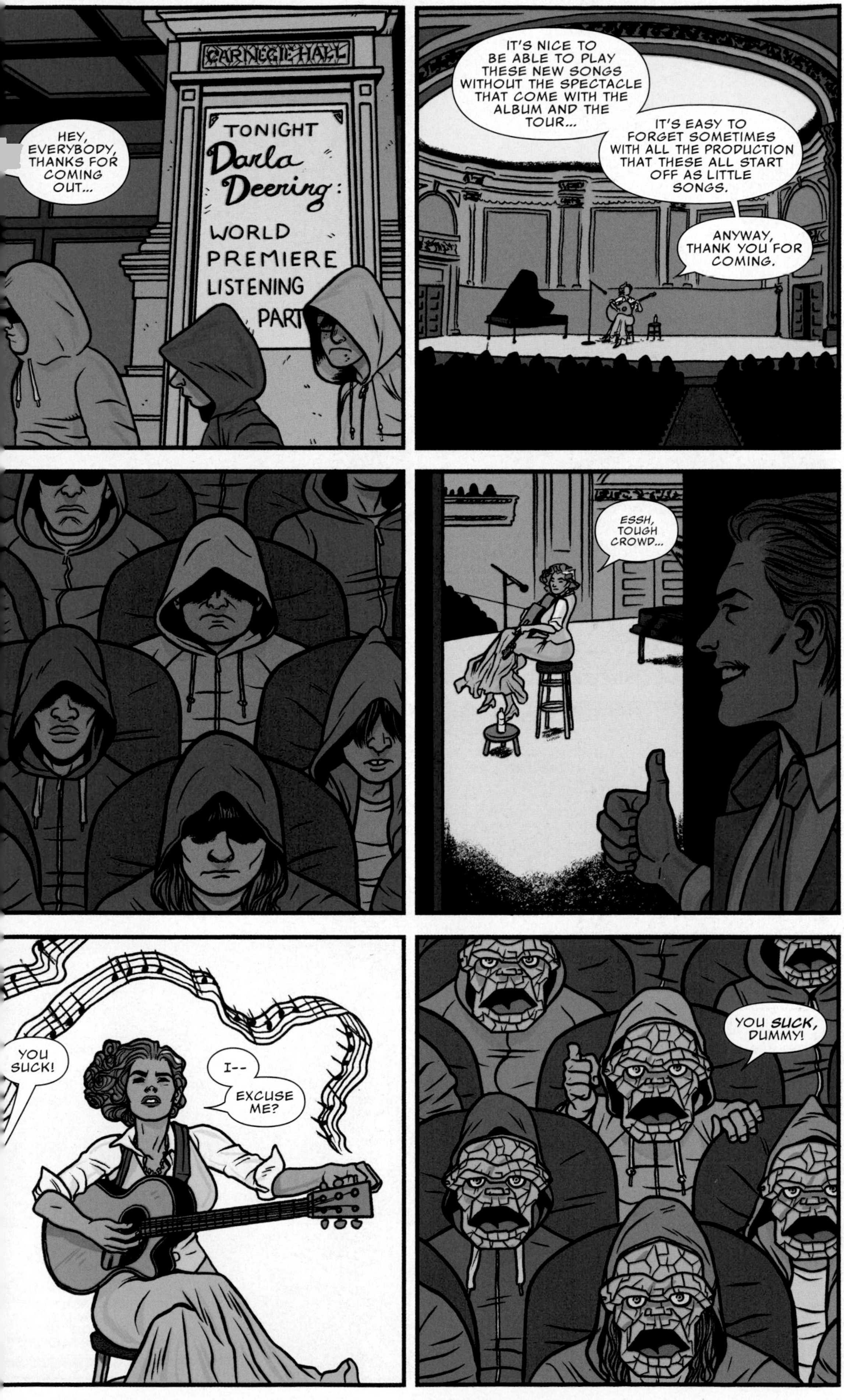
CARNEGIE HALL
TONIGHT Darla Deering: WORLD PREMIERE LISTENING PART
HEY, EVERYBODY, THANKS FOR COMING OUT...
IT'S NICE TO BE ABLE TO PLAY THESE NEW SONGS WITHOUT THE SPECTACLE THAT COME WITH THE ALBUM AND THE TOUR...
IT'S EASY TO FORGET SOMETIMES WITH ALL THE PRODUCTION THAT THESE ALL START OFF AS LITTLE SONGS.
ANYWAY, THANK YOU FOR COMING.
ESSH, TOUGH CROWD...
YOU SUCK!
I--
EXCUSE ME?
YOU SUCK, DUMMY!

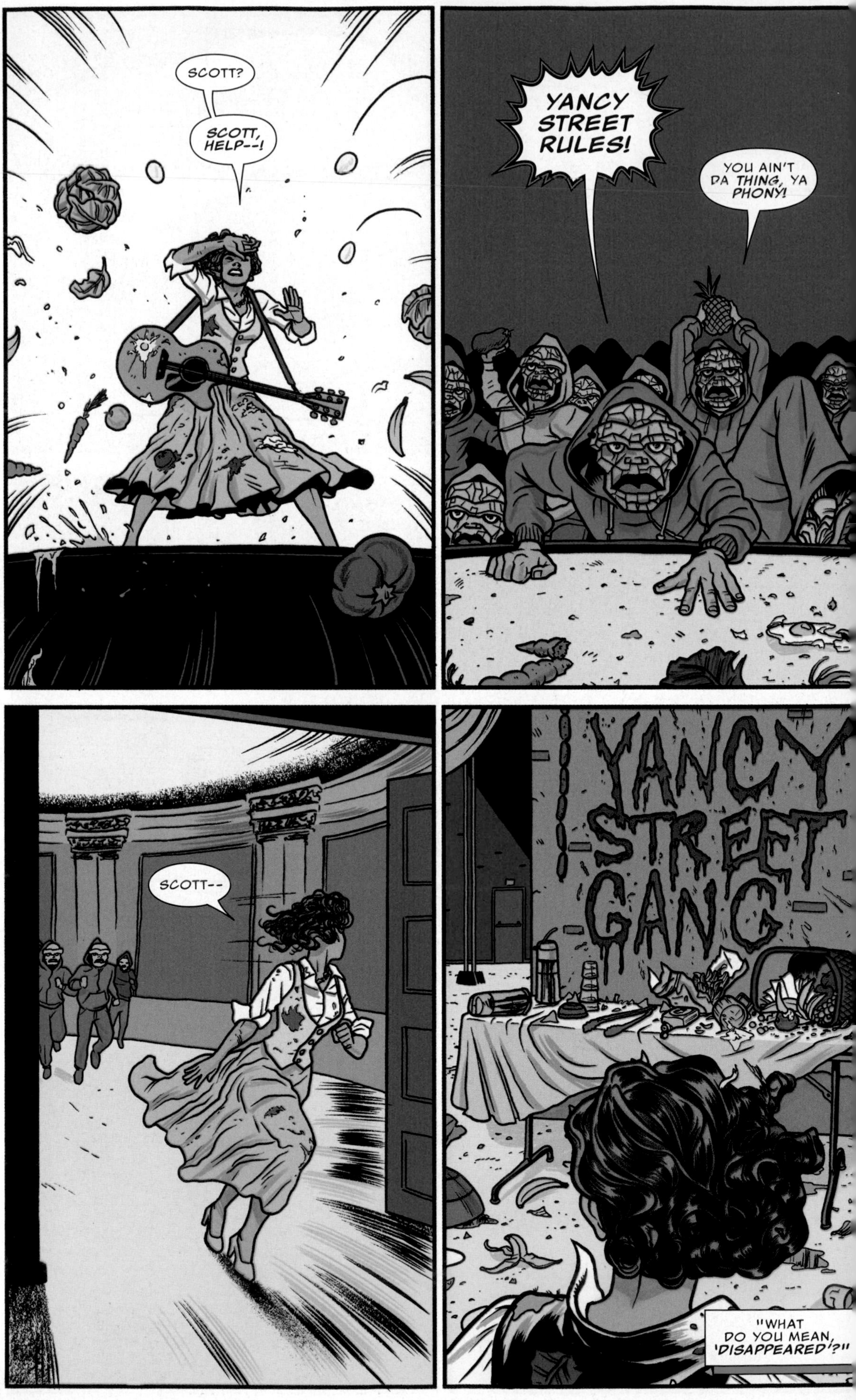
SCOTT?
SCOTT, HELP--!
YANCY STREET RULES!
YOU AIN'T DA THING, YA PHONY!
SCOTT--
YANCY STREET GANG
"WHAT DO YOU MEAN, 'DISAPPEARED'?"

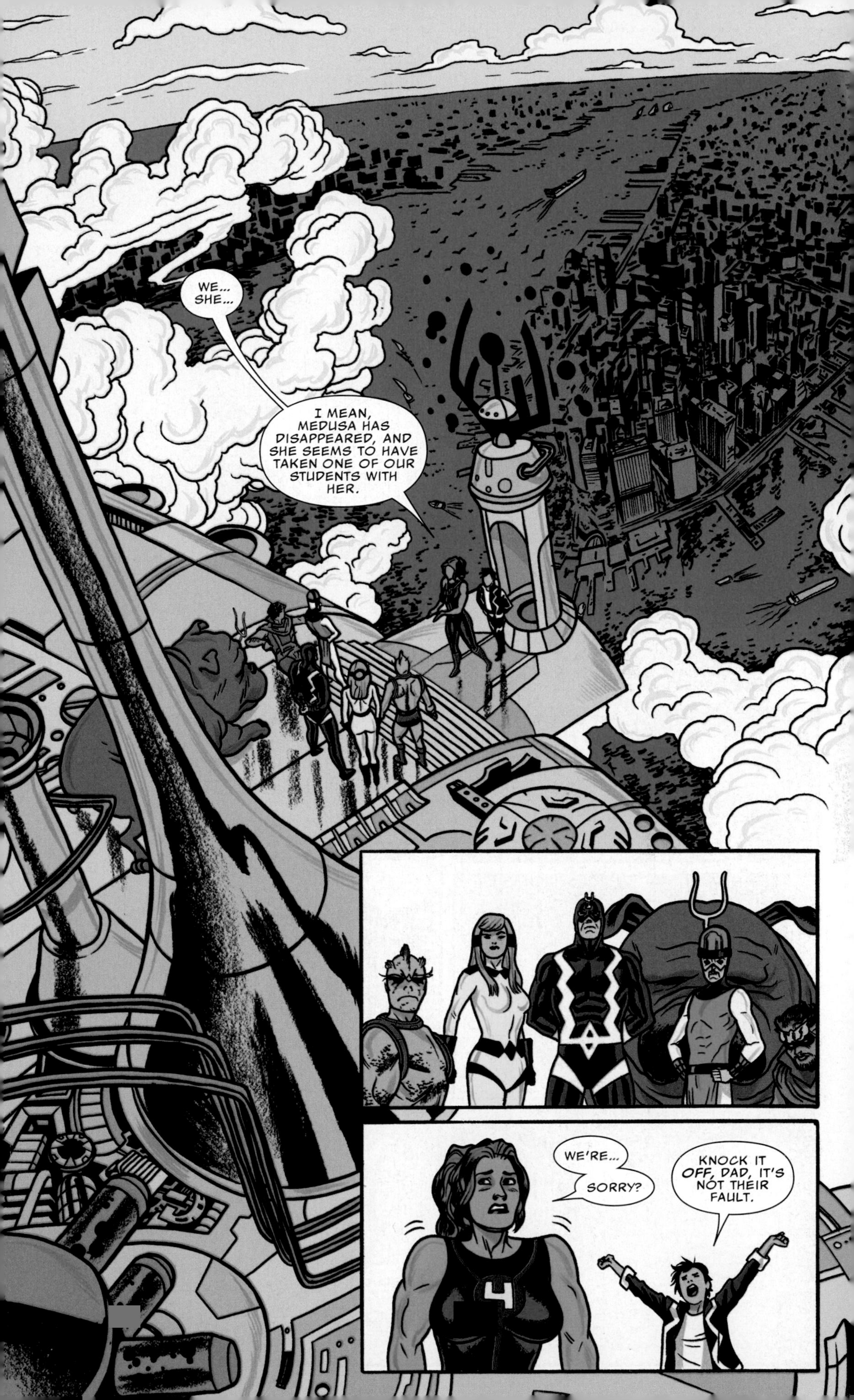
WE... SHE...
I MEAN, MEDUSA HAS DISAPPEARED, AND SHE SEEMS TO HAVE TAKEN ONE OF OUR STUDENTS WITH HER.
WE'RE...
SORRY?
KNOCK IT OFF, DAD, IT'S NOT THEIR FAULT.

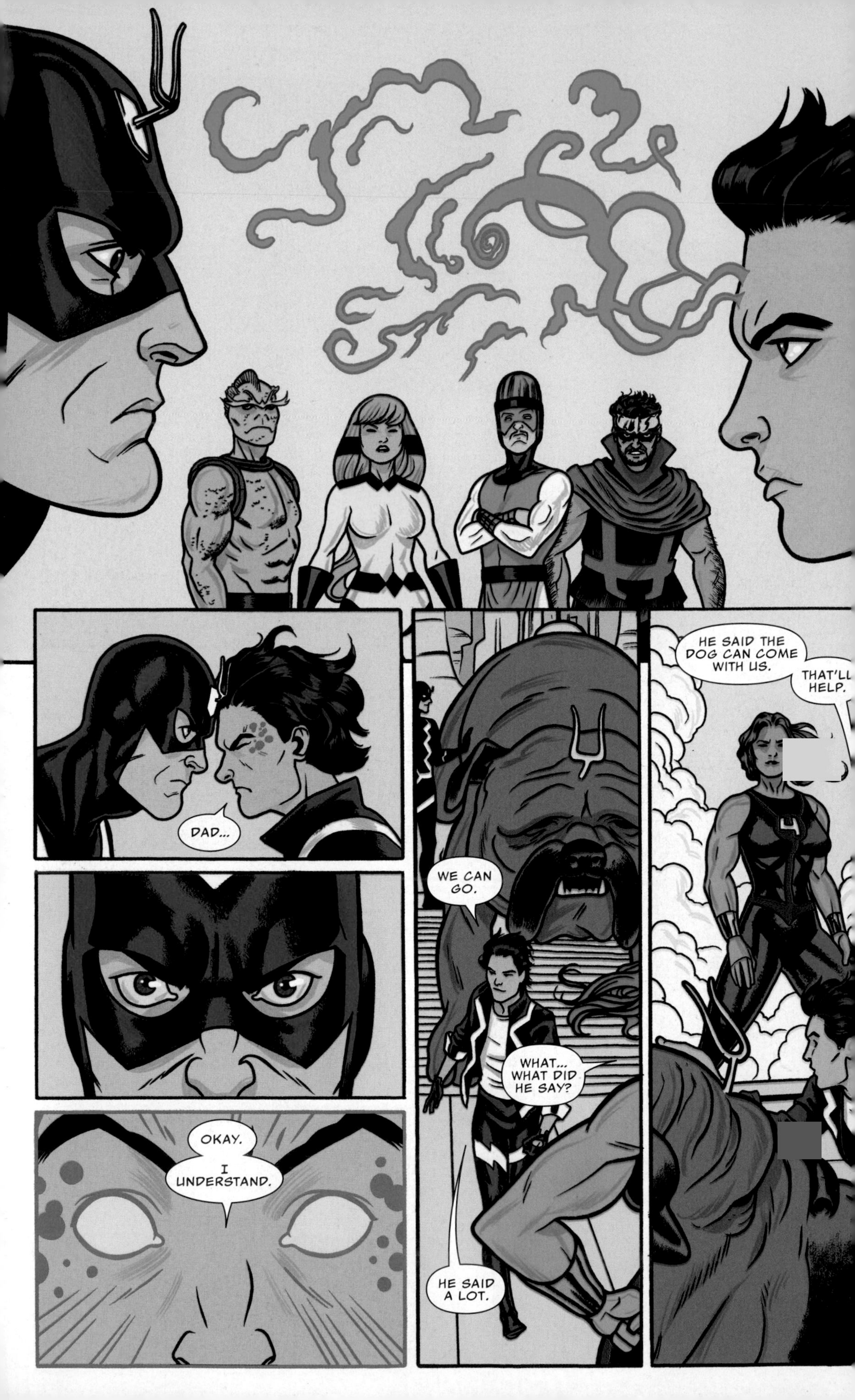

DAD...
OKAY.
I UNDERSTAND.
WE CAN GO.
WHAT... WHAT DID HE SAY?
HE SAID A LOT.
HE SAID THE DOG CAN COME WITH US.
THAT'LL HELP.

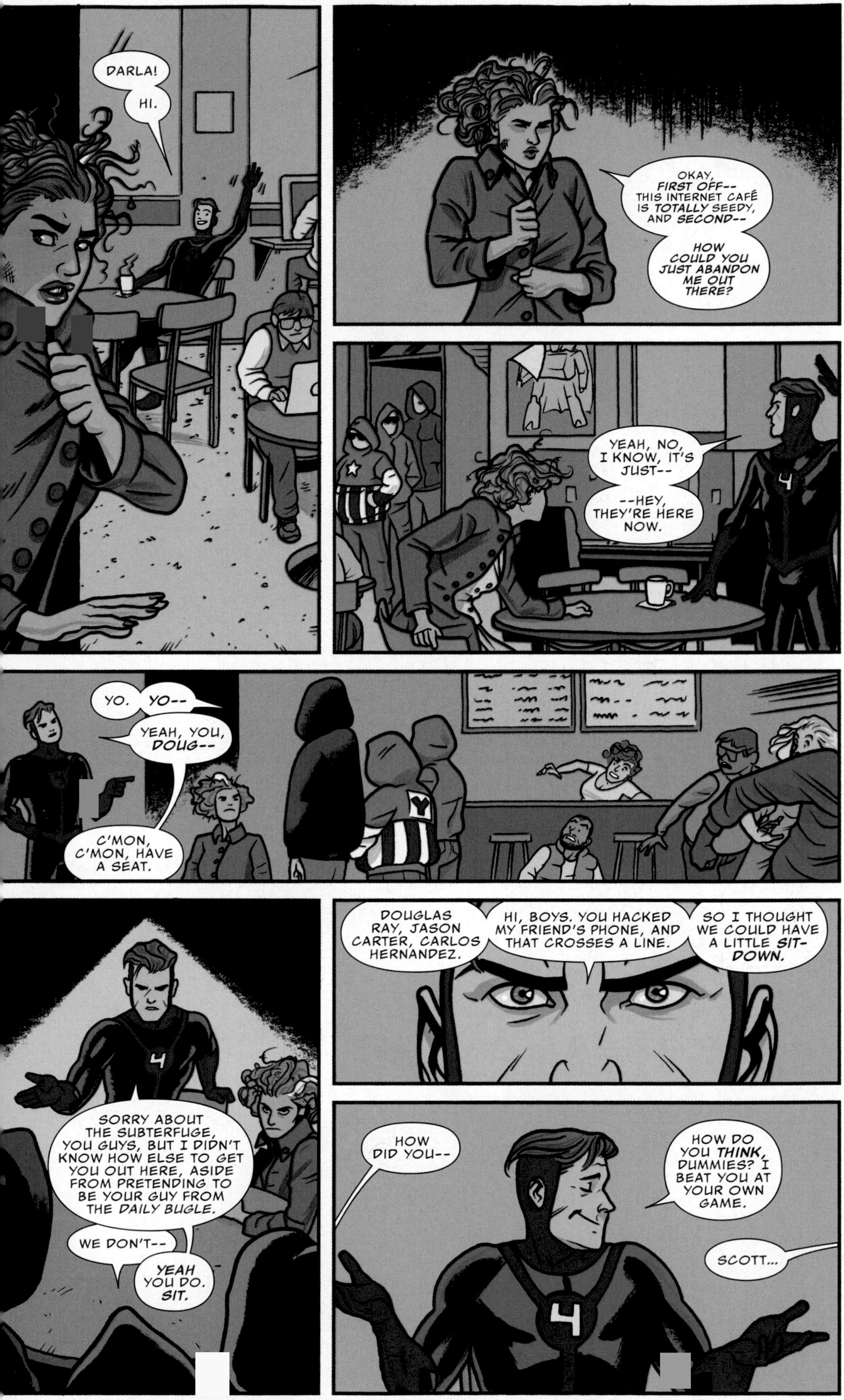
DARLA!
HI.
OKAY, FIRST OFF-- THIS INTERNET CAFÉ IS TOTALLY SEEDY, AND SECOND--
HOW COULD YOU JUST ABANDON ME OUT THERE?
YEAH, NO, I KNOW, IT'S JUST--
--HEY, THEY'RE HERE NOW.
YO.
YO--
YEAH, YOU, DOUG--
C'MON, C'MON, HAVE A SEAT.
SORRY ABOUT THE SUBTERFUGE, YOU GUYS, BUT I DIDN'T KNOW HOW ELSE TO GET YOU OUT HERE, ASIDE FROM PRETENDING TO BE YOUR GUY FROM THE DAILY BUGLE.
WE DON'T--
YEAH YOU DO. SIT.
DOUGLAS RAY, JASON CARTER, CARLOS HERNANDEZ.
HI, BOYS. YOU HACKED MY FRIEND'S PHONE, AND THAT CROSSES A LINE.
SO I THOUGHT WE COULD HAVE A LITTLE SIT-DOWN.
HOW DID YOU--
HOW DO YOU THINK, DUMMIES? I BEAT YOU AT YOUR OWN GAME.
SCOTT...

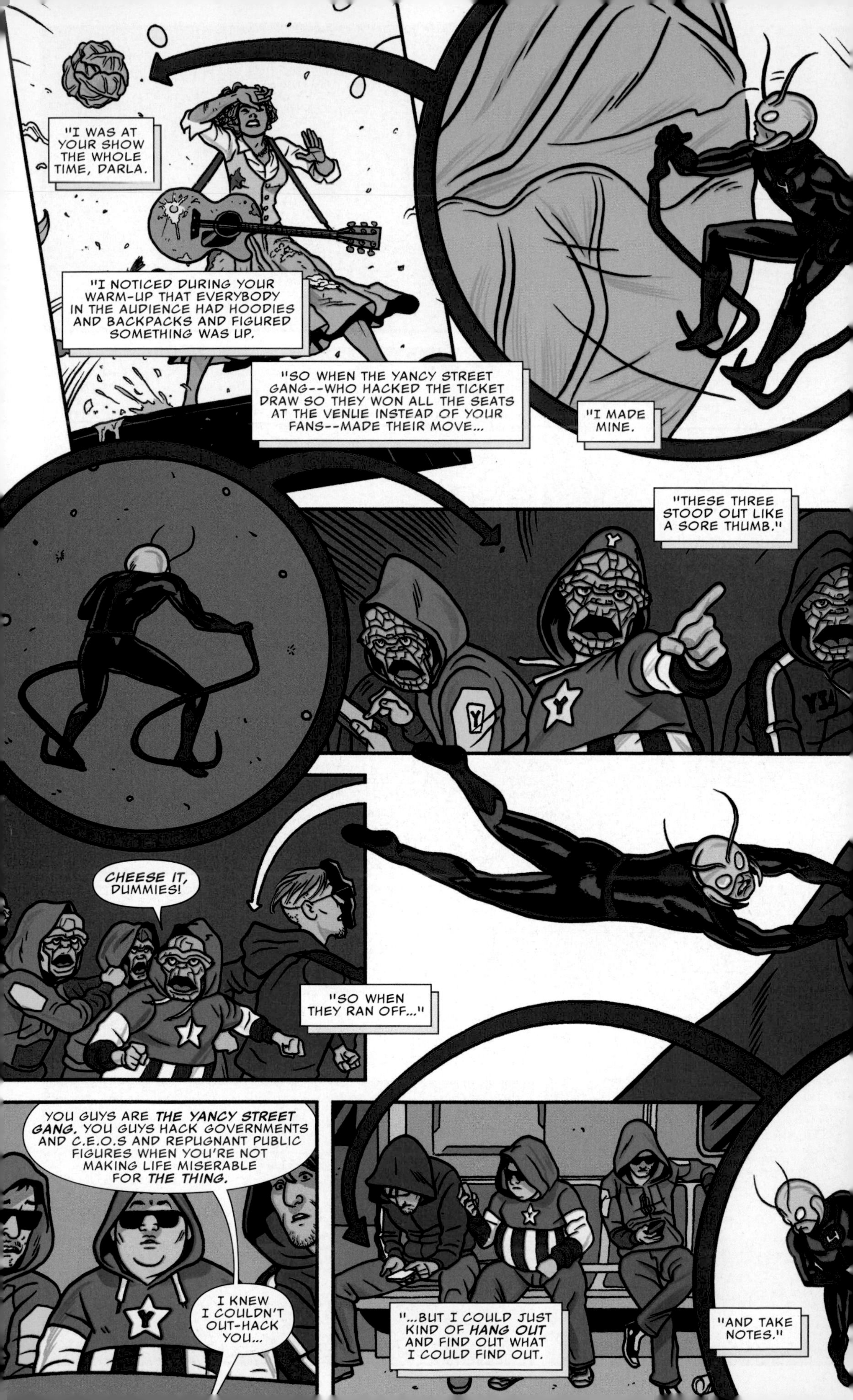

"I WAS AT YOUR SHOW THE WHOLE TIME, DARLA.
"I NOTICED DURING YOUR WARM-UP THAT EVERYBODY IN THE AUDIENCE HAD HOODIES AND BACKPACKS AND FIGURED SOMETHING WAS UP.
"SO WHEN THE YANCY STREET GANG--WHO HACKED THE TICKET DRAW SO THEY WON ALL THE SEATS AT THE VENUE INSTEAD OF YOUR FANS--MADE THEIR MOVE...
"I MADE MINE.
"THESE THREE STOOD OUT LIKE A SORE THUMB."
CHEESE IT, DUMMIES!
"SO WHEN THEY RAN OFF..."
YOU GUYS ARE THE YANCY STREET GANG. YOU GUYS HACK GOVERNMENTS AND C.E.O.S AND REPUGNANT PUBLIC FIGURES WHEN YOU'RE NOT MAKING LIFE MISERABLE FOR THE THING.
I KNEW I COULDN'T OUT-HACK YOU...
"...BUT I COULD JUST KIND OF HANG OUT AND FIND OUT WHAT I COULD FIND OUT.
"AND TAKE NOTES."

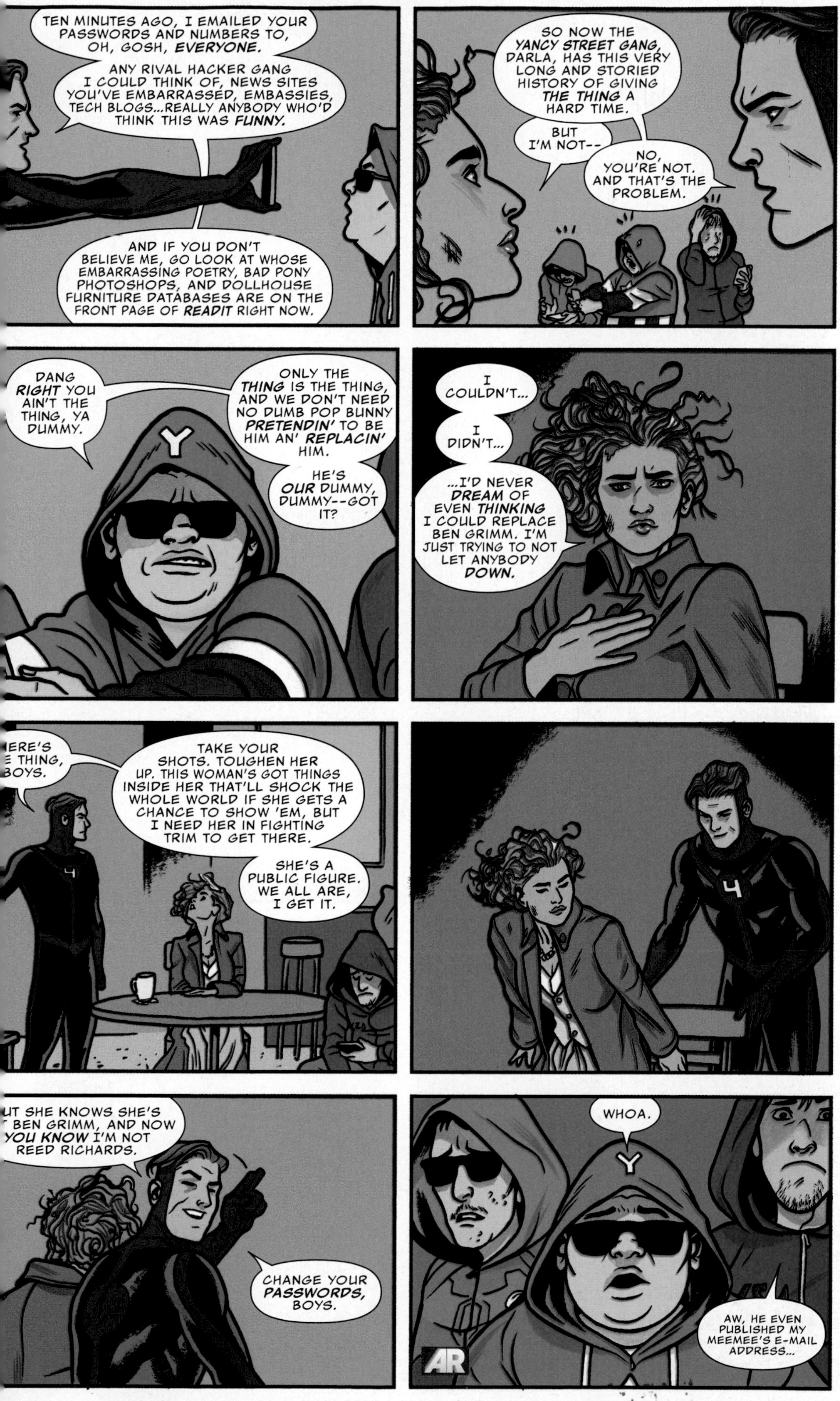
TEN MINUTES AGO, I EMAILED YOUR PASSWORDS AND NUMBERS TO, OH, GOSH, EVERYONE.
ANY RIVAL HACKER GANG I COULD THINK OF, NEWS SITES YOU'VE EMBARRASSED, EMBASSIES, TECH BLOGS...REALLY ANYBODY WHO'D THINK THIS WAS FUNNY.
AND IF YOU DON'T BELIEVE ME, GO LOOK AT WHOSE EMBARRASSING POETRY, BAD PONY PHOTOSHOPS, AND DOLLHOUSE FURNITURE DATABASES ARE ON THE FRONT PAGE OF READIT RIGHT NOW.
SO NOW THE YANCY STREET GANG, DARLA, HAS THIS VERY LONG AND STORIED HISTORY OF GIVING THE THING A HARD TIME.
BUT I'M NOT--
NO, YOU'RE NOT. AND THAT'S THE PROBLEM.
DANG RIGHT YOU AIN'T THE THING, YA DUMMY.
ONLY THE THING IS THE THING, AND WE DON'T NEED NO DUMB POP BUNNY PRETENDIN' TO BE HIM AN' REPLACIN' HIM.
HE'S OUR DUMMY, DUMMY--GOT IT?
I COULDN'T...
I DIDN'T...
...I'D NEVER DREAM OF EVEN THINKING I COULD REPLACE BEN GRIMM. I'M JUST TRYING TO NOT LET ANYBODY DOWN.
ERE'S THING, OYS.
TAKE YOUR SHOTS. TOUGHEN HER UP. THIS WOMAN'S GOT THINGS INSIDE HER THAT'LL SHOCK THE WHOLE WORLD IF SHE GETS A CHANCE TO SHOW 'EM, BUT I NEED HER IN FIGHTING TRIM TO GET THERE.
SHE'S A PUBLIC FIGURE. WE ALL ARE, I GET IT.
UT SHE KNOWS SHE'S BEN GRIMM, AND NOW YOU KNOW I'M NOT REED RICHARDS.
CHANGE YOUR PASSWORDS, BOYS.
WHOA.
AW, HE EVEN PUBLISHED MY MEEMEE'S E-MAIL ADDRESS...

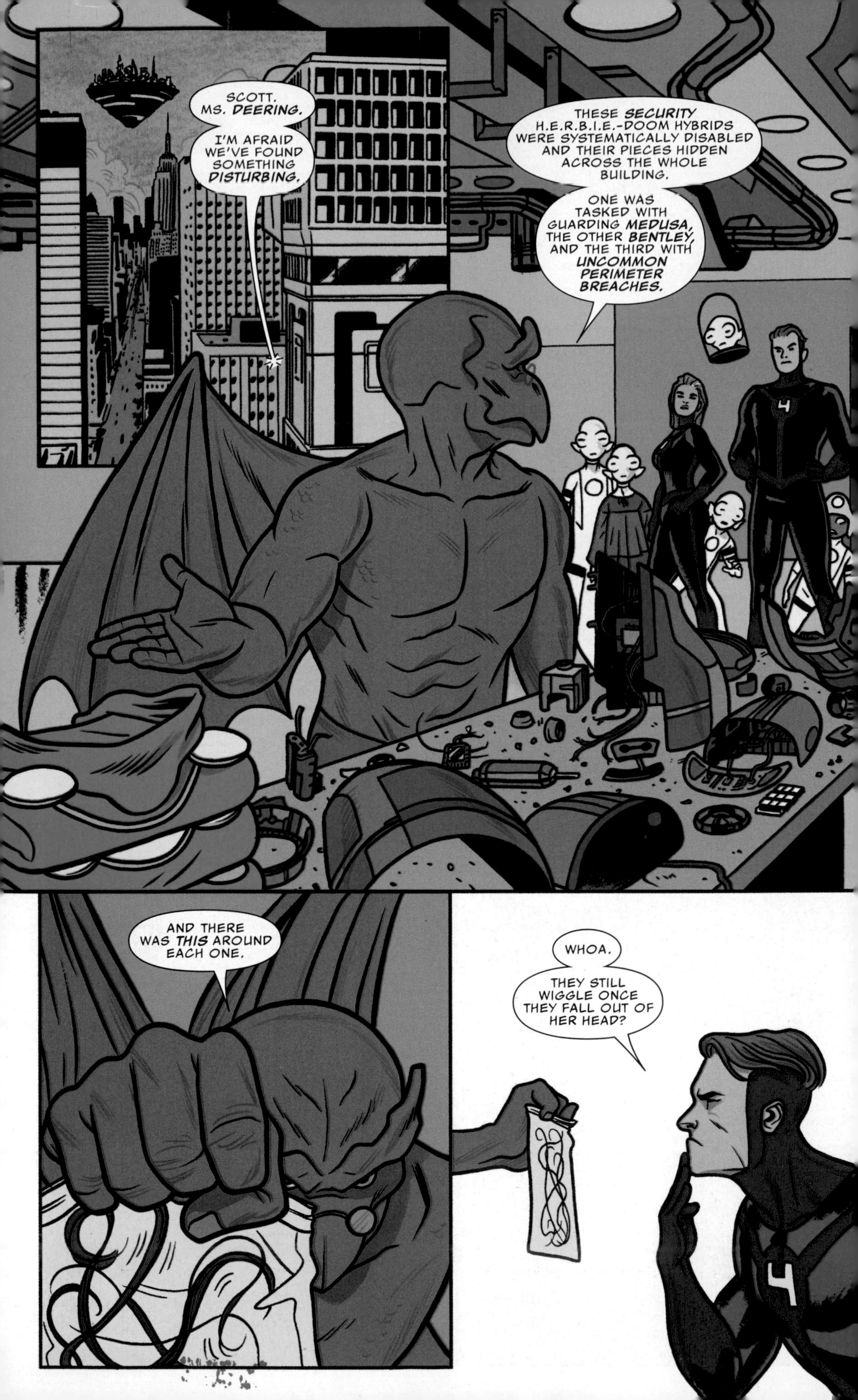
SCOTT. MS. DEERING.
I'M AFRAID WE'VE FOUND SOMETHING DISTURBING.
THESE SECURITY H.E.R.B.I.E.-DOOM HYBRIDS WERE SYSTEMATICALLY DISABLED AND THEIR PIECES HIDDEN ACROSS THE WHOLE BUILDING.
ONE WAS TASKED WITH GUARDING MEDUSA, THE OTHER BENTLEY, AND THE THIRD WITH UNCOMMON PERIMETER BREACHES.
AND THERE WAS THIS AROUND EACH ONE.
WHOA.
THEY STILL WIGGLE ONCE THEY FALL OUT OF HER HEAD?

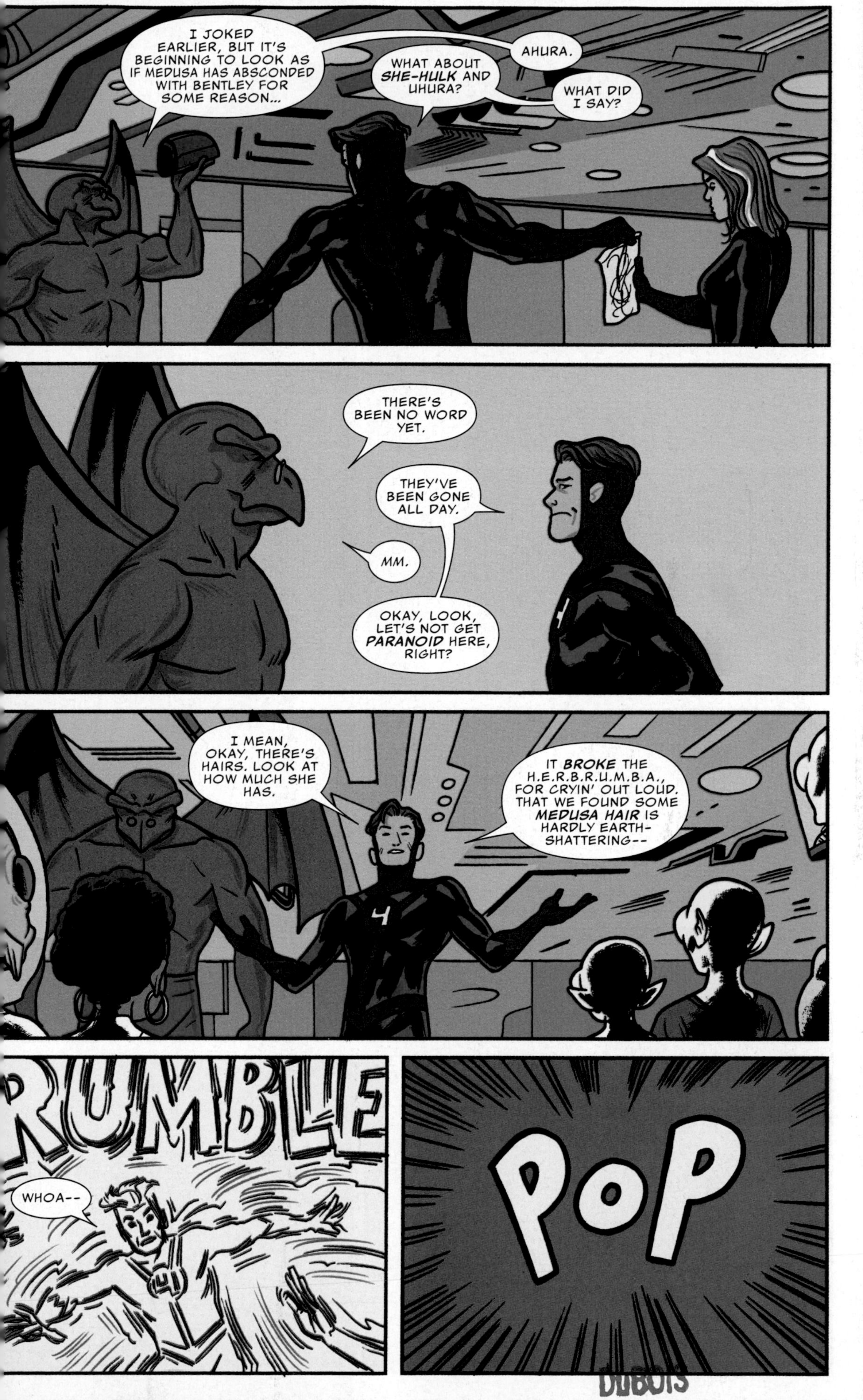
I JOKED EARLIER, BUT IT'S BEGINNING TO LOOK AS IF MEDUSA HAS ABSCONDED WITH BENTLEY FOR SOME REASON...
WHAT ABOUT SHE-HULK AND UHURA?
AHURA.
WHAT DID I SAY?
THERE'S BEEN NO WORD YET.
THEY'VE BEEN GONE ALL DAY.
MM.
OKAY, LOOK, LET'S NOT GET PARANOID HERE, RIGHT?
I MEAN, OKAY, THERE'S HAIRS. LOOK AT HOW MUCH SHE HAS.
IT BROKE THE H.E.R.B.R.U.M.B.A., FOR CRYIN' OUT LOUD. THAT WE FOUND SOME MEDUSA HAIR IS HARDLY EARTH-SHATTERING--
RUMBLE
WHOA--
POP

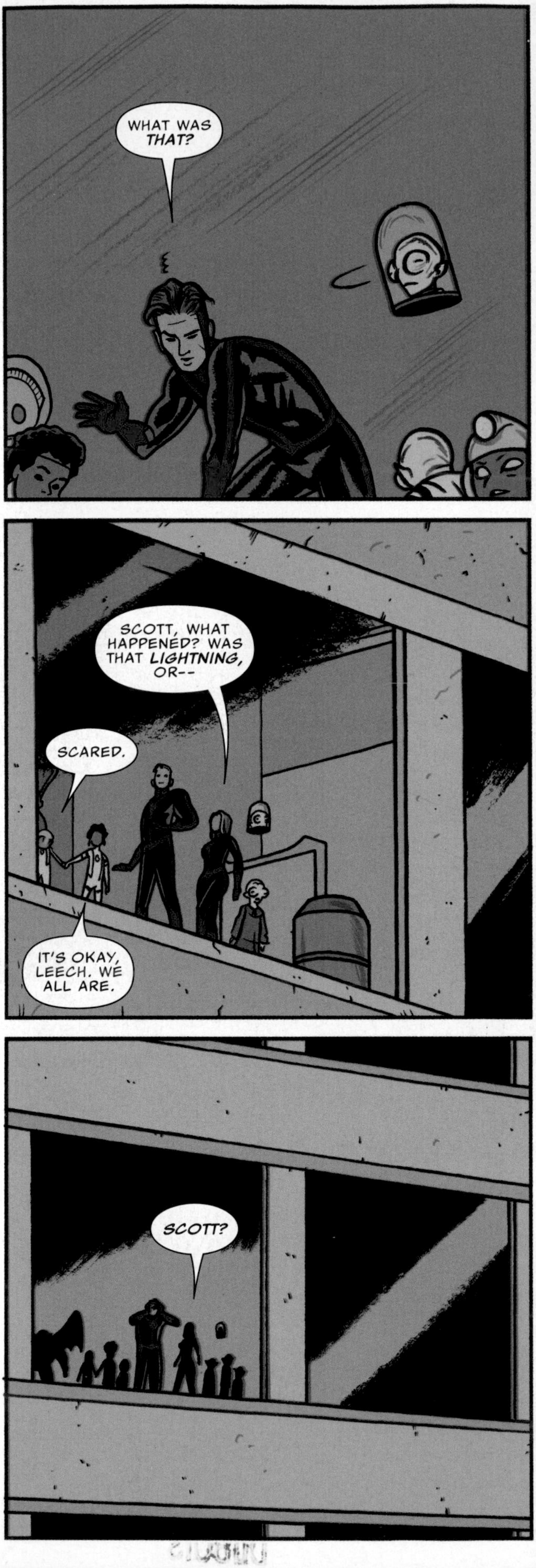
WHAT WAS THAT?
SCOTT, WHAT HAPPENED? WAS THAT LIGHTNING, OR--
SCARED.
IT'S OKAY, LEECH. WE ALL ARE.
SCOTT?

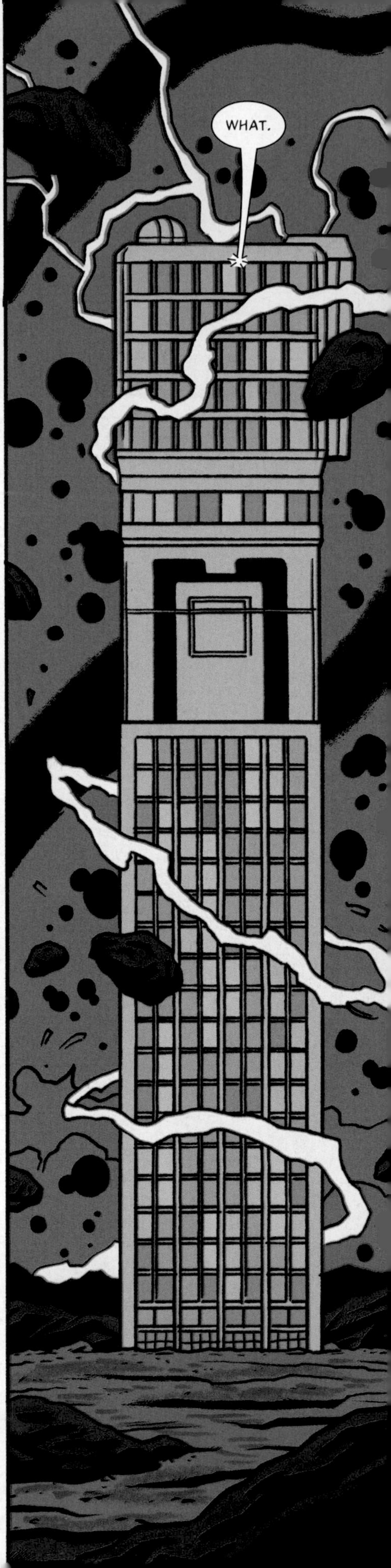
WHAT.

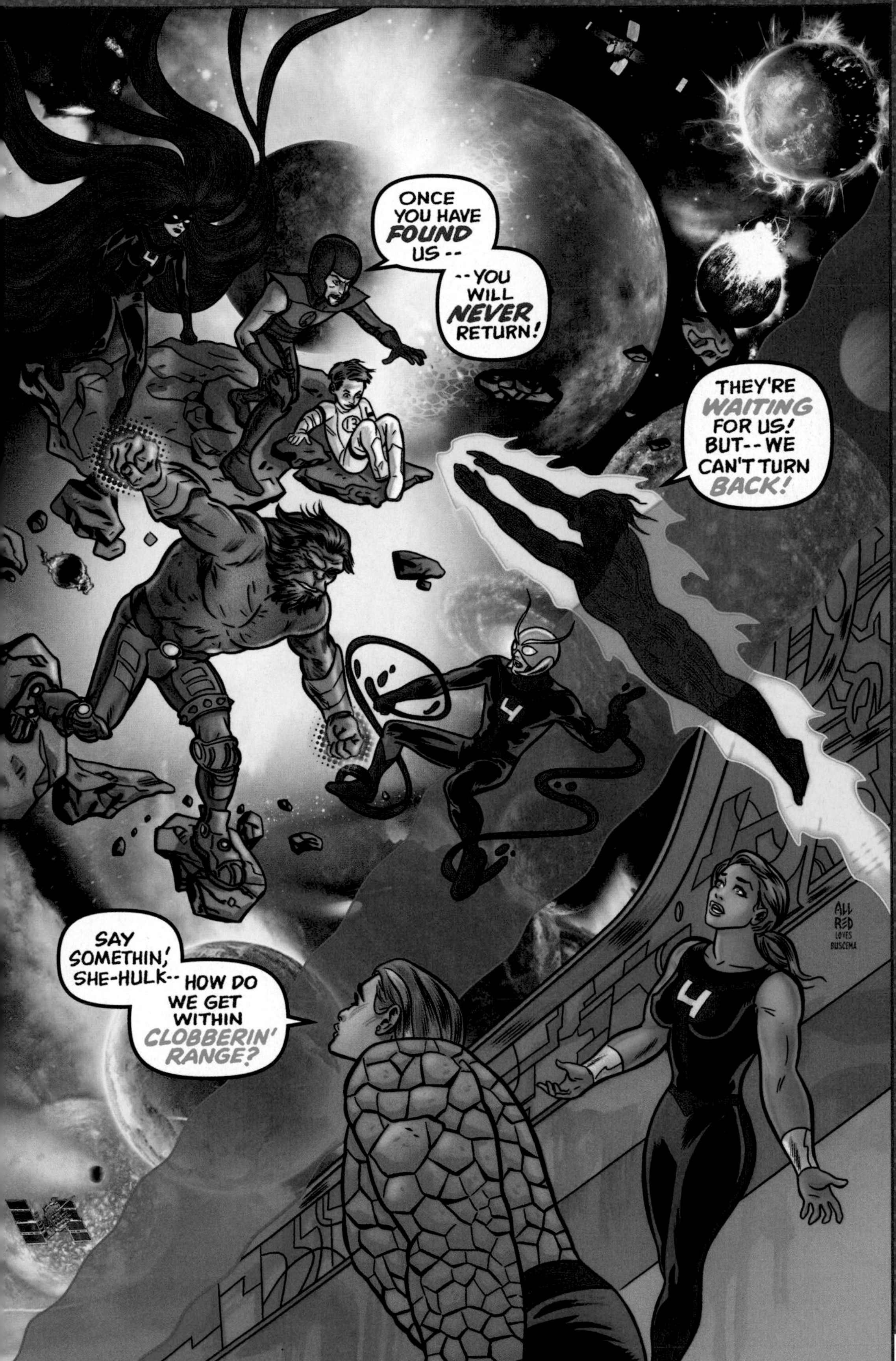
ONCE YOU HAVE FOUND US --
--YOU WILL NEVER RETURN!
THEY'RE WAITING FOR US! BUT-- WE CAN'T TURN BACK!
ALLRED LOVES BUSCEMA
SAY SOMETHIN', SHE-HULK--
HOW DO WE GET WITHIN CLOBBERIN' RANGE?

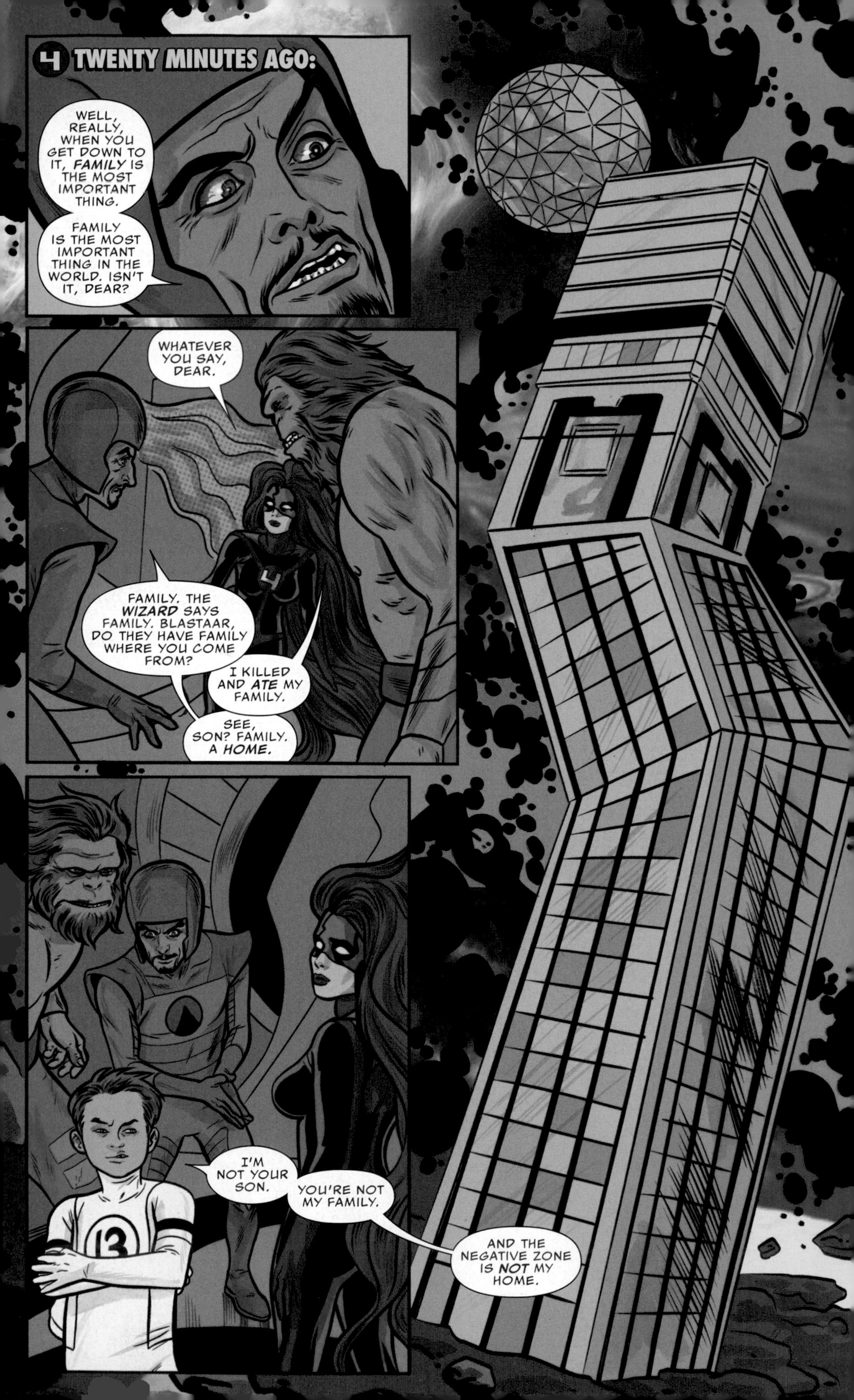
TWENTY MINUTES AGO:
WELL, REALLY, WHEN YOU GET DOWN TO IT, FAMILY IS THE MOST IMPORTANT THING.
FAMILY IS THE MOST IMPORTANT THING IN THE WORLD. ISN'T IT, DEAR?
WHATEVER YOU SAY, DEAR.
FAMILY. THE WIZARD SAYS FAMILY. BLASTAAR, DO THEY HAVE FAMILY WHERE YOU COME FROM?
I KILLED AND ATE MY FAMILY.
SEE, SON? FAMILY. A HOME.
I'M NOT YOUR SON.
YOU'RE NOT MY FAMILY.
AND THE NEGATIVE ZONE IS NOT MY HOME.

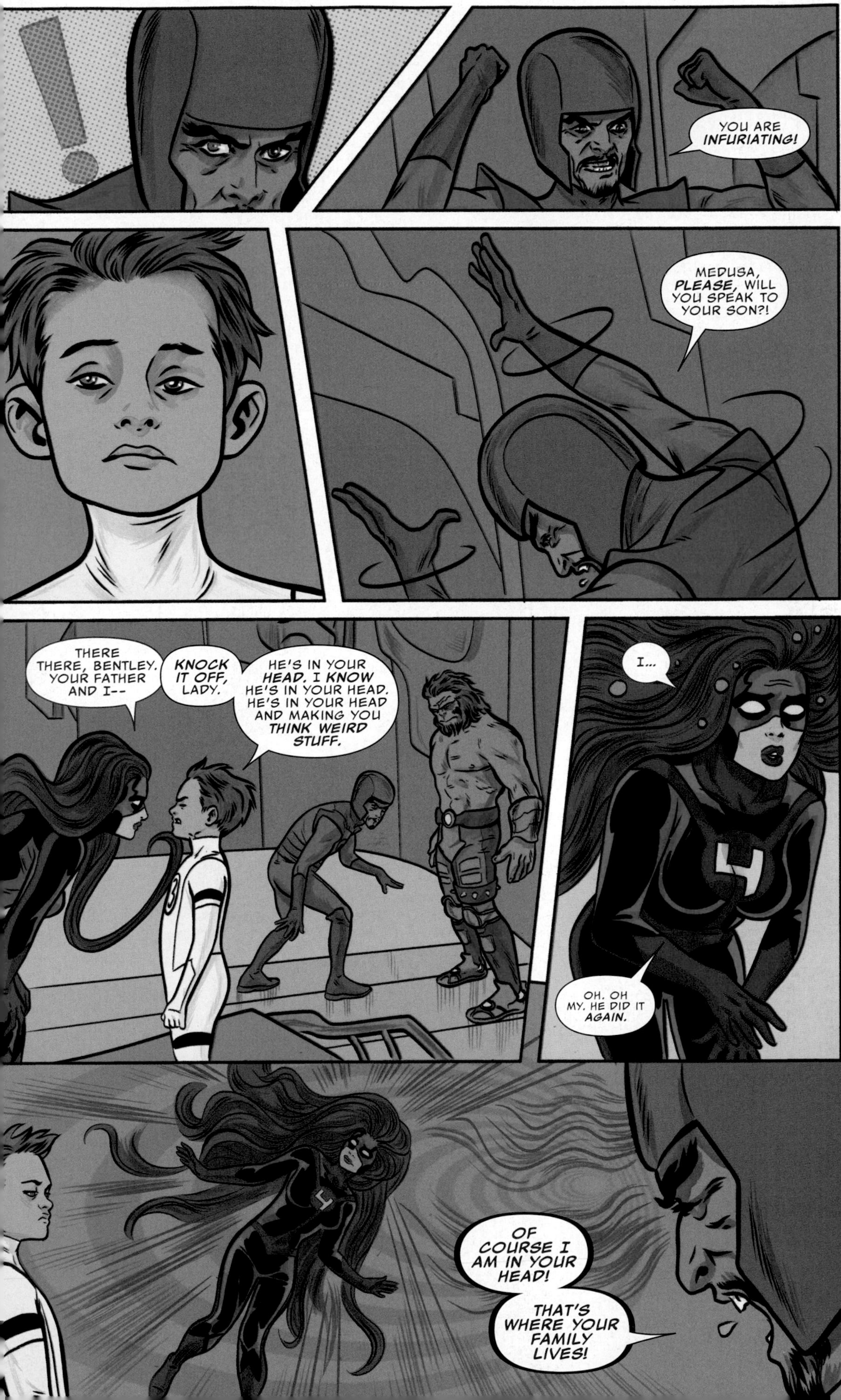

!
YOU ARE INFURIATING!
MEDUSA, PLEASE, WILL YOU SPEAK TO YOUR SON?!
THERE THERE, BENTLEY. YOUR FATHER AND I--
KNOCK IT OFF, LADY.
HE'S IN YOUR HEAD. I KNOW HE'S IN YOUR HEAD. HE'S IN YOUR HEAD AND MAKING YOU THINK WEIRD STUFF.
I...
OH. OH MY. HE DID IT AGAIN.
OF COURSE I AM IN YOUR HEAD!
THAT'S WHERE YOUR FAMILY LIVES!

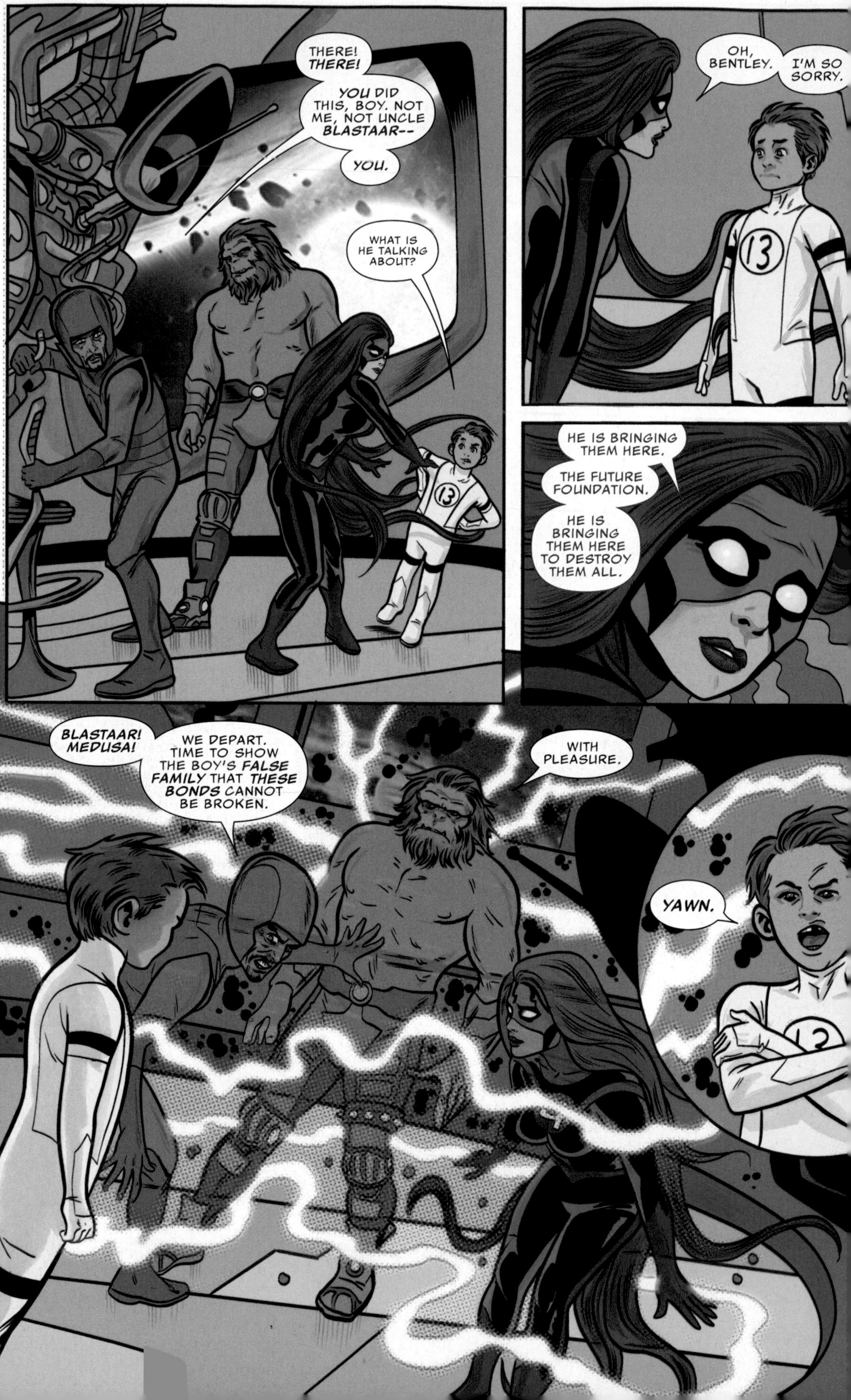
THERE! THERE!
YOU DID THIS, BOY. NOT ME, NOT UNCLE BLASTAAR--
YOU.
WHAT IS HE TALKING ABOUT?
OH, BENTLEY.
I'M SO SORRY.
HE IS BRINGING THEM HERE.
THE FUTURE FOUNDATION.
HE IS BRINGING THEM HERE TO DESTROY THEM ALL.
BLASTAAR! MEDUSA!
WE DEPART. TIME TO SHOW THE BOY'S FALSE FAMILY THAT THESE BONDS CANNOT BE BROKEN.
WITH PLEASURE.
YAWN.

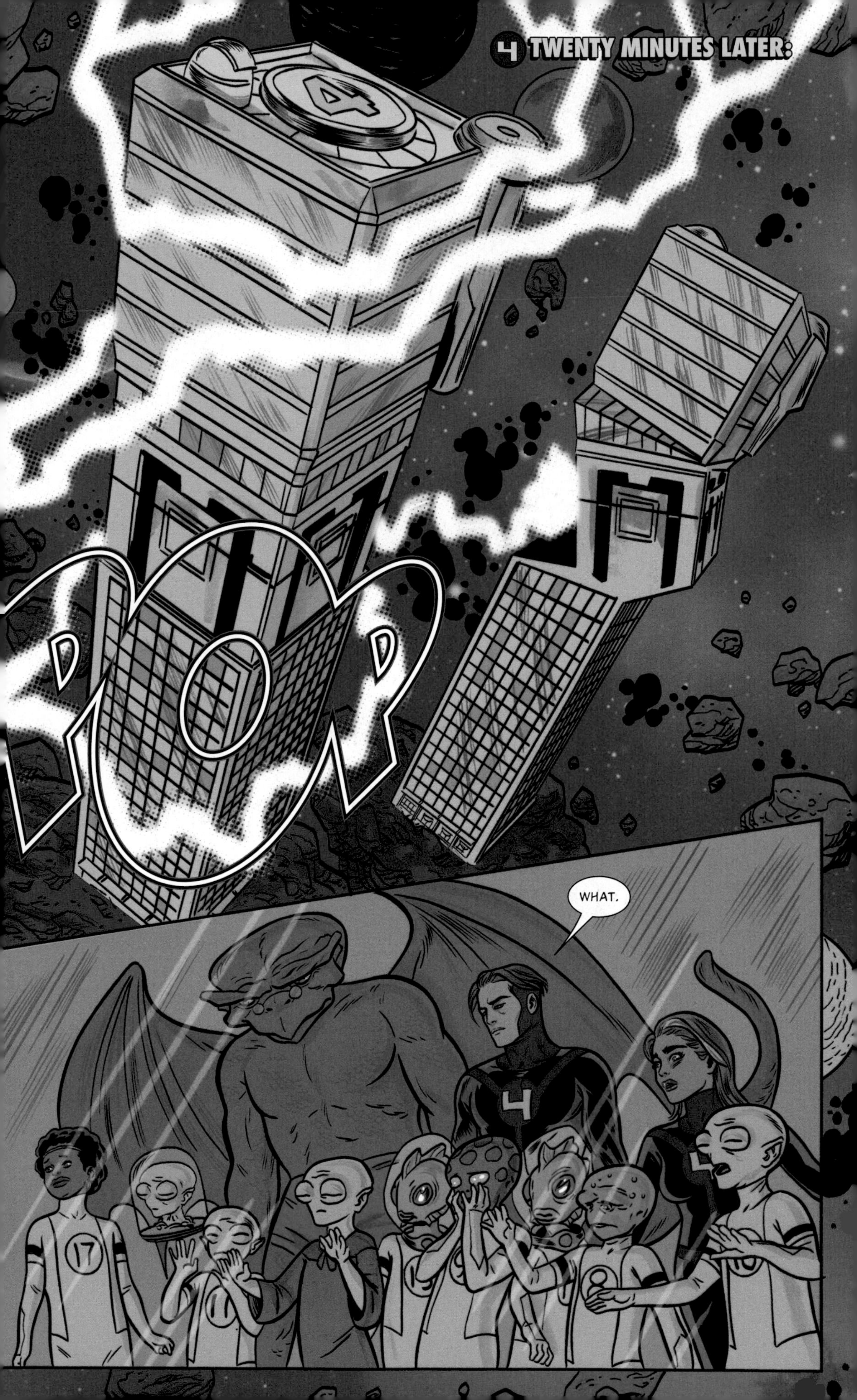
4 TWENTY MINUTES LATER:
POP
WHAT.

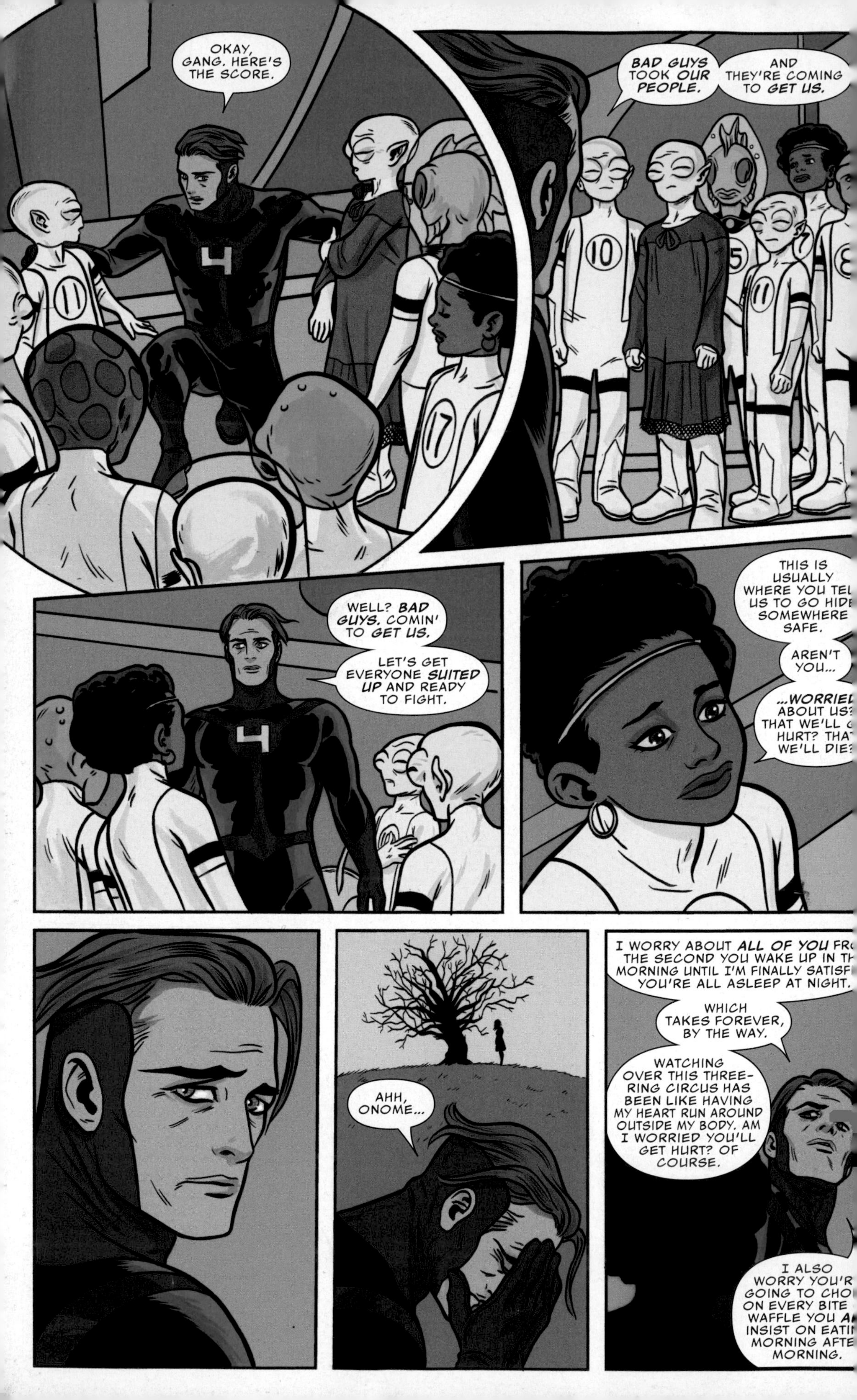
OKAY, GANG. HERE'S THE SCORE.
BAD GUYS TOOK OUR PEOPLE.
AND THEY'RE COMING TO GET US.
WELL? BAD GUYS. COMIN' TO GET US.
LET'S GET EVERYONE SUITED UP AND READY TO FIGHT.
THIS IS USUALLY WHERE YOU TEL US TO GO HIDE SOMEWHERE SAFE.
AREN'T YOU...
...WORRIEI ABOUT US? THAT WE'LL HURT? THAT WE'LL DIE?
AHH, ONOME...
I WORRY ABOUT ALL OF YOU FR THE SECOND YOU WAKE UP IN TH MORNING UNTIL I'M FINALLY SATISF YOU'RE ALL ASLEEP AT NIGHT.
WHICH TAKES FOREVER, BY THE WAY.
WATCHING OVER THIS THREE-RING CIRCUS HAS BEEN LIKE HAVING MY HEART RUN AROUND OUTSIDE MY BODY. AM I WORRIED YOU'LL GET HURT? OF COURSE.
I ALSO WORRY YOU'R GOING TO CHO ON EVERY BITE WAFFLE YOU A INSIST ON EATI MORNING AFTE MORNING.

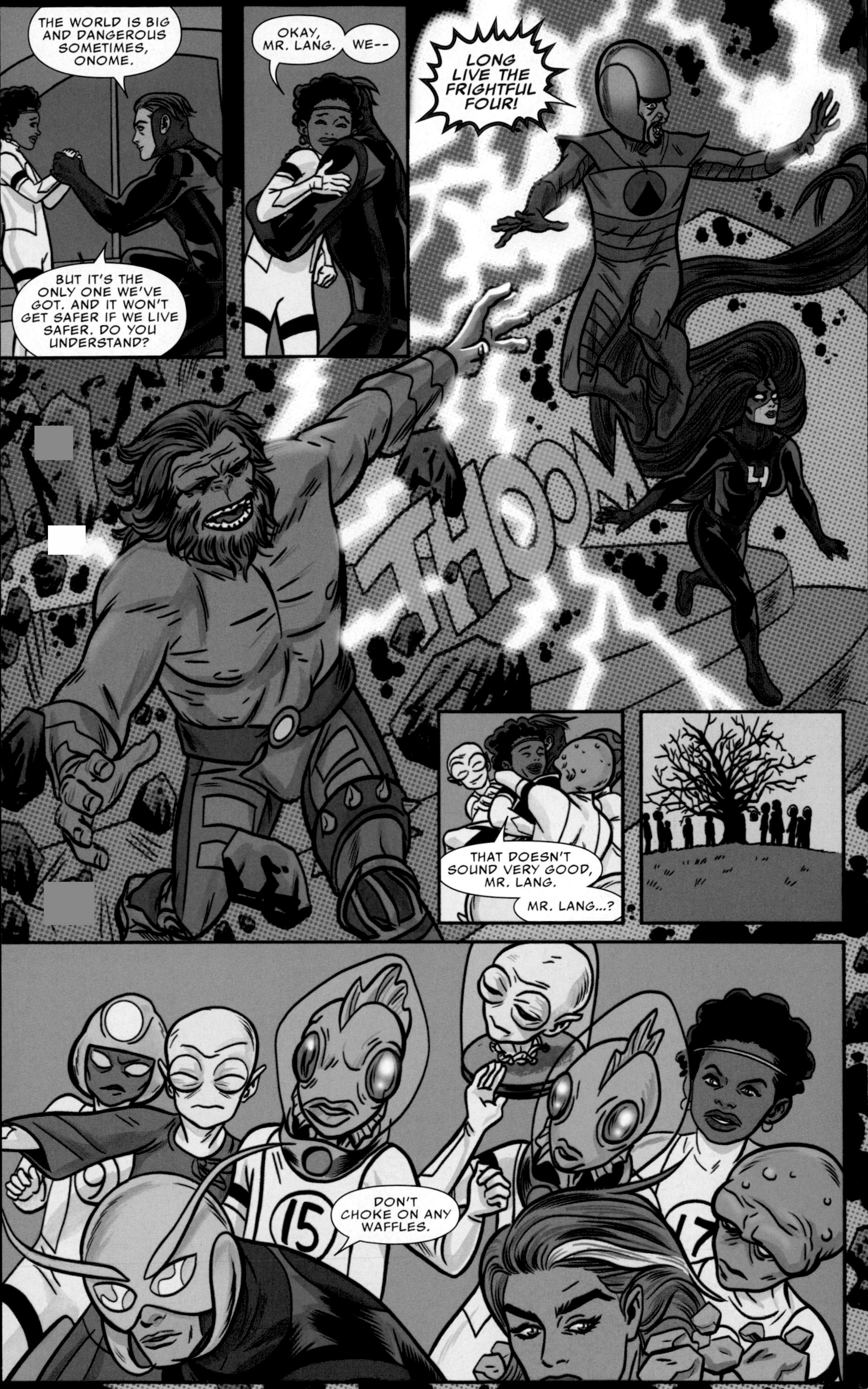
THE WORLD IS BIG AND DANGEROUS SOMETIMES, ONOME.
BUT IT'S THE ONLY ONE WE'VE GOT. AND IT WON'T GET SAFER IF WE LIVE SAFER. DO YOU UNDERSTAND?
OKAY, MR. LANG.
WE--
LONG LIVE THE FRIGHTFUL FOUR!
THOOM
THAT DOESN'T SOUND VERY GOOD, MR. LANG.
MR. LANG...?
DON'T CHOKE ON ANY WAFFLES.

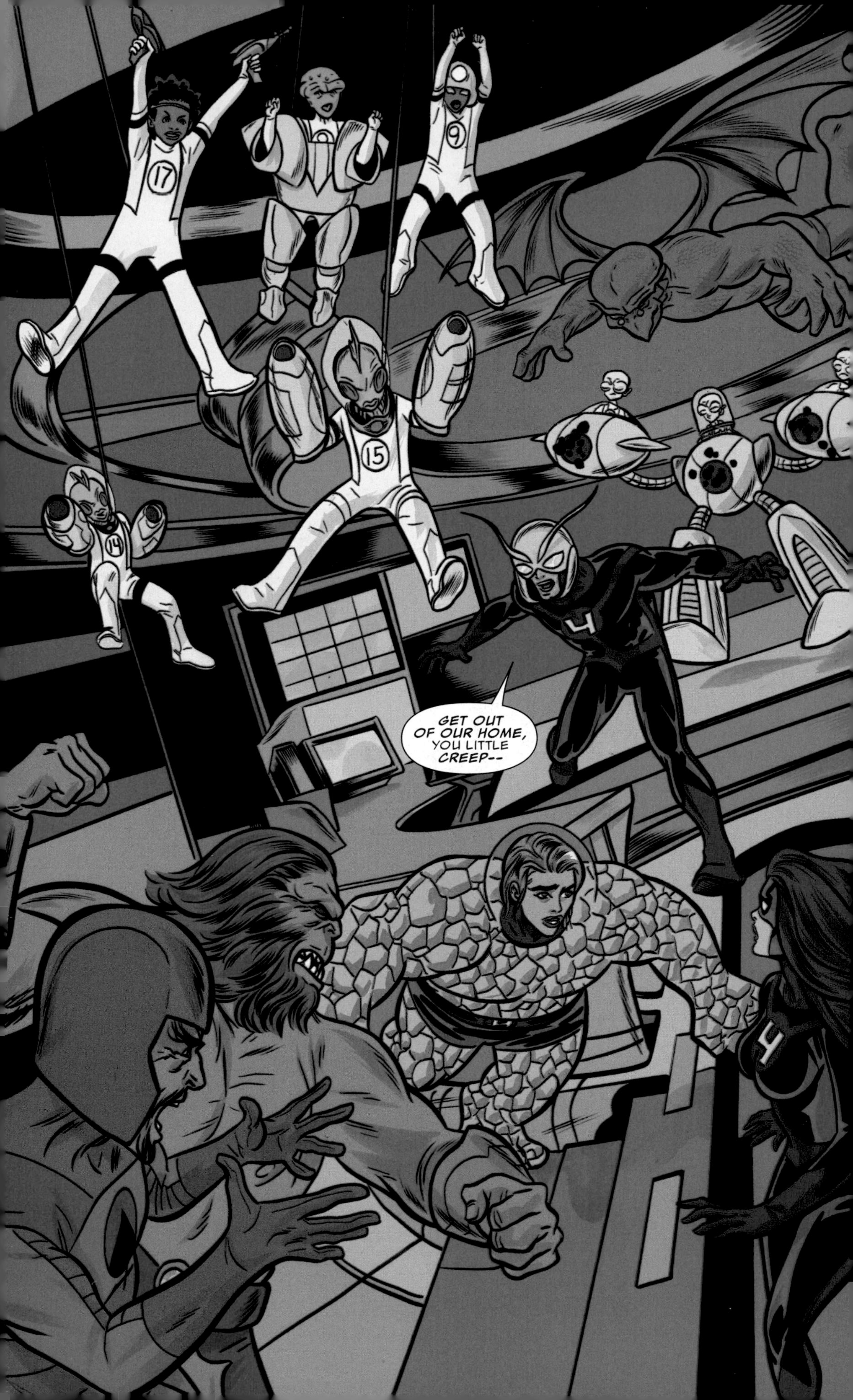
GET OUT OF OUR HOME, YOU LITTLE CREEP--

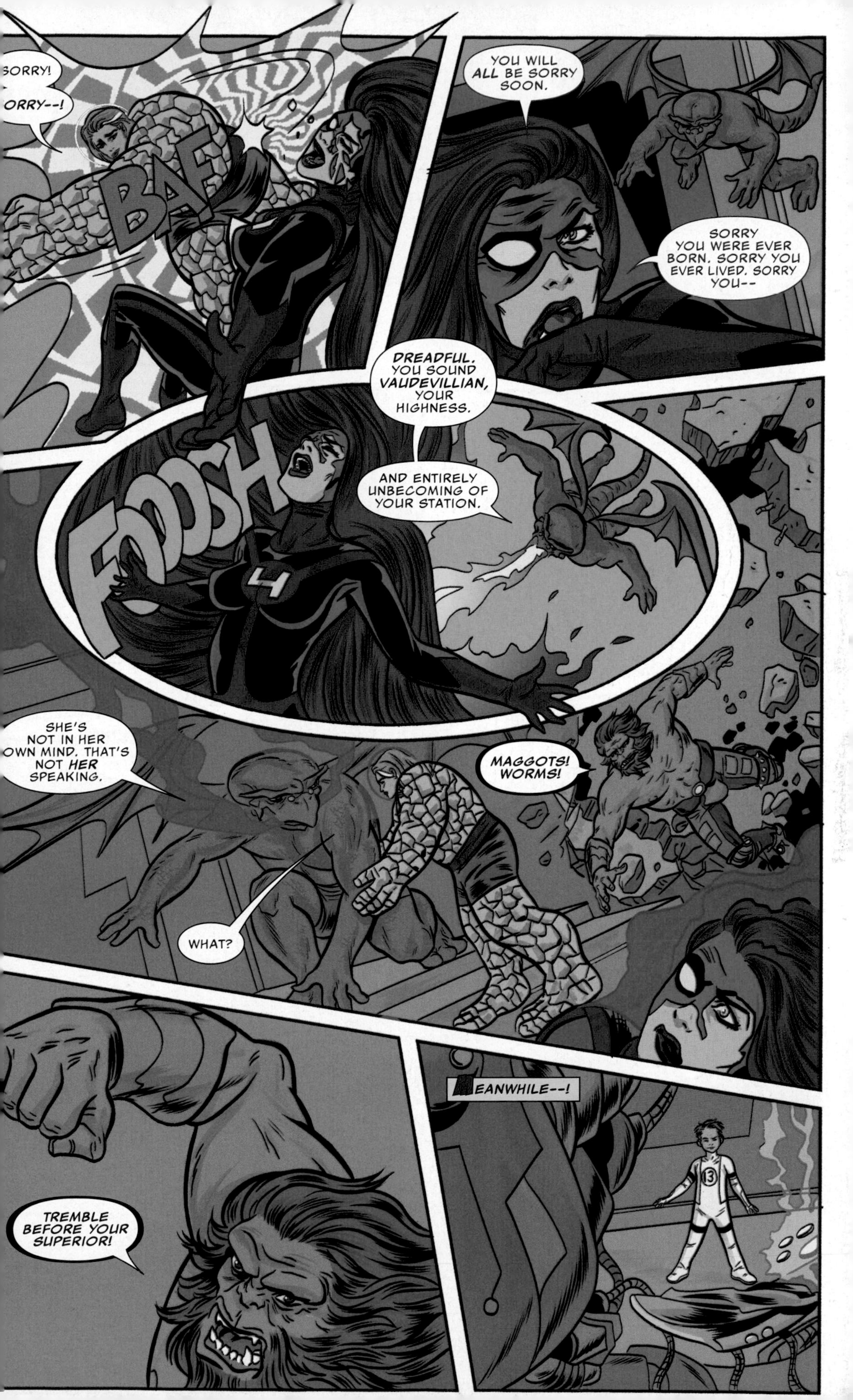
SORRY!
ORRY--!
BAF
YOU WILL ALL BE SORRY SOON.
SORRY YOU WERE EVER BORN. SORRY YOU EVER LIVED. SORRY YOU--
DREADFUL. YOU SOUND VAUDEVILLIAN, YOUR HIGHNESS.
AND ENTIRELY UNBECOMING OF YOUR STATION.
FOOOSH
SHE'S NOT IN HER OWN MIND. THAT'S NOT HER SPEAKING.
MAGGOTS! WORMS!
WHAT?
TREMBLE BEFORE YOUR SUPERIOR!
MEANWHILE--!

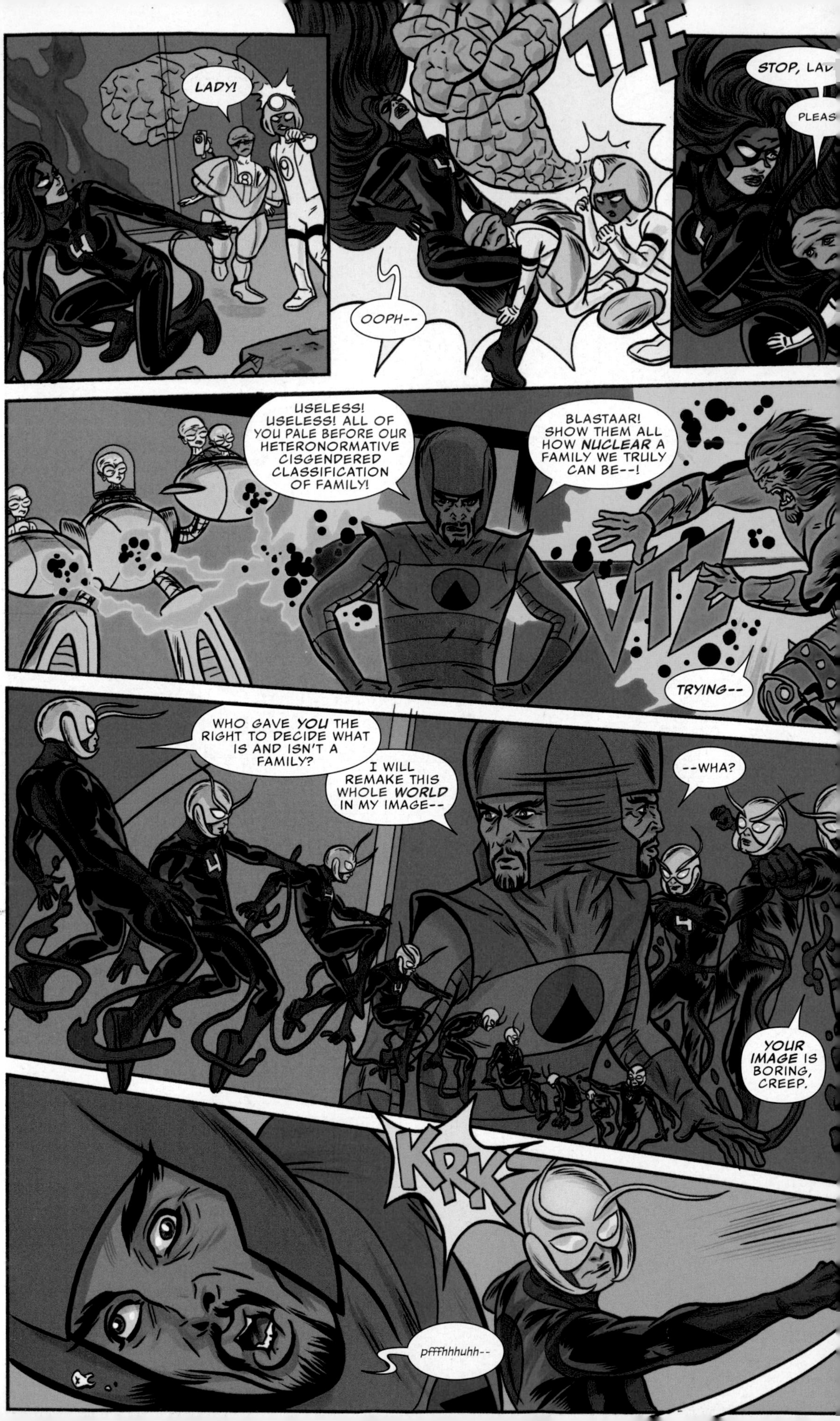
LADY!
TFF
OOPH--
STOP, LAD
PLEAS
USELESS! USELESS! ALL OF YOU PALE BEFORE OUR HETERONORMATIVE CISGENDERED CLASSIFICATION OF FAMILY!
BLASTAAR! SHOW THEM ALL HOW NUCLEAR A FAMILY WE TRULY CAN BE--!
VTZ
TRYING--
WHO GAVE YOU THE RIGHT TO DECIDE WHAT IS AND ISN'T A FAMILY?
I WILL REMAKE THIS WHOLE WORLD IN MY IMAGE--
--WHA?
YOUR IMAGE IS BORING, CREEP.
KRK
pfffhhhuhh--

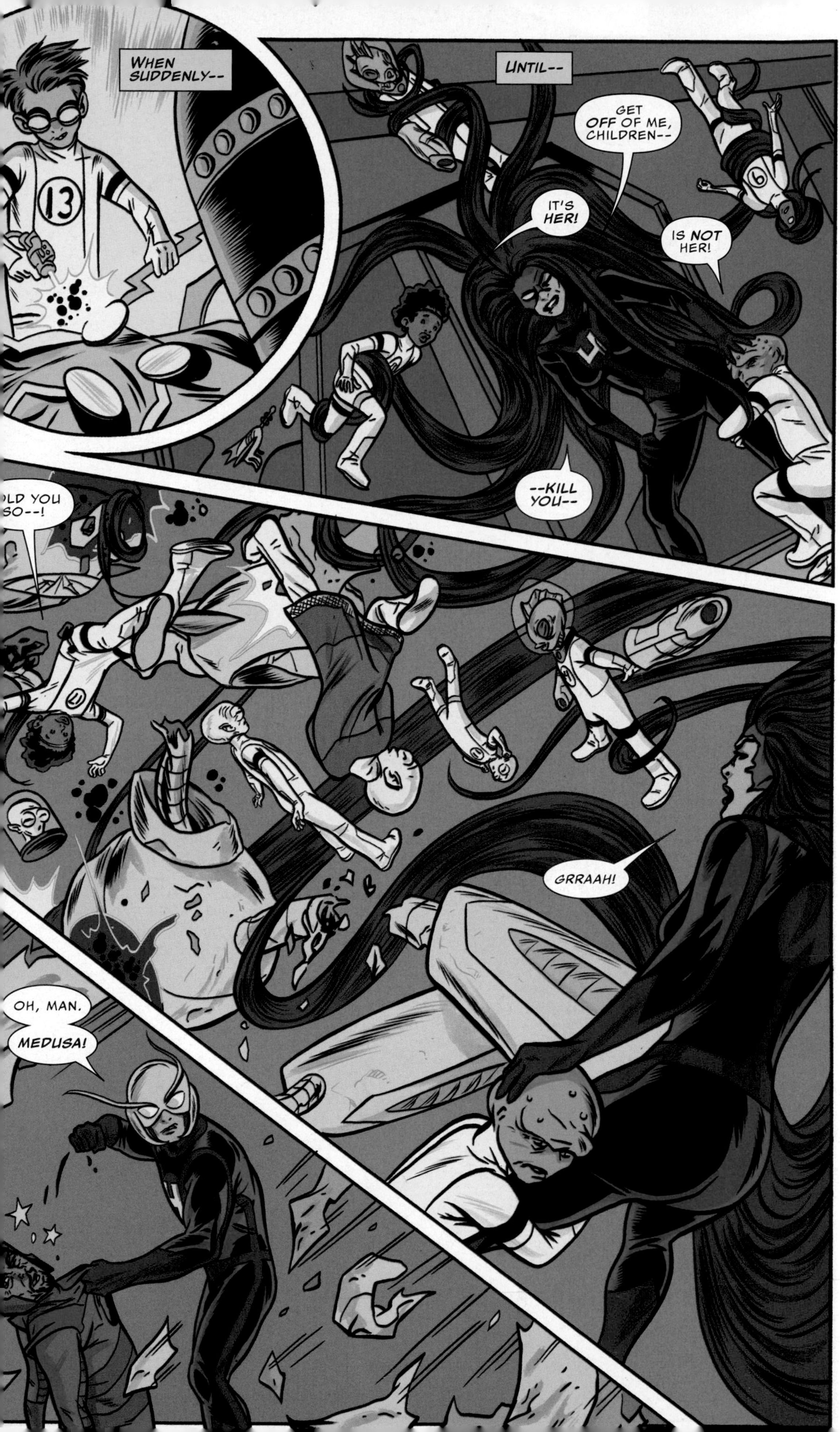

WHEN SUDDENLY--
UNTIL--
GET OFF OF ME, CHILDREN--
IT'S HER!
IS NOT HER!
--KILL YOU--
OLD YOU SO--!
GRRAAH!
OH, MAN.
MEDUSA!

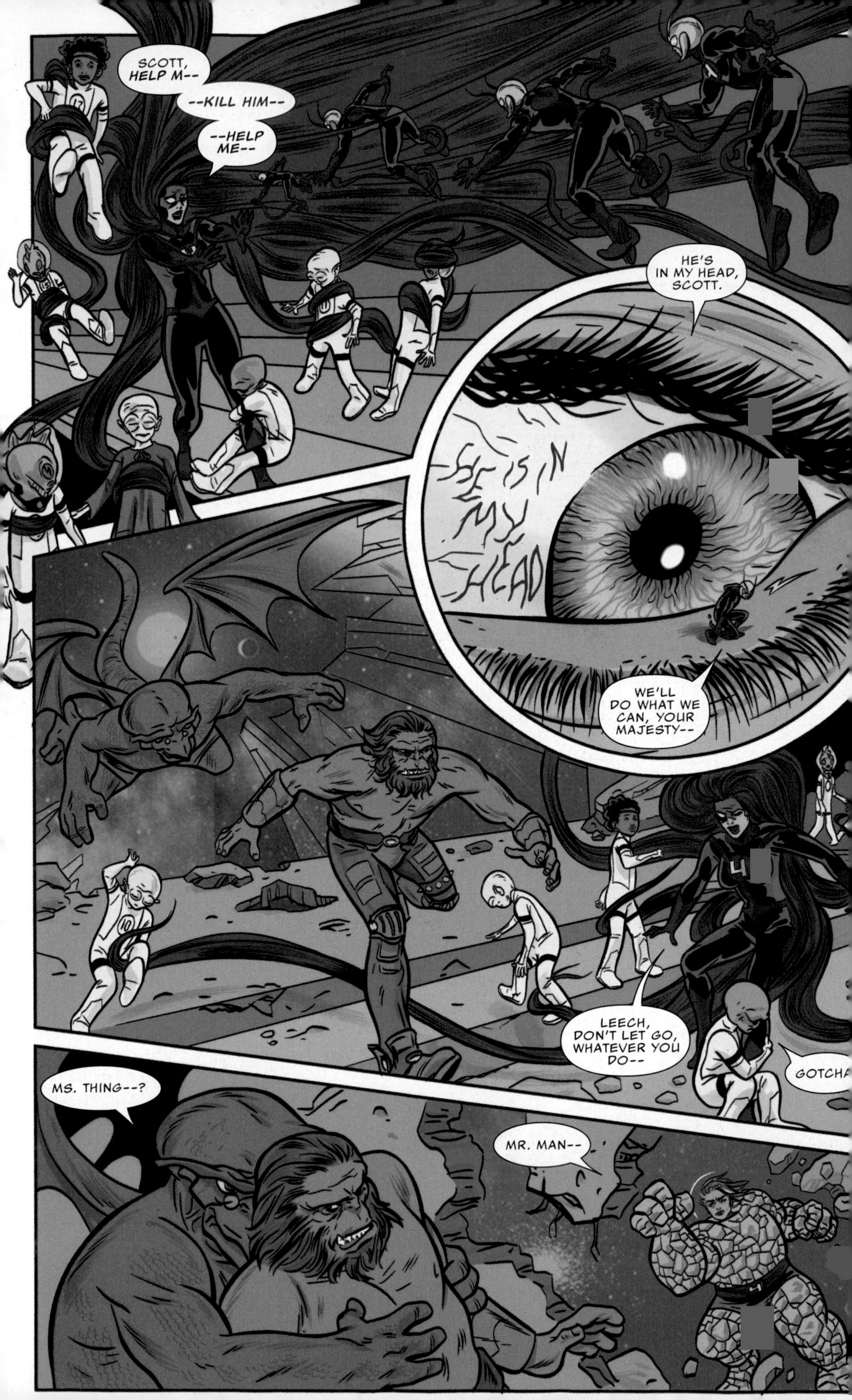
SCOTT, HELP M--
--KILL HIM--
--HELP ME--
HE'S IN MY HEAD, SCOTT.
HE IS IN MY HEAD
WE'LL DO WHAT WE CAN, YOUR MAJESTY--
LEECH, DON'T LET GO, WHATEVER YOU DO--
GOTCHA
MS. THING--?
MR. MAN--

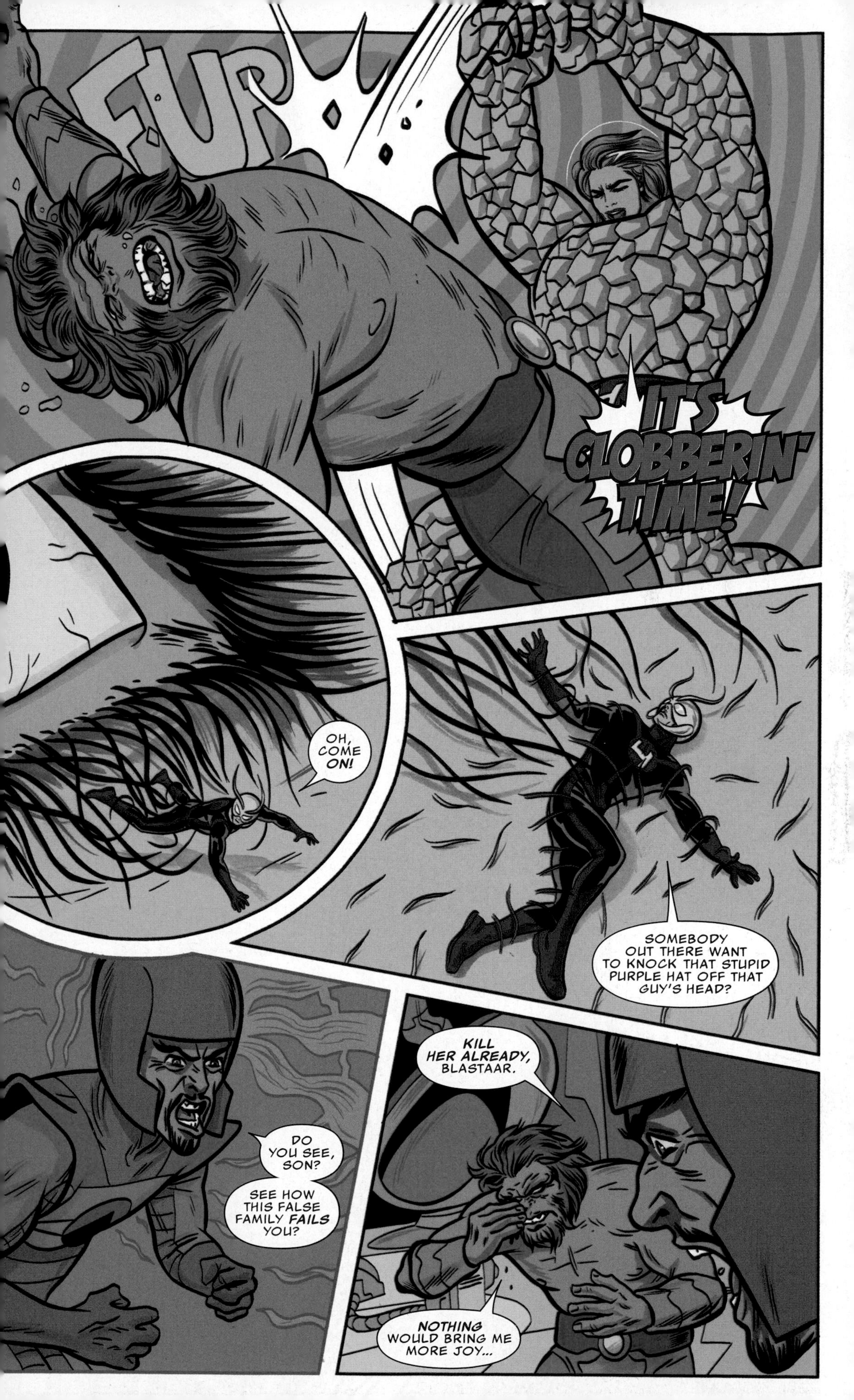
FUP
IT'S CLOBBERIN' TIME!
OH, COME ON!
SOMEBODY OUT THERE WANT TO KNOCK THAT STUPID PURPLE HAT OFF THAT GUY'S HEAD?
DO YOU SEE, SON?
SEE HOW THIS FALSE FAMILY FAILS YOU?
KILL HER ALREADY, BLASTAAR.
NOTHING WOULD BRING ME MORE JOY...

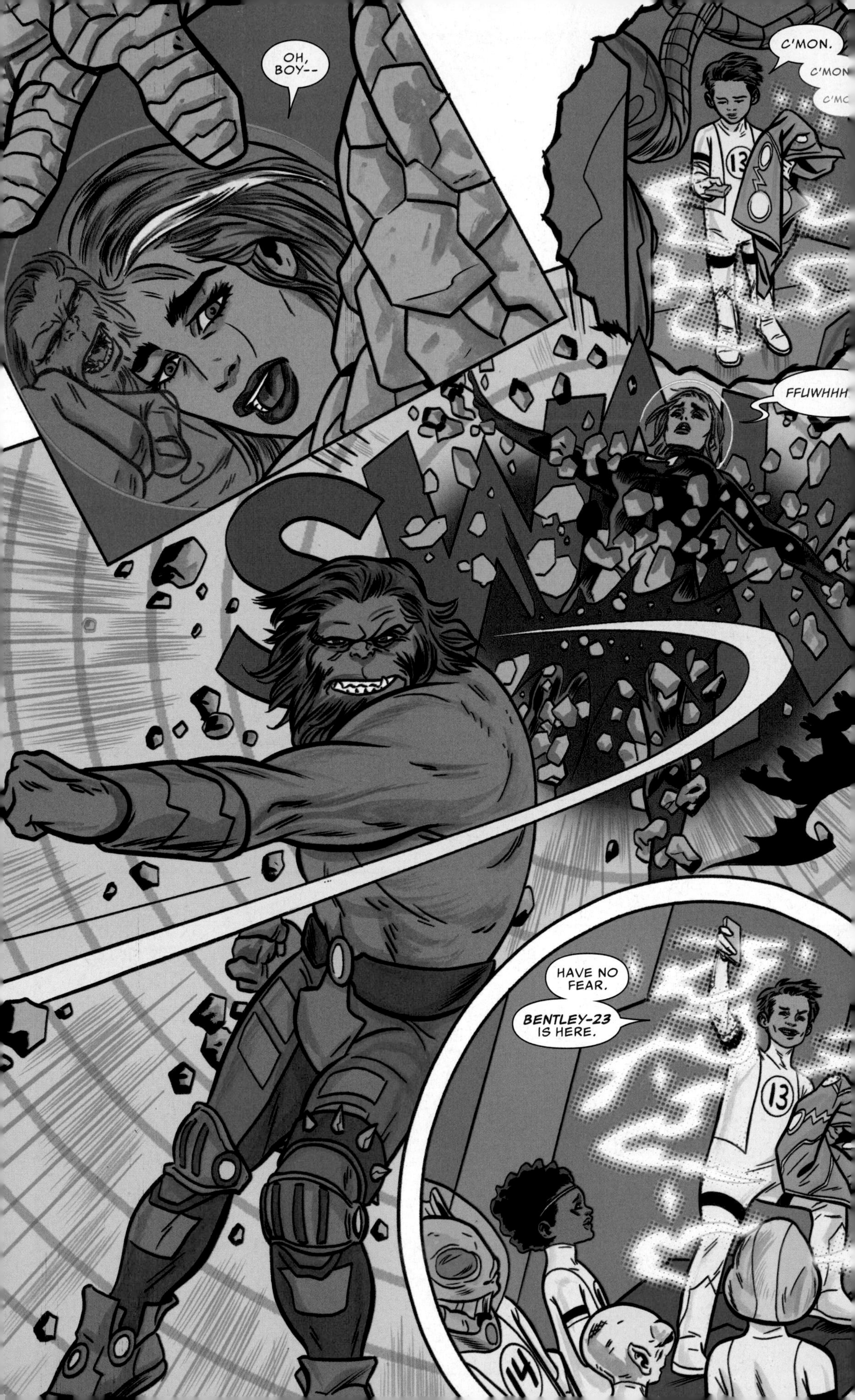
OH, BOY--
C'MON.
C'MON
C'MC
FFUWHHH
HAVE NO FEAR.
BENTLEY-23 IS HERE.

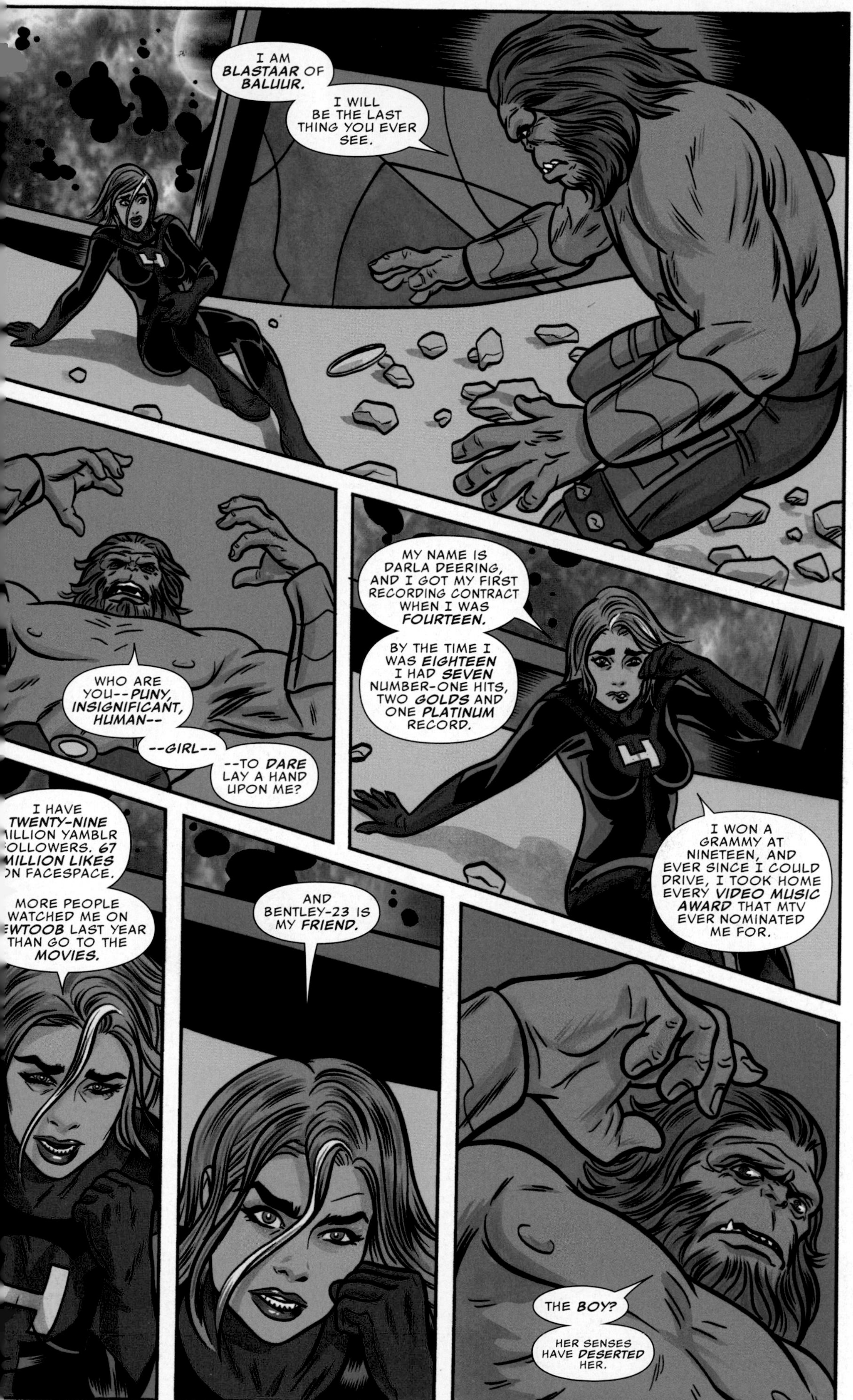
I AM BLASTAAR OF BALUUR.
I WILL BE THE LAST THING YOU EVER SEE.
WHO ARE YOU--PUNY, INSIGNIFICANT, HUMAN--
--GIRL--
--TO DARE LAY A HAND UPON ME?
MY NAME IS DARLA DEERING, AND I GOT MY FIRST RECORDING CONTRACT WHEN I WAS FOURTEEN.
BY THE TIME I WAS EIGHTEEN I HAD SEVEN NUMBER-ONE HITS, TWO GOLDS AND ONE PLATINUM RECORD.
I WON A GRAMMY AT NINETEEN, AND EVER SINCE I COULD DRIVE, I TOOK HOME EVERY VIDEO MUSIC AWARD THAT MTV EVER NOMINATED ME FOR.
I HAVE TWENTY-NINE MILLION YAMBLR FOLLOWERS. 67 MILLION LIKES ON FACESPACE.
MORE PEOPLE WATCHED ME ON EWTOOB LAST YEAR THAN GO TO THE MOVIES.
AND BENTLEY-23 IS MY FRIEND.
THE BOY?
HER SENSES HAVE DESERTED HER.

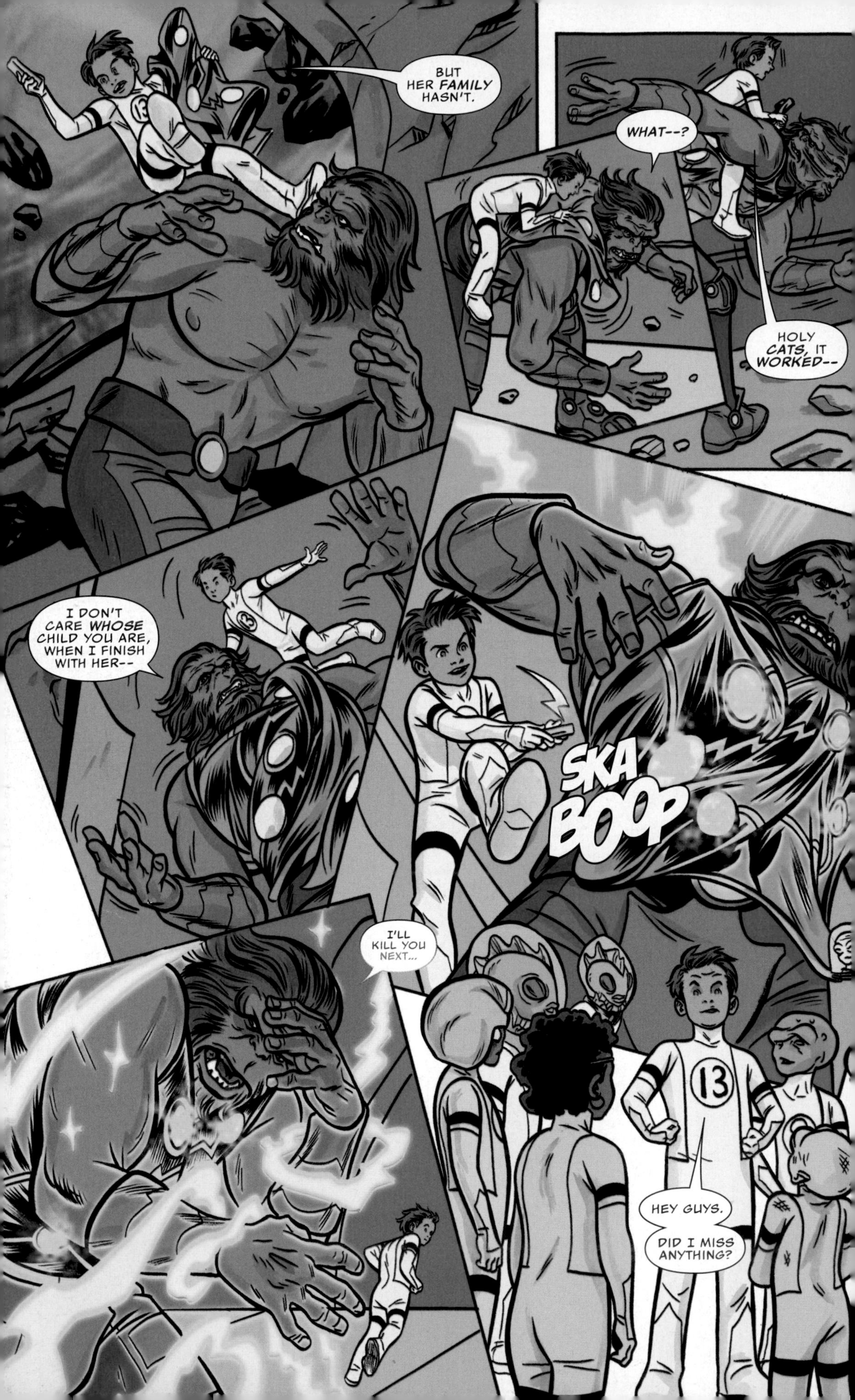
BUT HER FAMILY HASN'T.
WHAT--?
HOLY CATS, IT WORKED--
I DON'T CARE WHOSE CHILD YOU ARE, WHEN I FINISH WITH HER--
SKA BOOP
I'LL KILL YOU NEXT...
HEY GUYS.
DID I MISS ANYTHING?

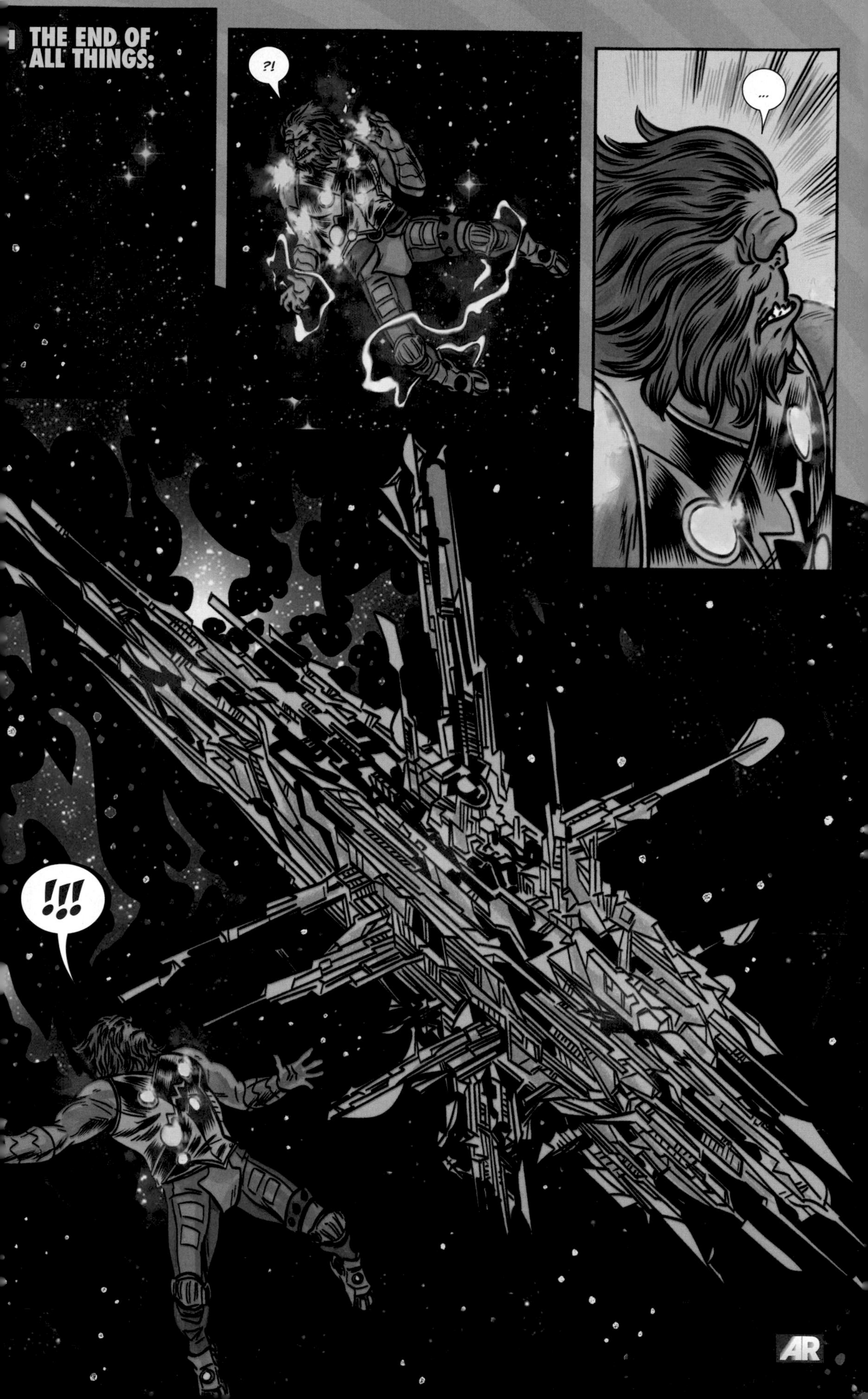
THE END OF ALL THINGS:
?!
...
!!!
AR

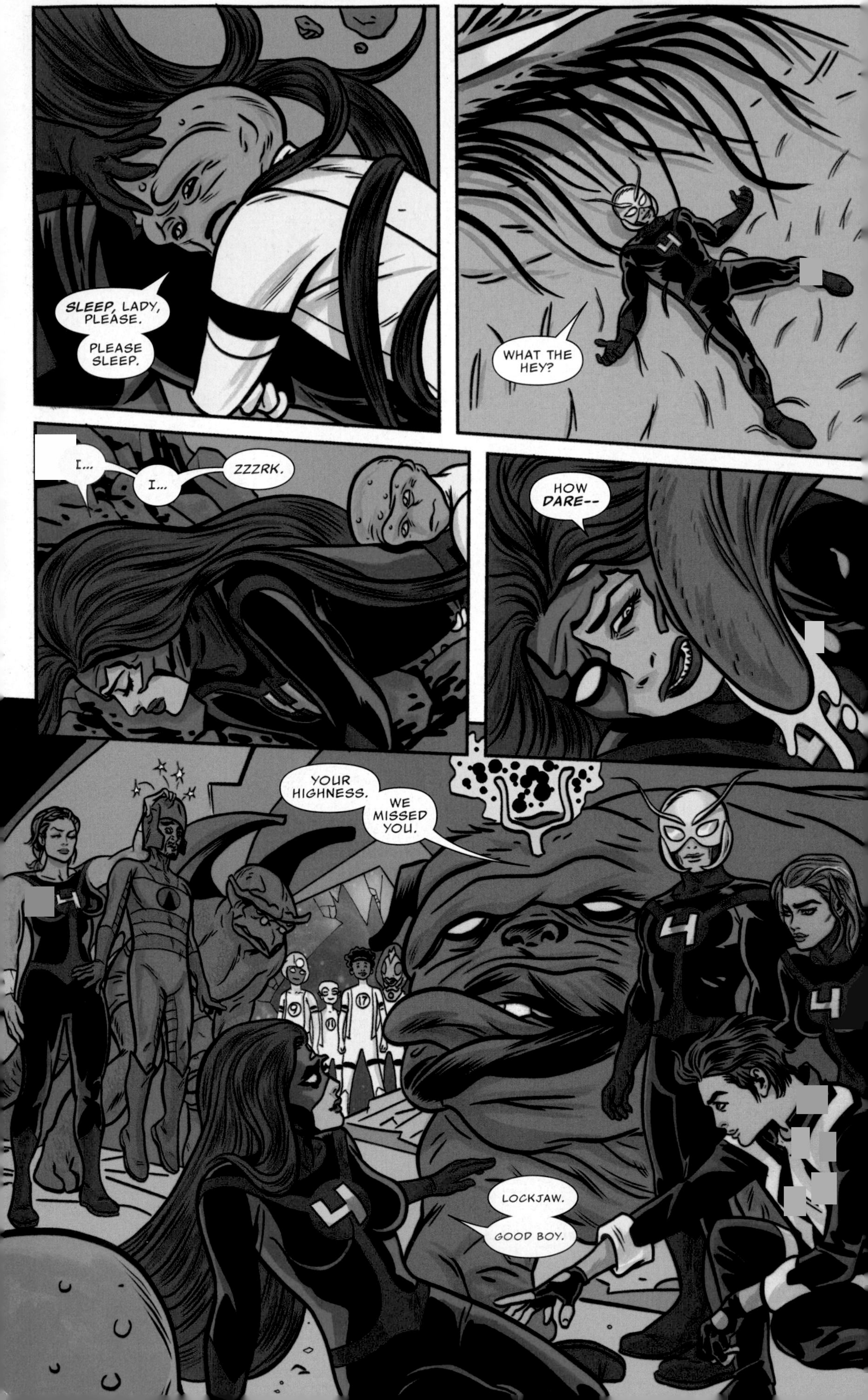
SLEEP, LADY, PLEASE.
PLEASE SLEEP.
WHAT THE HEY?
I...
I...
ZZZRK.
HOW DARE--
YOUR HIGHNESS.
WE MISSED YOU.
LOCKJAW.
GOOD BOY.

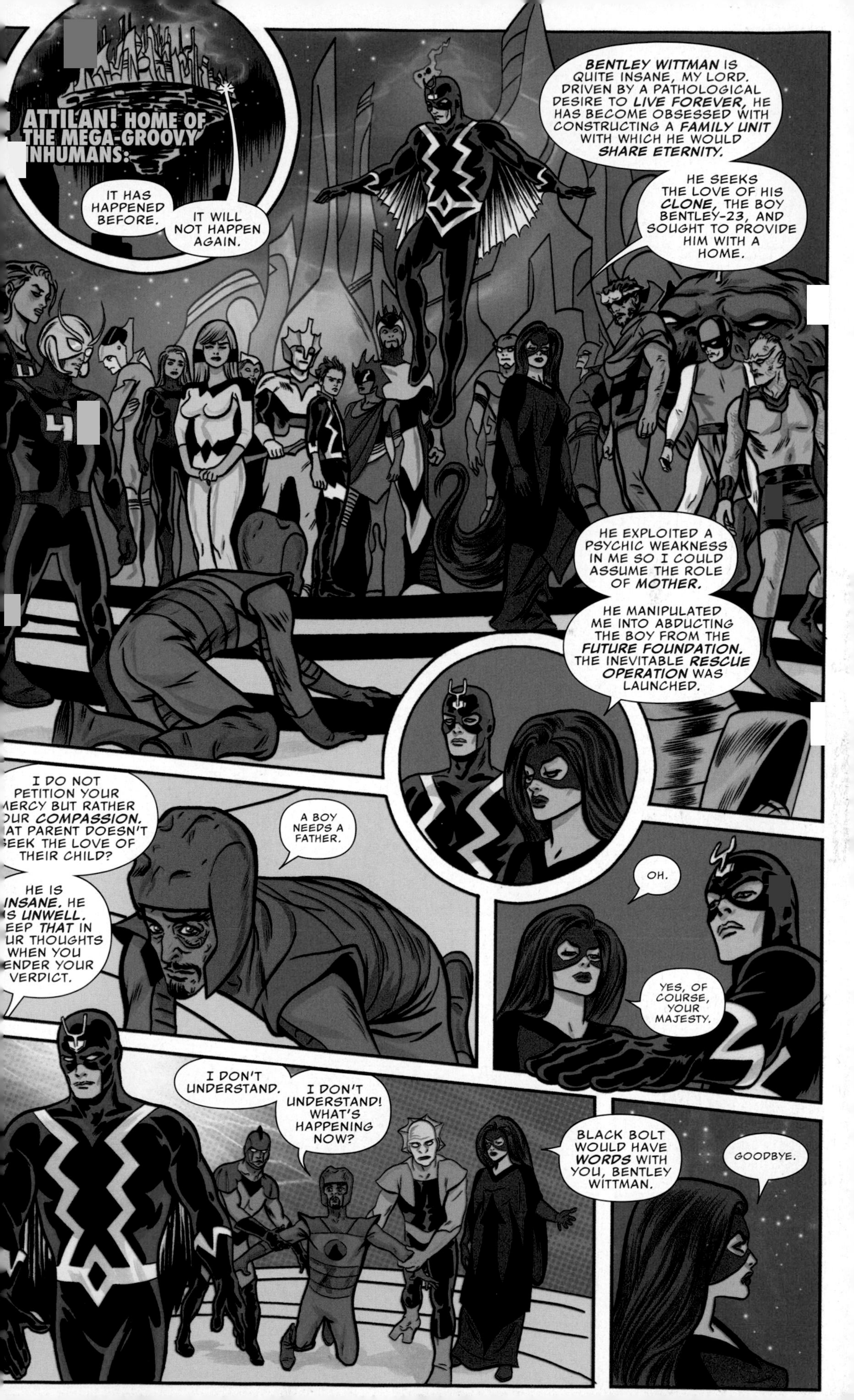
ATTILAN! HOME OF THE MEGA-GROOVY INHUMANS:
IT HAS HAPPENED BEFORE.
IT WILL NOT HAPPEN AGAIN.
BENTLEY WITTMAN IS QUITE INSANE, MY LORD. DRIVEN BY A PATHOLOGICAL DESIRE TO LIVE FOREVER, HE HAS BECOME OBSESSED WITH CONSTRUCTING A FAMILY UNIT WITH WHICH HE WOULD SHARE ETERNITY.
HE SEEKS THE LOVE OF HIS CLONE, THE BOY BENTLEY-23, AND SOUGHT TO PROVIDE HIM WITH A HOME.
HE EXPLOITED A PSYCHIC WEAKNESS IN ME SO I COULD ASSUME THE ROLE OF MOTHER.
HE MANIPULATED ME INTO ABDUCTING THE BOY FROM THE FUTURE FOUNDATION. THE INEVITABLE RESCUE OPERATION WAS LAUNCHED.
I DO NOT PETITION YOUR ERCY BUT RATHER OUR COMPASSION. AT PARENT DOESN'T EEK THE LOVE OF THEIR CHILD?
A BOY NEEDS A FATHER.
HE IS INSANE. HE S UNWELL. EEP THAT IN UR THOUGHTS WHEN YOU ENDER YOUR VERDICT.
OH.
YES, OF COURSE, YOUR MAJESTY.
I DON'T UNDERSTAND.
I DON'T UNDERSTAND! WHAT'S HAPPENING NOW?
BLACK BOLT WOULD HAVE WORDS WITH YOU, BENTLEY WITTMAN.
GOODBYE.

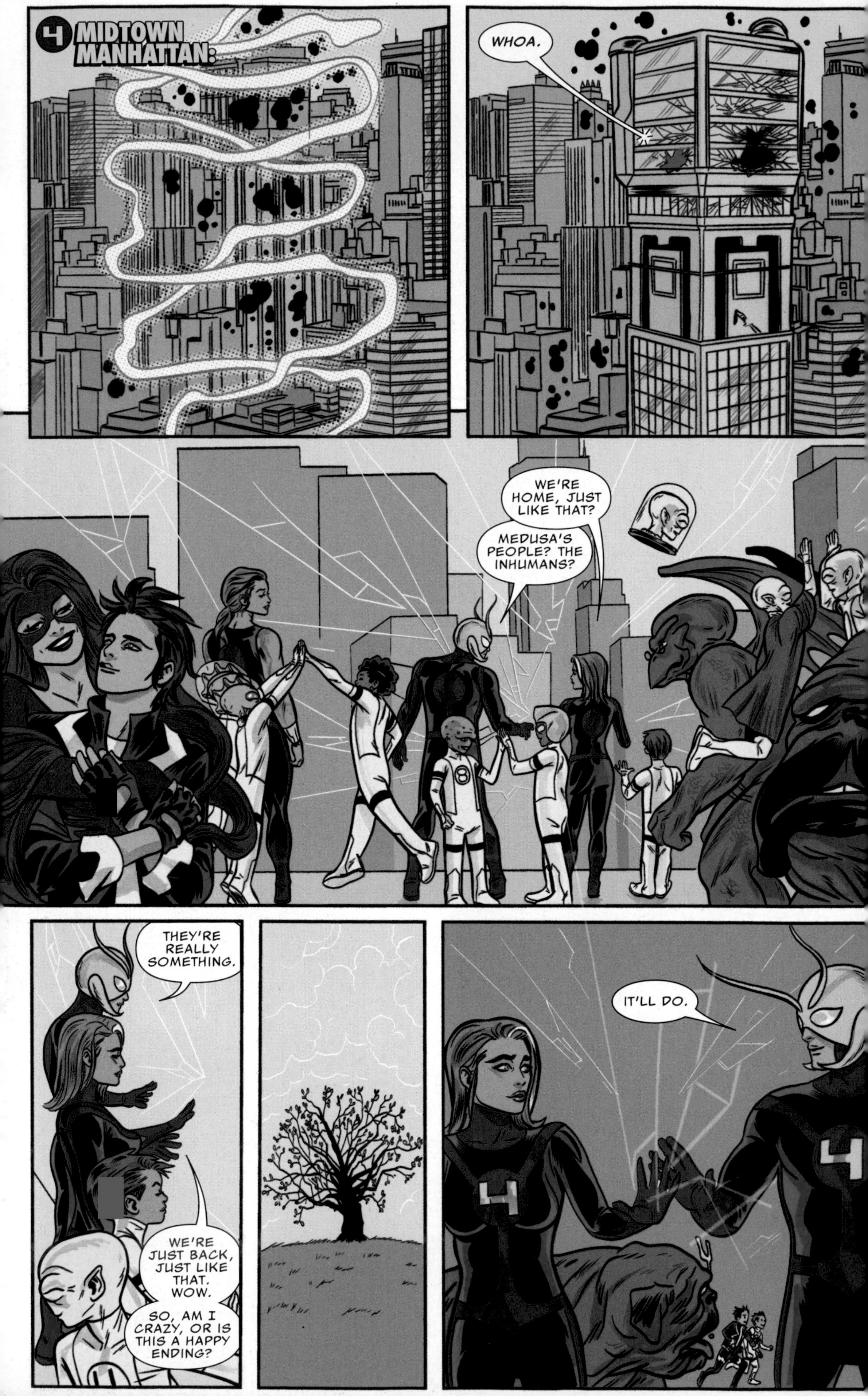
4 MIDTOWN MANHATTAN:
WHOA.
WE'RE HOME, JUST LIKE THAT?
MEDUSA'S PEOPLE? THE INHUMANS?
THEY'RE REALLY SOMETHING.
WE'RE JUST BACK, JUST LIKE THAT. WOW.
SO, AM I CRAZY, OR IS THIS A HAPPY ENDING?
IT'LL DO.

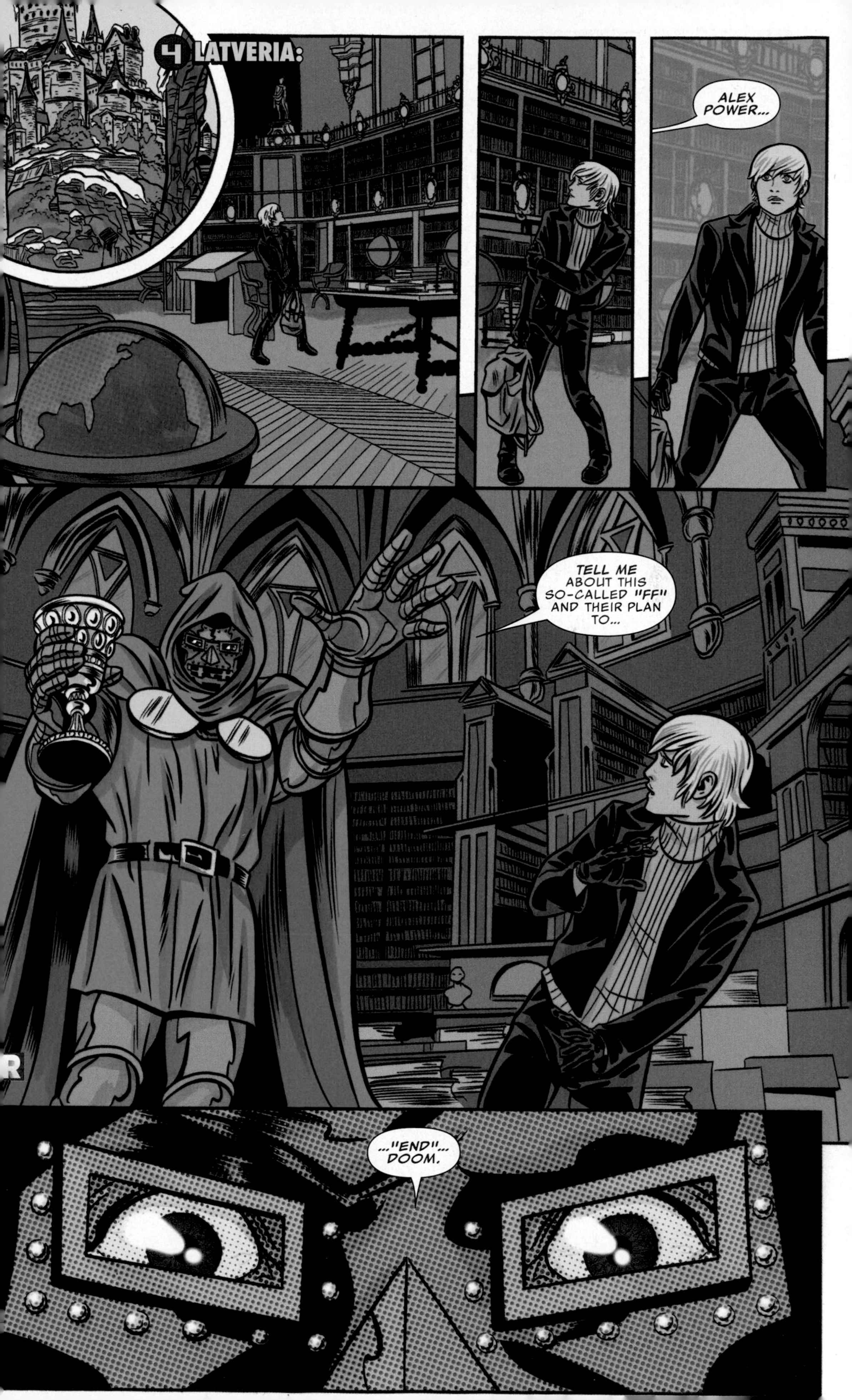
4 LATVERIA:
ALEX POWER...
TELL ME ABOUT THIS SO-CALLED "FF" AND THEIR PLAN TO...
..."END"... DOOM.

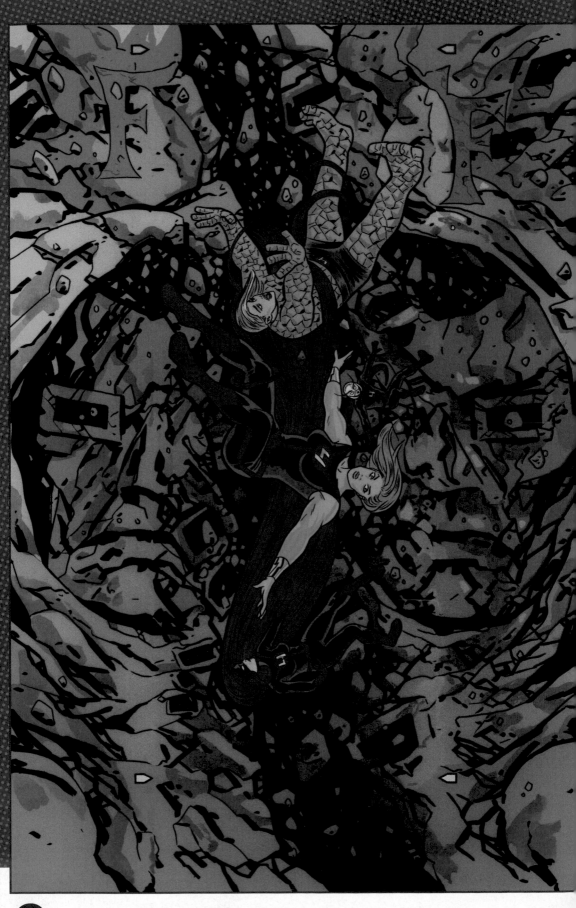

8 CAN'T GO HOME AGAIN

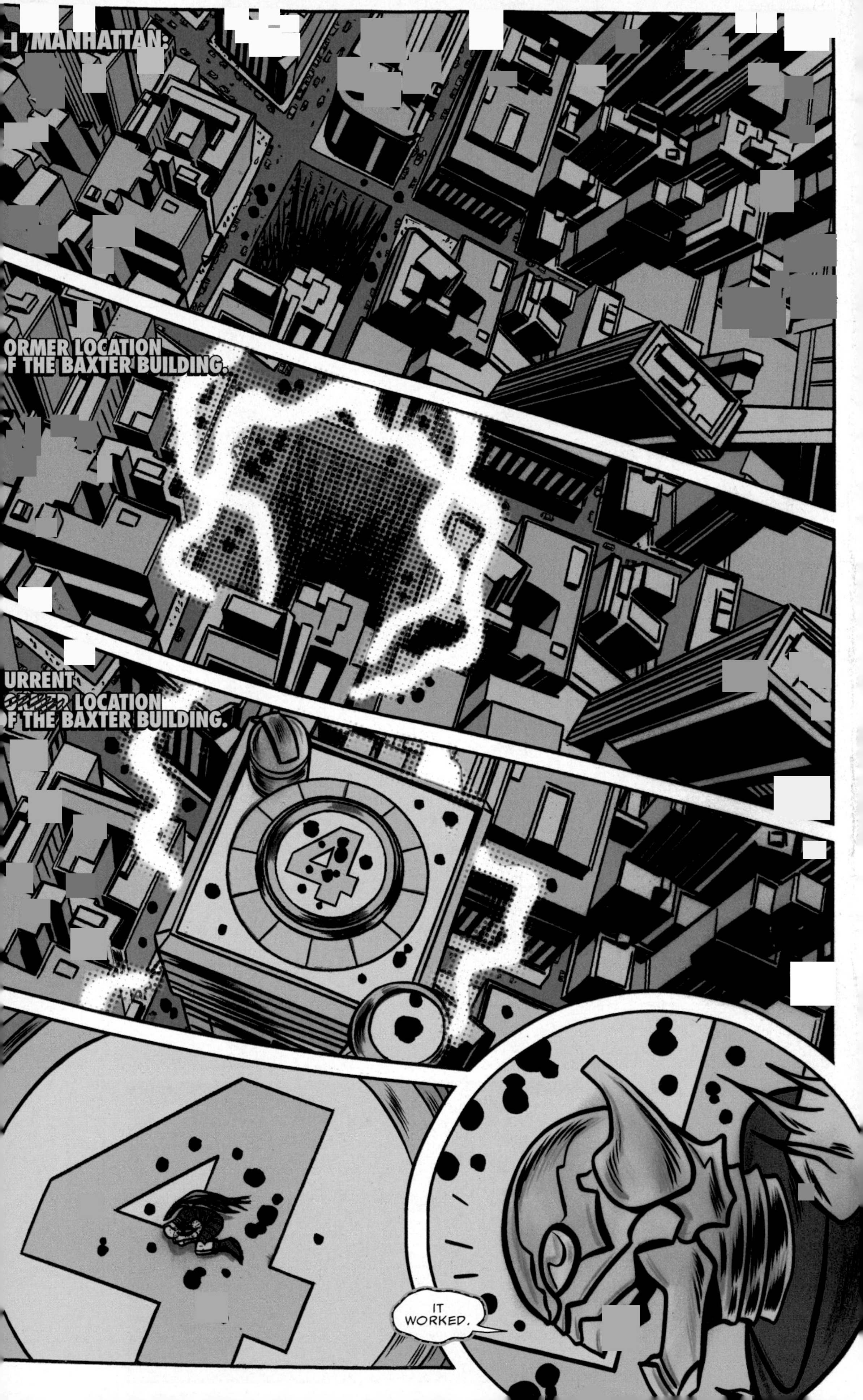

H MANHATTAN:
ORMER LOCATION
F THE BAXTER BUILDING.
URRENT
~~ORMER~~ LOCATION
F THE BAXTER BUILDING.
IT WORKED.

FINAL

DAILY BUGLE

NEW YORK'S FINEST DAILY NEWSPAPER

SINCE 1

$1.00 (in

$1.50 (outside

THERE GOES THE NEIGHBORHOO

"F.F." RETURN FROM GOD KNOWS WHERE, ALAS

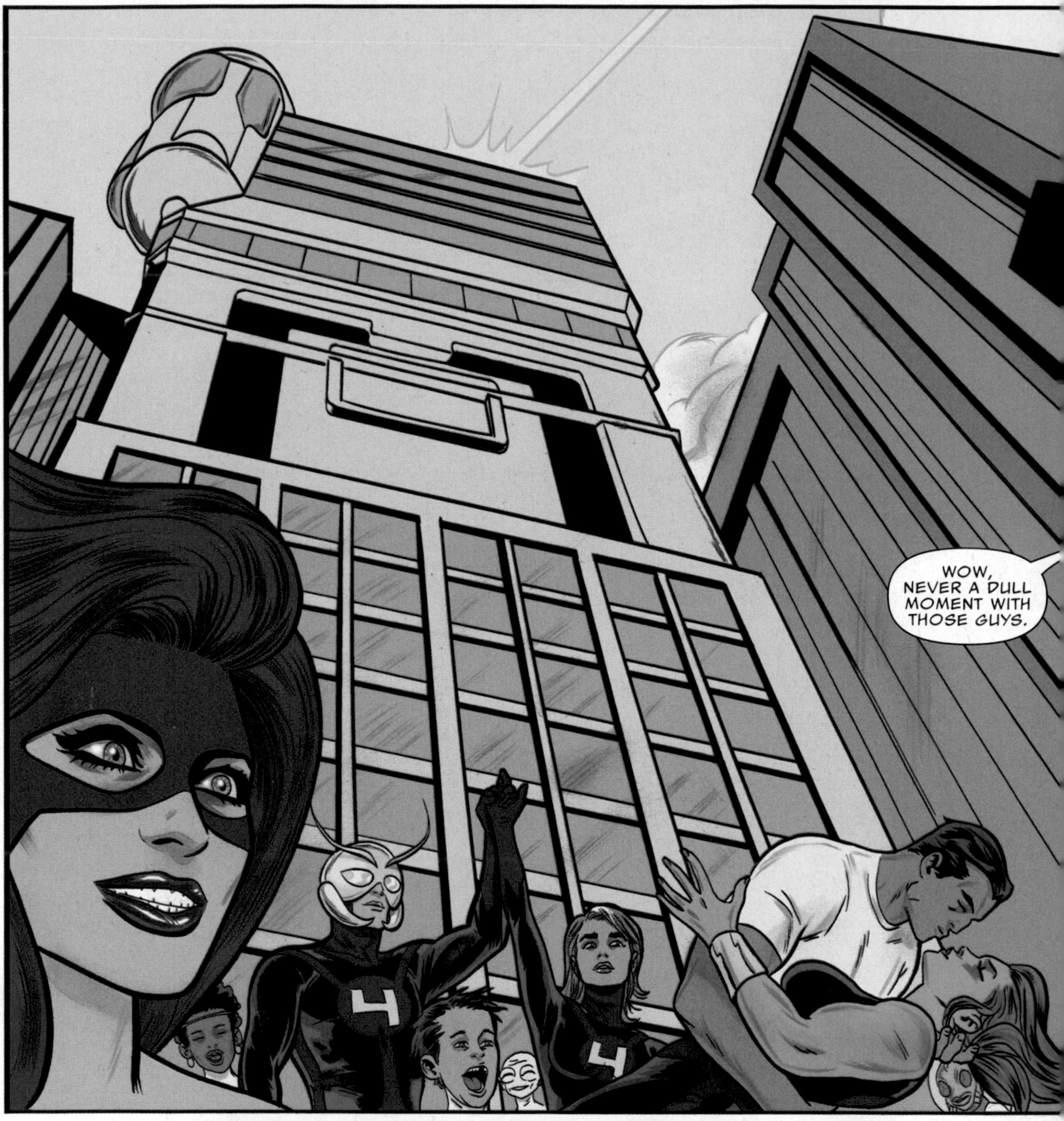
WOW, NEVER A DULL MOMENT WITH THOSE GUYS.

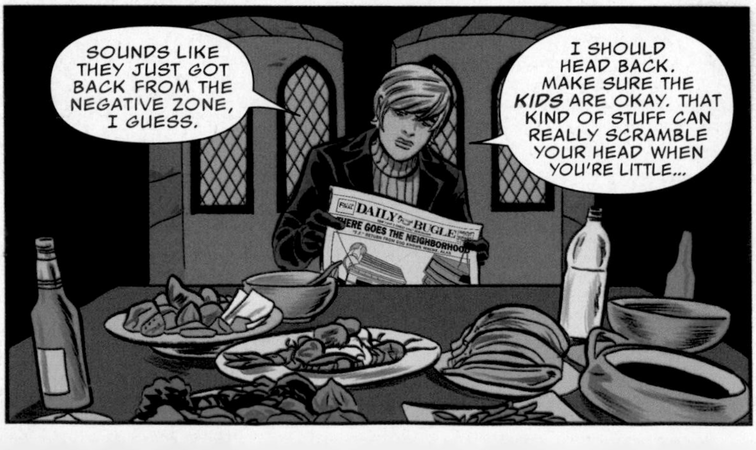
SOUNDS LIKE THEY JUST GOT BACK FROM THE NEGATIVE ZONE, I GUESS.
I SHOULD HEAD BACK. MAKE SURE THE *KIDS* ARE OKAY. THAT KIND OF STUFF CAN REALLY SCRAMBLE YOUR HEAD WHEN YOU'RE LITTLE...

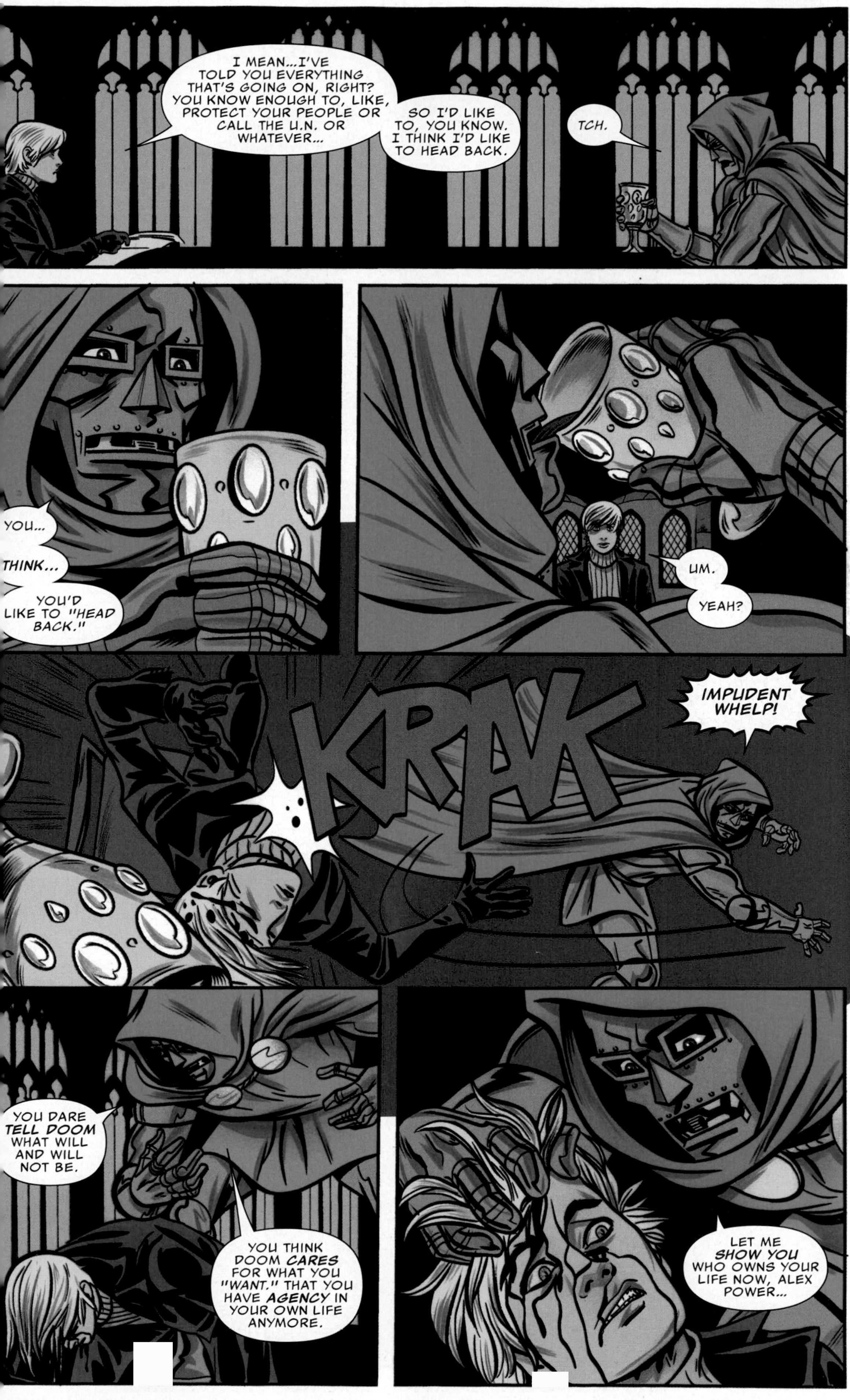

I MEAN...I'VE TOLD YOU EVERYTHING THAT'S GOING ON, RIGHT? YOU KNOW ENOUGH TO, LIKE, PROTECT YOUR PEOPLE OR CALL THE U.N. OR WHATEVER...
SO I'D LIKE TO, YOU KNOW. I THINK I'D LIKE TO HEAD BACK.
TCH.
YOU...
THINK...
YOU'D LIKE TO "HEAD BACK."
UM.
YEAH?
KRAK
IMPUDENT WHELP!
YOU DARE TELL DOOM WHAT WILL AND WILL NOT BE.
YOU THINK DOOM CARES FOR WHAT YOU "WANT." THAT YOU HAVE AGENCY IN YOUR OWN LIFE ANYMORE.
LET ME SHOW YOU WHO OWNS YOUR LIFE NOW, ALEX POWER...

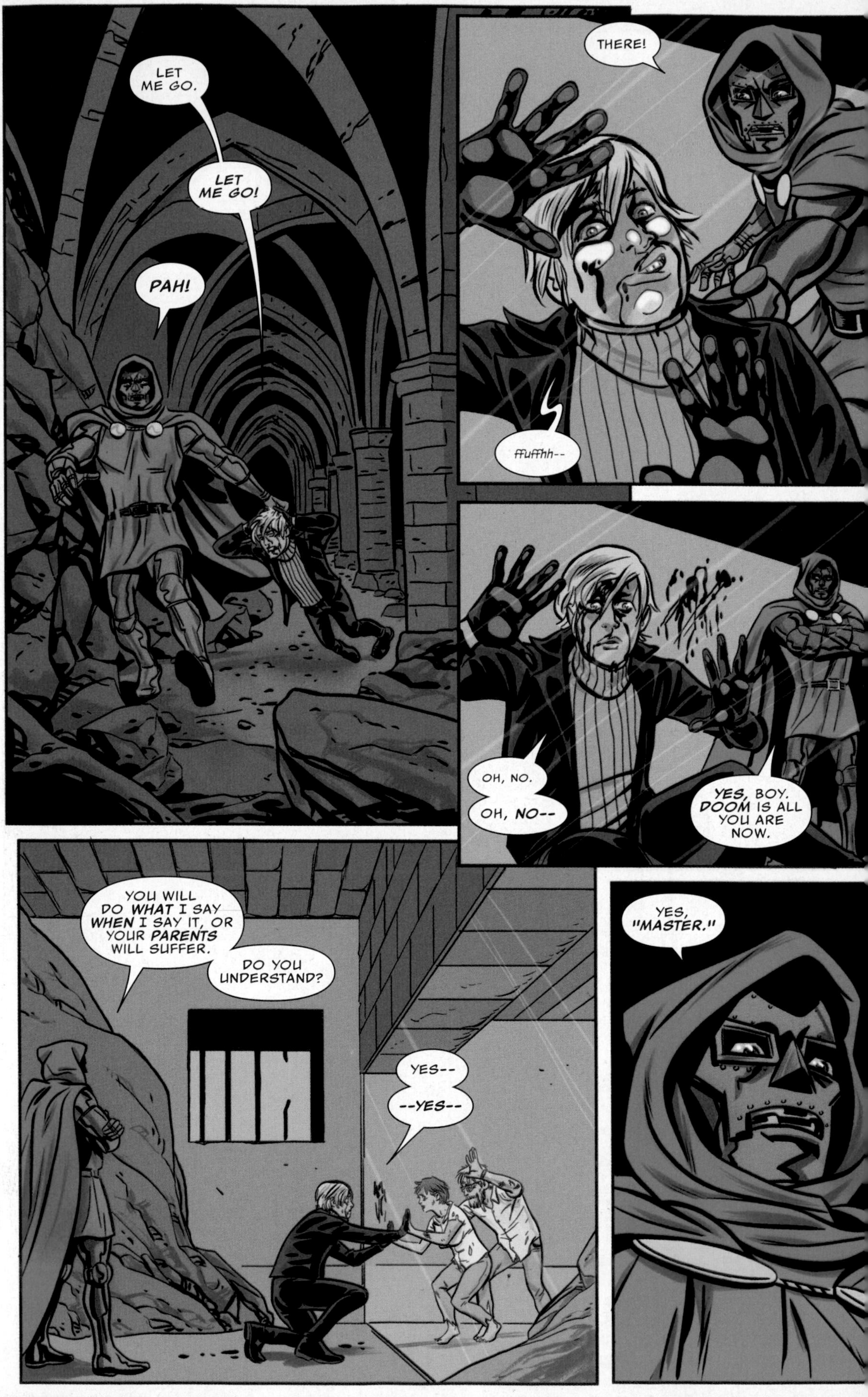

LET ME GO.
LET ME GO!
PAH!
THERE!
ffuffhh--
OH, NO.
OH, NO--
YES, BOY. DOOM IS ALL YOU ARE NOW.
YOU WILL DO WHAT I SAY WHEN I SAY IT, OR YOUR PARENTS WILL SUFFER.
DO YOU UNDERSTAND?
YES--
--YES--
YES, "MASTER."

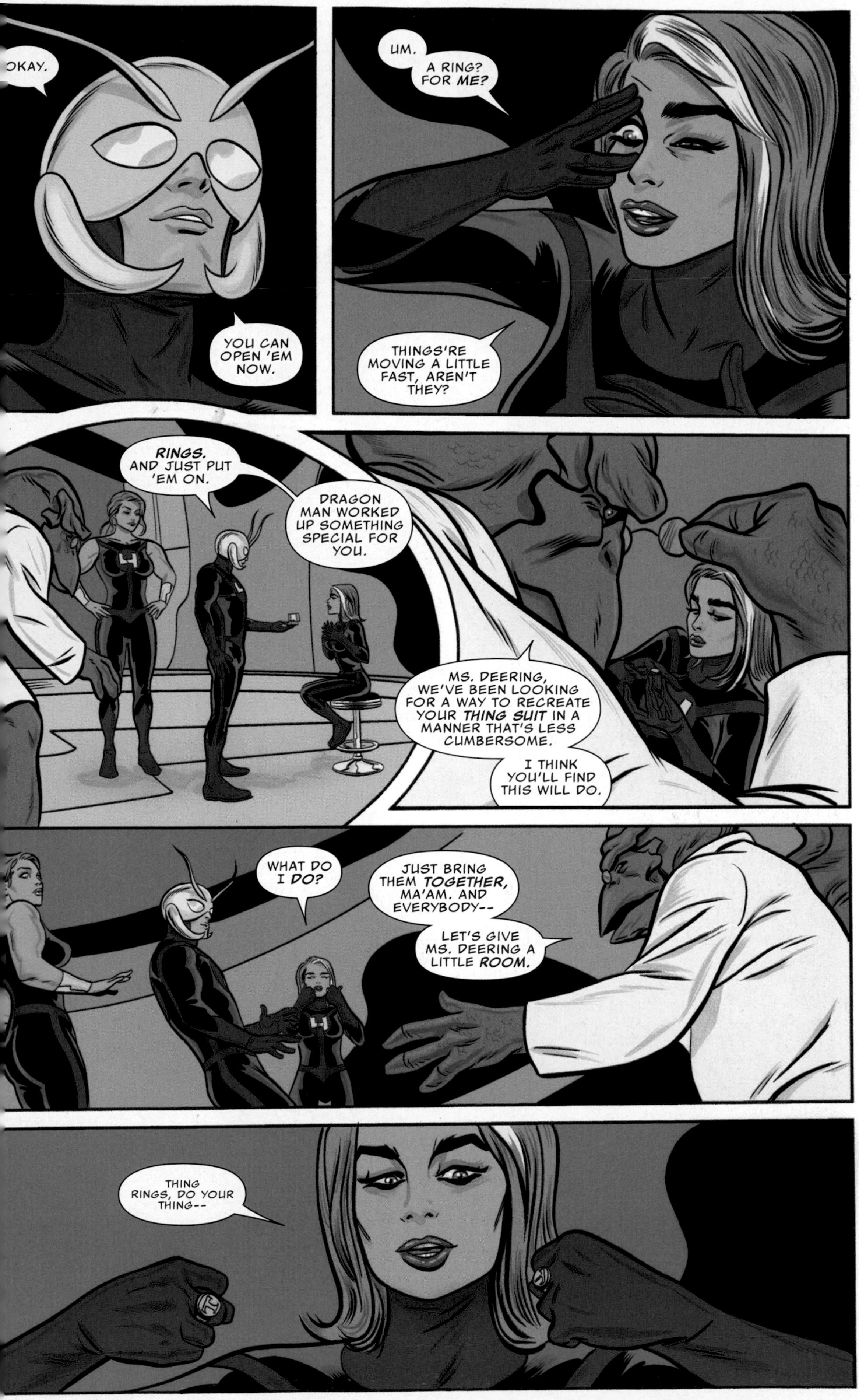
OKAY.
YOU CAN OPEN 'EM NOW.
UM.
A RING? FOR ME?
THINGS'RE MOVING A LITTLE FAST, AREN'T THEY?
RINGS. AND JUST PUT 'EM ON.
DRAGON MAN WORKED UP SOMETHING SPECIAL FOR YOU.
MS. DEERING, WE'VE BEEN LOOKING FOR A WAY TO RECREATE YOUR THING SUIT IN A MANNER THAT'S LESS CUMBERSOME.
I THINK YOU'LL FIND THIS WILL DO.
WHAT DO I DO?
JUST BRING THEM TOGETHER, MA'AM. AND EVERYBODY--
LET'S GIVE MS. DEERING A LITTLE ROOM.
THING RINGS, DO YOUR THING--

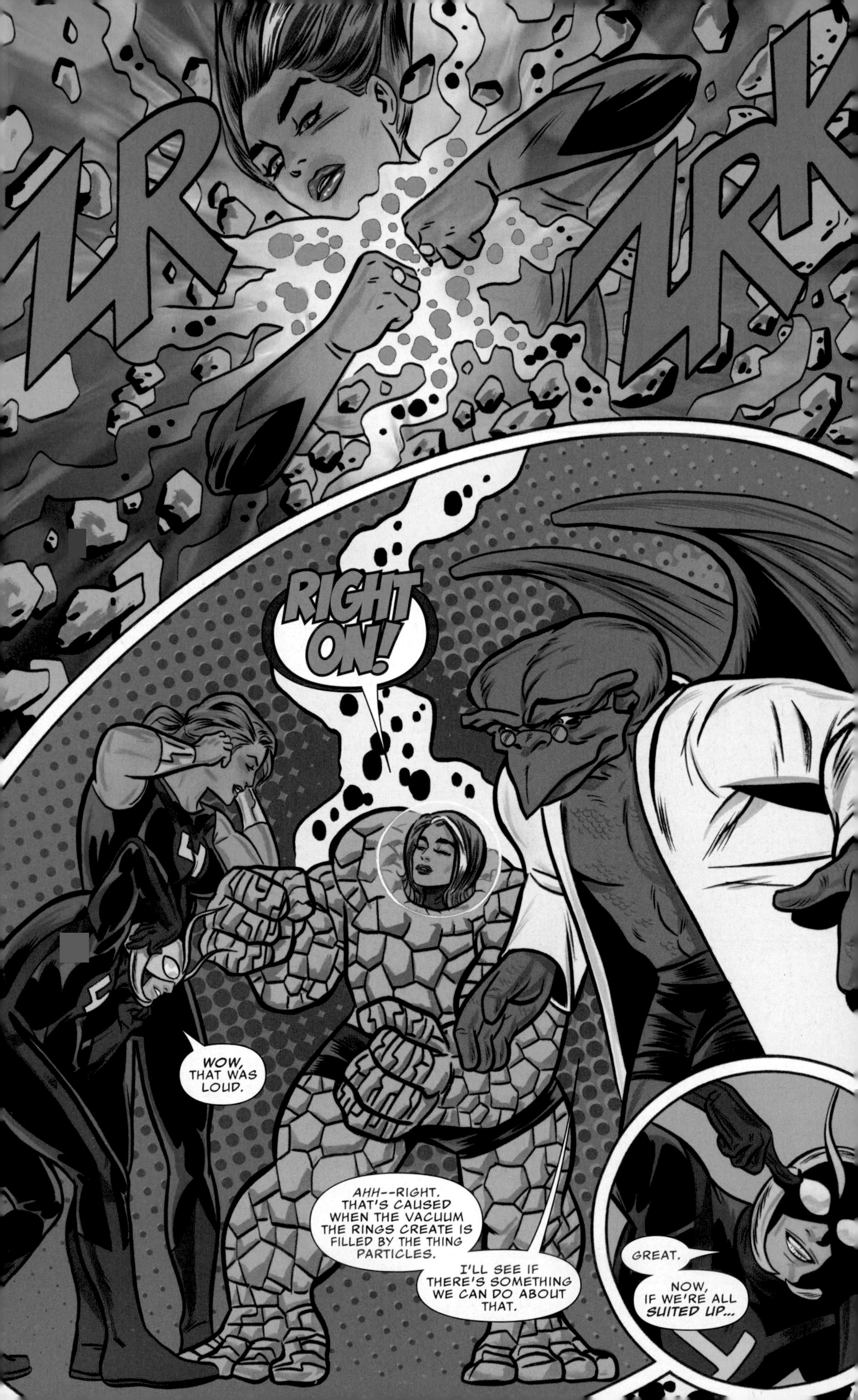
RIGHT ON!
WOW, THAT WAS LOUD.
AHH--RIGHT. THAT'S CAUSED WHEN THE VACUUM THE RINGS CREATE IS FILLED BY THE THING PARTICLES.
I'LL SEE IF THERE'S SOMETHING WE CAN DO ABOUT THAT.
GREAT.
NOW, IF WE'RE ALL SUITED UP...

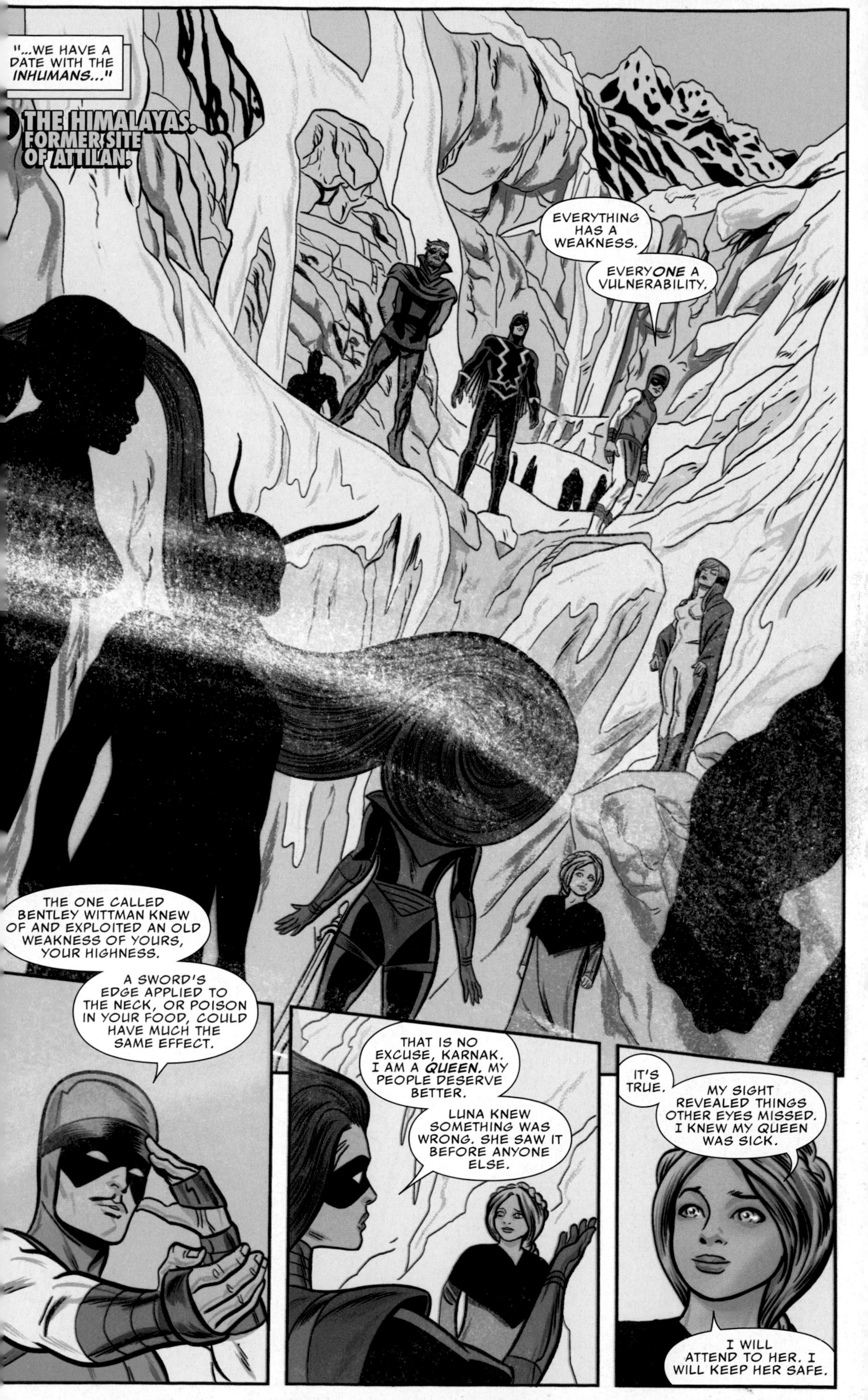
"...WE HAVE A DATE WITH THE INHUMANS..."
THE HIMALAYAS. FORMER SITE OF ATTILAN.
EVERYTHING HAS A WEAKNESS.
EVERYONE A VULNERABILITY.
THE ONE CALLED BENTLEY WITTMAN KNEW OF AND EXPLOITED AN OLD WEAKNESS OF YOURS, YOUR HIGHNESS.
A SWORD'S EDGE APPLIED TO THE NECK, OR POISON IN YOUR FOOD, COULD HAVE MUCH THE SAME EFFECT.
THAT IS NO EXCUSE, KARNAK. I AM A QUEEN. MY PEOPLE DESERVE BETTER.
LUNA KNEW SOMETHING WAS WRONG. SHE SAW IT BEFORE ANYONE ELSE.
IT'S TRUE.
MY SIGHT REVEALED THINGS OTHER EYES MISSED. I KNEW MY QUEEN WAS SICK.
I WILL ATTEND TO HER. I WILL KEEP HER SAFE.

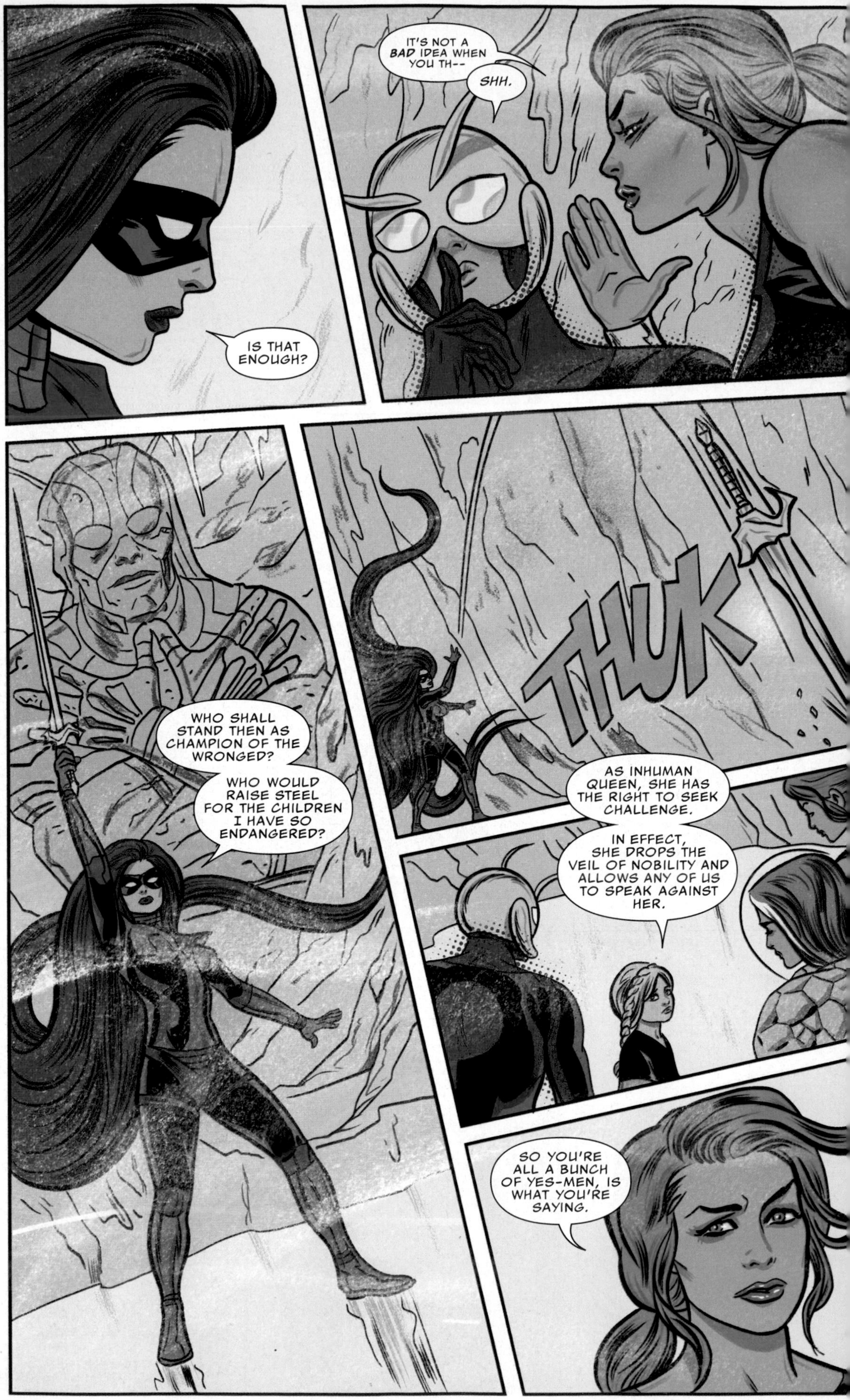
IS THAT ENOUGH?
IT'S NOT A BAD IDEA WHEN YOU TH--
SHH.
WHO SHALL STAND THEN AS CHAMPION OF THE WRONGED?
WHO WOULD RAISE STEEL FOR THE CHILDREN I HAVE SO ENDANGERED?
THUK
AS INHUMAN QUEEN, SHE HAS THE RIGHT TO SEEK CHALLENGE.
IN EFFECT, SHE DROPS THE VEIL OF NOBILITY AND ALLOWS ANY OF US TO SPEAK AGAINST HER.
SO YOU'RE ALL A BUNCH OF YES-MEN, IS WHAT YOU'RE SAYING.

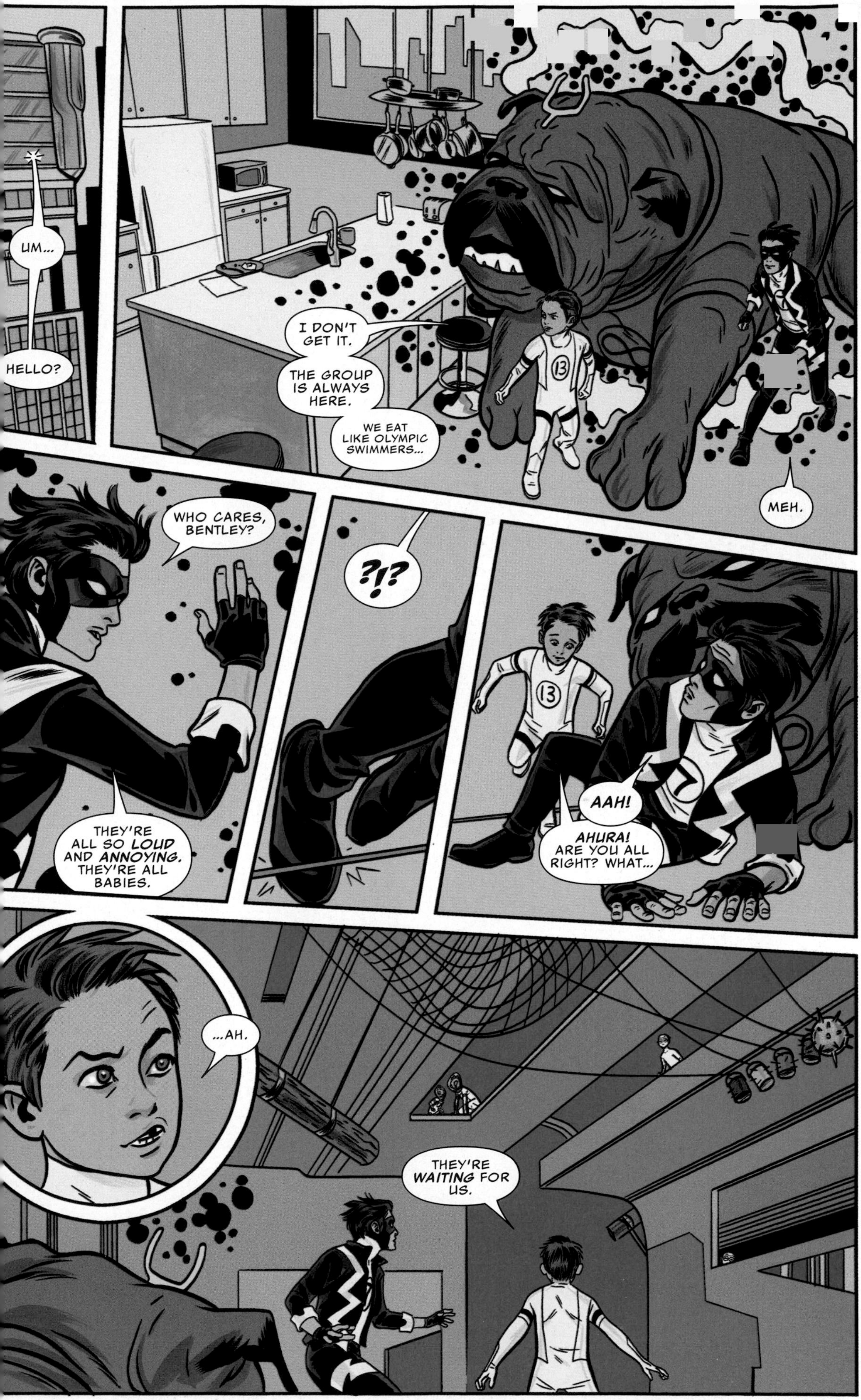
UM...
HELLO?
I DON'T GET IT.
THE GROUP IS ALWAYS HERE.
WE EAT LIKE OLYMPIC SWIMMERS...
MEH.
WHO CARES, BENTLEY?
THEY'RE ALL SO LOUD AND ANNOYING. THEY'RE ALL BABIES.
?!?
AAH!
AHURA! ARE YOU ALL RIGHT? WHAT...
...AH.
THEY'RE WAITING FOR US.

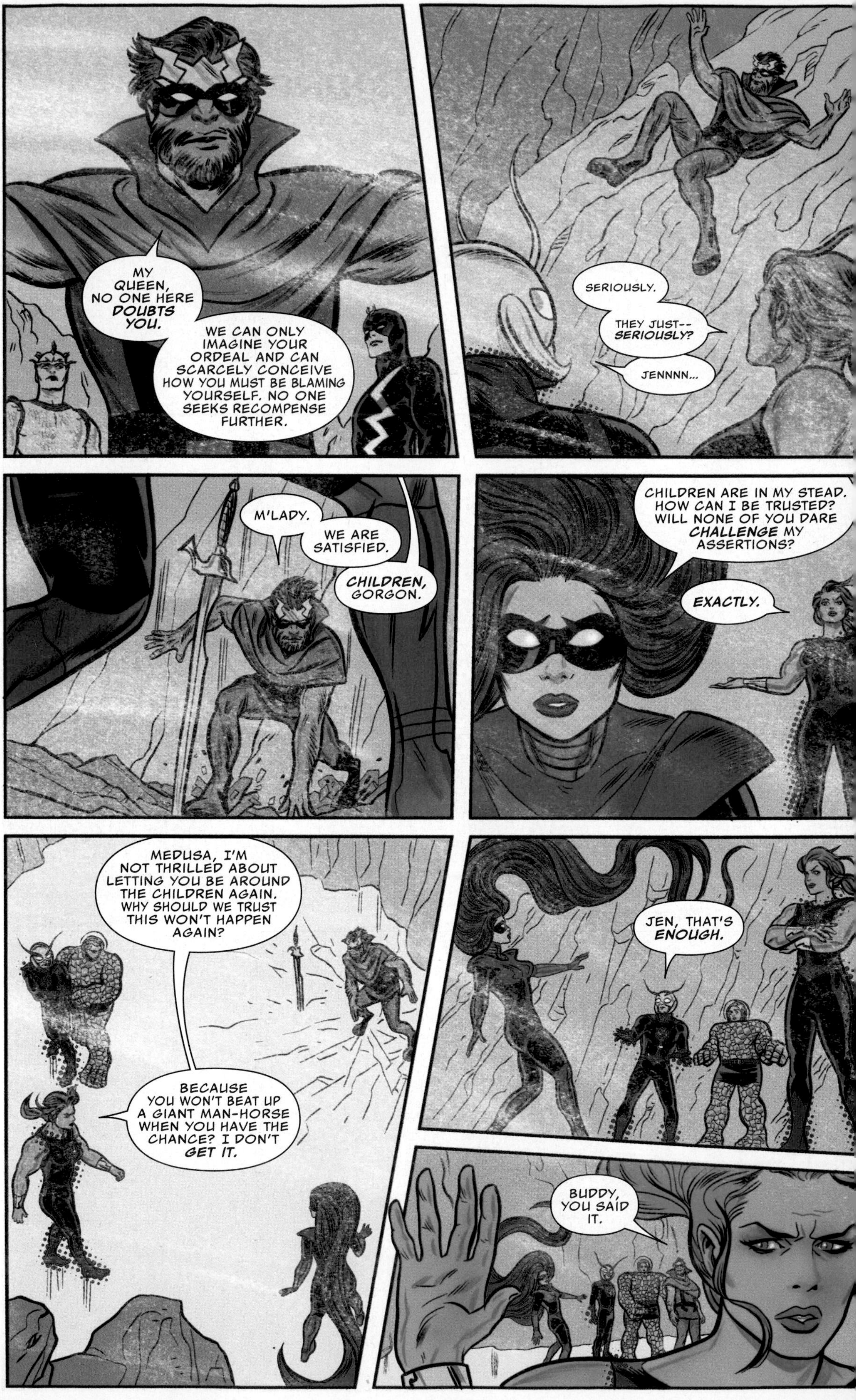

MY QUEEN, NO ONE HERE DOUBTS YOU.
WE CAN ONLY IMAGINE YOUR ORDEAL AND CAN SCARCELY CONCEIVE HOW YOU MUST BE BLAMING YOURSELF. NO ONE SEEKS RECOMPENSE FURTHER.
SERIOUSLY.
THEY JUST-- SERIOUSLY?
JENNNN...
M'LADY.
WE ARE SATISFIED.
CHILDREN, GORGON.
CHILDREN ARE IN MY STEAD. HOW CAN I BE TRUSTED? WILL NONE OF YOU DARE CHALLENGE MY ASSERTIONS?
EXACTLY.
MEDUSA, I'M NOT THRILLED ABOUT LETTING YOU BE AROUND THE CHILDREN AGAIN. WHY SHOULD WE TRUST THIS WON'T HAPPEN AGAIN?
BECAUSE YOU WON'T BEAT UP A GIANT MAN-HORSE WHEN YOU HAVE THE CHANCE? I DON'T GET IT.
JEN, THAT'S ENOUGH.
BUDDY, YOU SAID IT.

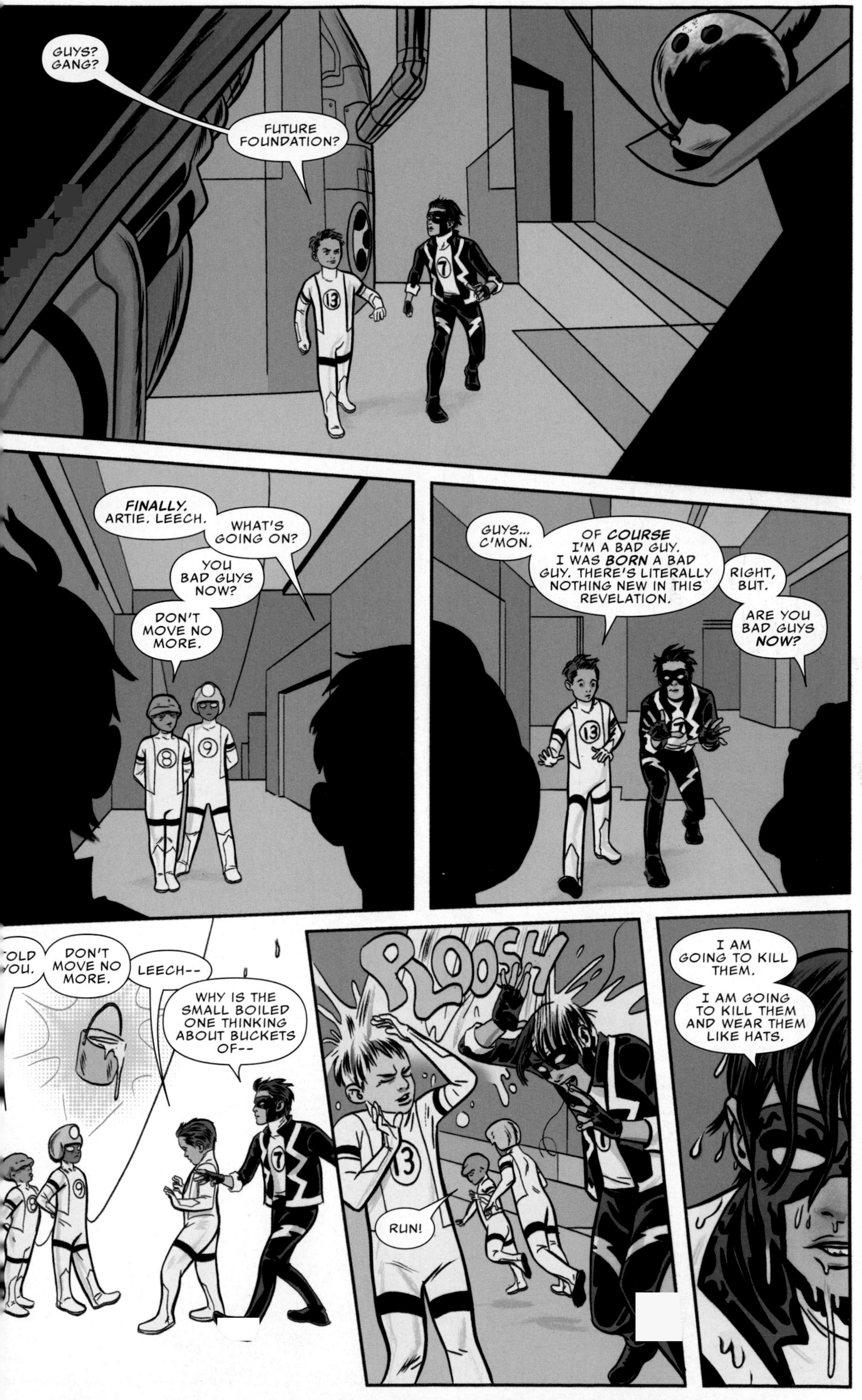

GUYS? GANG?
FUTURE FOUNDATION?
FINALLY. ARTIE. LEECH.
WHAT'S GOING ON?
YOU BAD GUYS NOW?
DON'T MOVE NO MORE.
GUYS... C'MON.
OF COURSE I'M A BAD GUY. I WAS BORN A BAD GUY. THERE'S LITERALLY NOTHING NEW IN THIS REVELATION.
RIGHT, BUT.
ARE YOU BAD GUYS NOW?
DON'T MOVE NO MORE.
LEECH--
WHY IS THE SMALL BOILED ONE THINKING ABOUT BUCKETS OF--
PLOOSH
RUN!
I AM GOING TO KILL THEM.
I AM GOING TO KILL THEM AND WEAR THEM LIKE HATS.

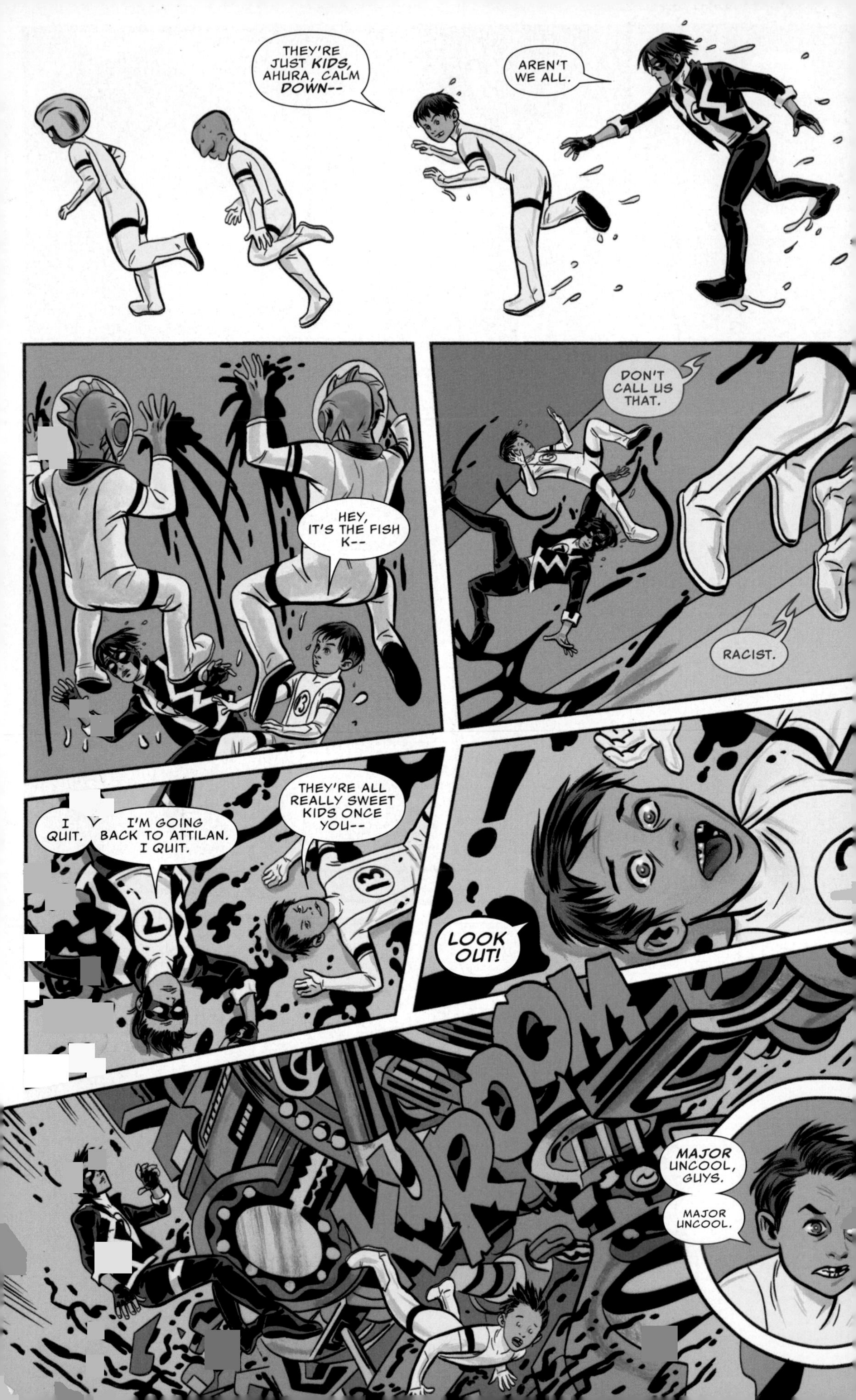

THEY'RE JUST KIDS, AHURA, CALM DOWN--
AREN'T WE ALL.
HEY, IT'S THE FISH K--
DON'T CALL US THAT.
RACIST.
I QUIT.
I'M GOING BACK TO ATTILAN. I QUIT.
THEY'RE ALL REALLY SWEET KIDS ONCE YOU--
LOOK OUT!
MAJOR UNCOOL, GUYS.
MAJOR UNCOOL.

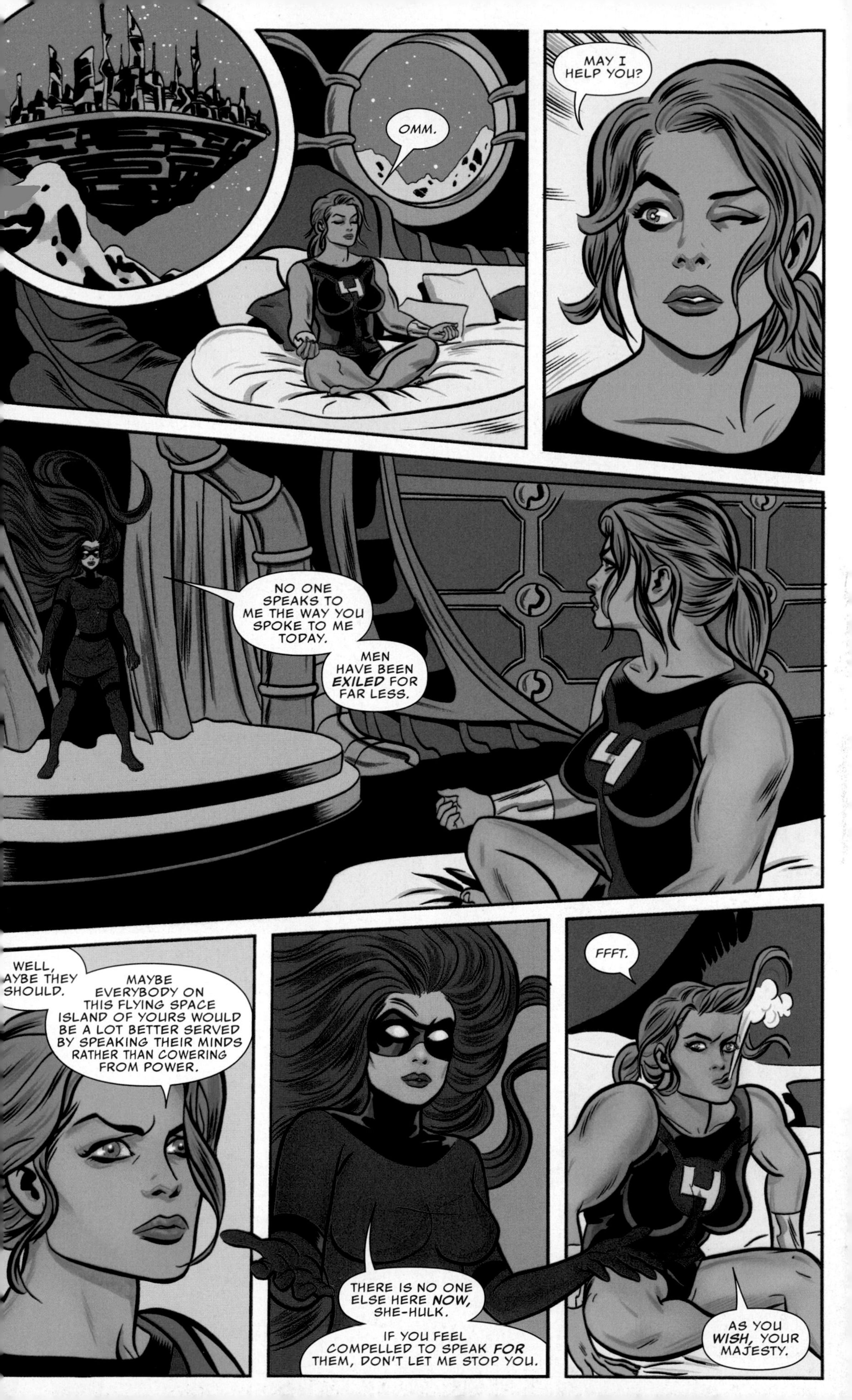
OMM.
MAY I HELP YOU?
NO ONE SPEAKS TO ME THE WAY YOU SPOKE TO ME TODAY.
MEN HAVE BEEN EXILED FOR FAR LESS.
WELL, AYBE THEY SHOULD.
MAYBE EVERYBODY ON THIS FLYING SPACE ISLAND OF YOURS WOULD BE A LOT BETTER SERVED BY SPEAKING THEIR MINDS RATHER THAN COWERING FROM POWER.
THERE IS NO ONE ELSE HERE NOW, SHE-HULK.
IF YOU FEEL COMPELLED TO SPEAK FOR THEM, DON'T LET ME STOP YOU.
FFFT.
AS YOU WISH, YOUR MAJESTY.

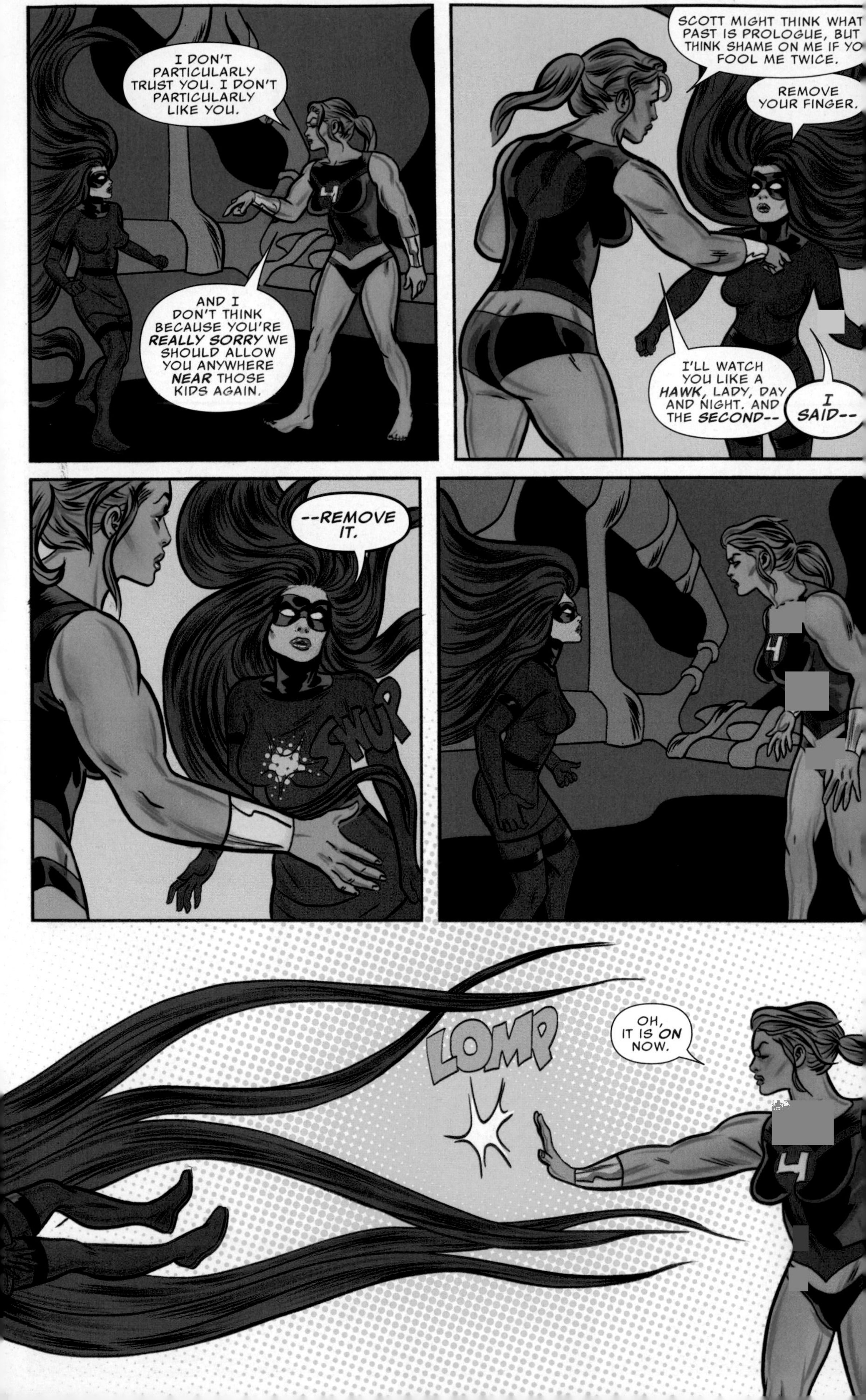
I DON'T PARTICULARLY TRUST YOU. I DON'T PARTICULARLY LIKE YOU.
AND I DON'T THINK BECAUSE YOU'RE *REALLY SORRY* WE SHOULD ALLOW YOU ANYWHERE *NEAR* THOSE KIDS AGAIN.
SCOTT MIGHT THINK WHAT PAST IS PROLOGUE, BUT THINK SHAME ON ME IF YO FOOL ME TWICE.
REMOVE YOUR FINGER.
I'LL WATCH YOU LIKE A *HAWK*, LADY, DAY AND NIGHT. AND THE *SECOND--*
I SAID--
--REMOVE IT.
SKUP
LOMP
OH, IT IS *ON* NOW.

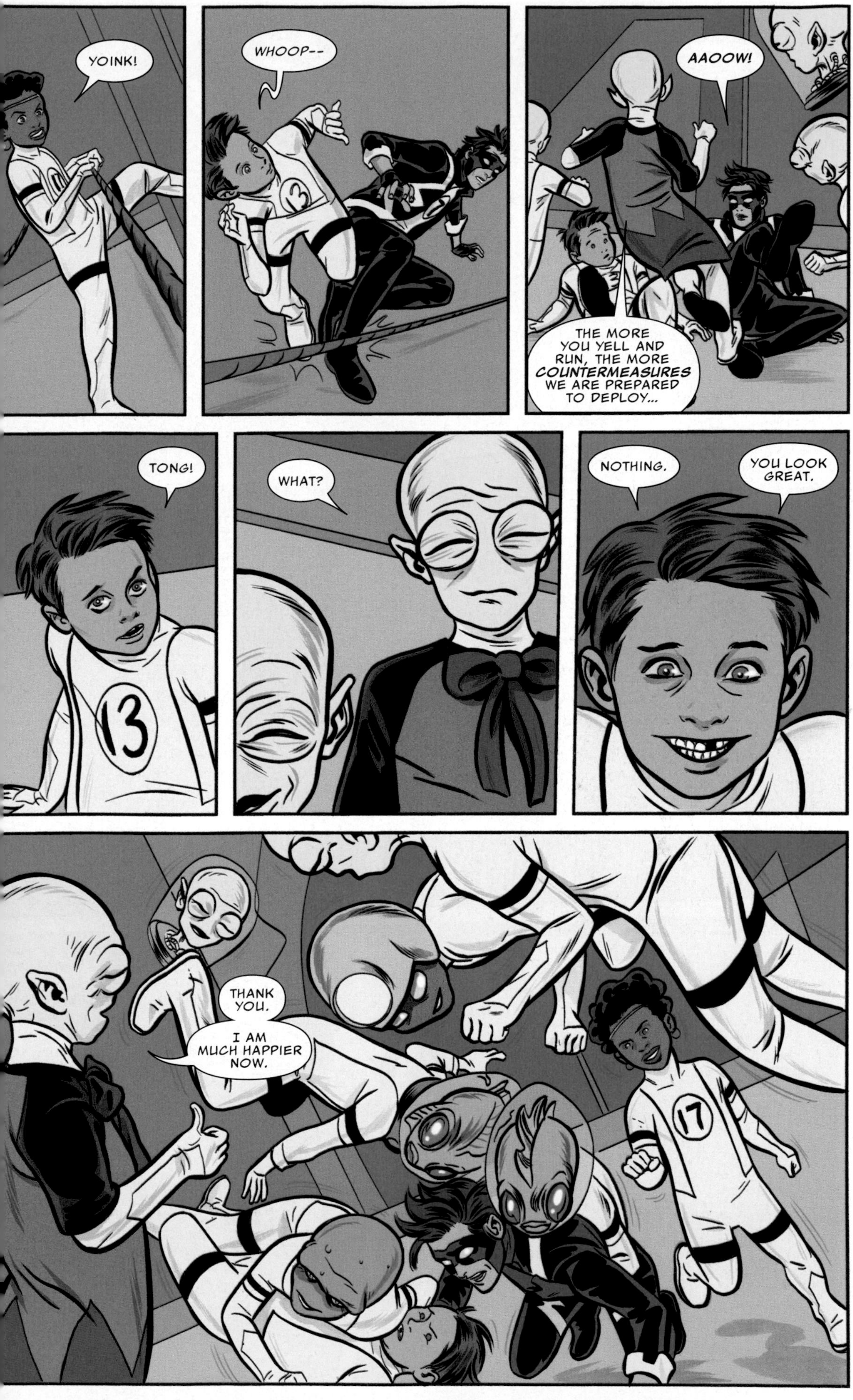
YOINK!
WHOOP--
AAOOW!
THE MORE YOU YELL AND RUN, THE MORE COUNTERMEASURES WE ARE PREPARED TO DEPLOY...
TONG!
WHAT?
NOTHING.
YOU LOOK GREAT.
THANK YOU.
I AM MUCH HAPPIER NOW.
13
13
17

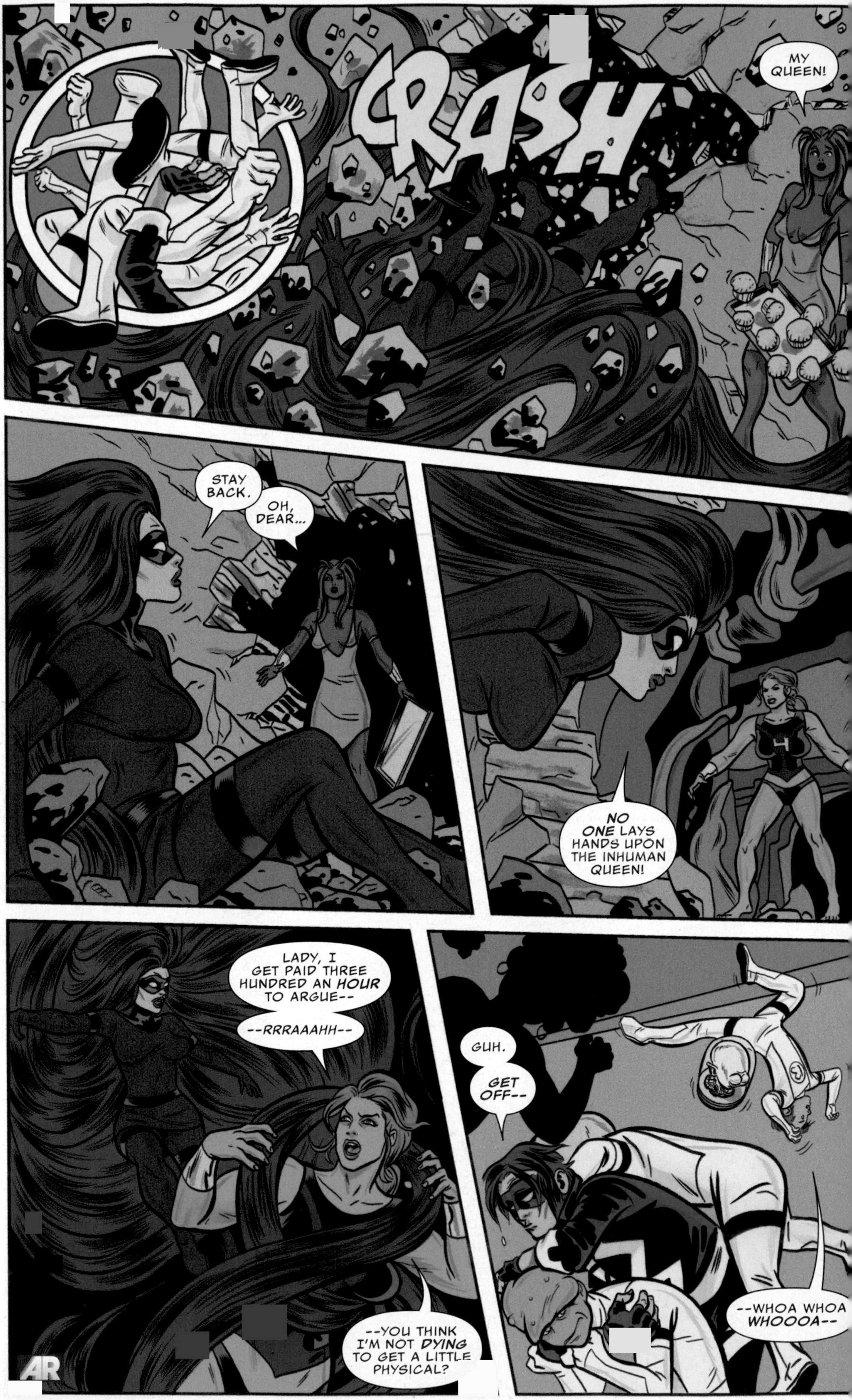
CRASH
MY QUEEN!
STAY BACK.
OH, DEAR...
NO ONE LAYS HANDS UPON THE INHUMAN QUEEN!
LADY, I GET PAID THREE HUNDRED AN HOUR TO ARGUE--
--RRRAAAHH--
--YOU THINK I'M NOT DYING TO GET A LITTLE PHYSICAL?
GUH.
GET OFF--
--WHOA WHOA WHOOOA--

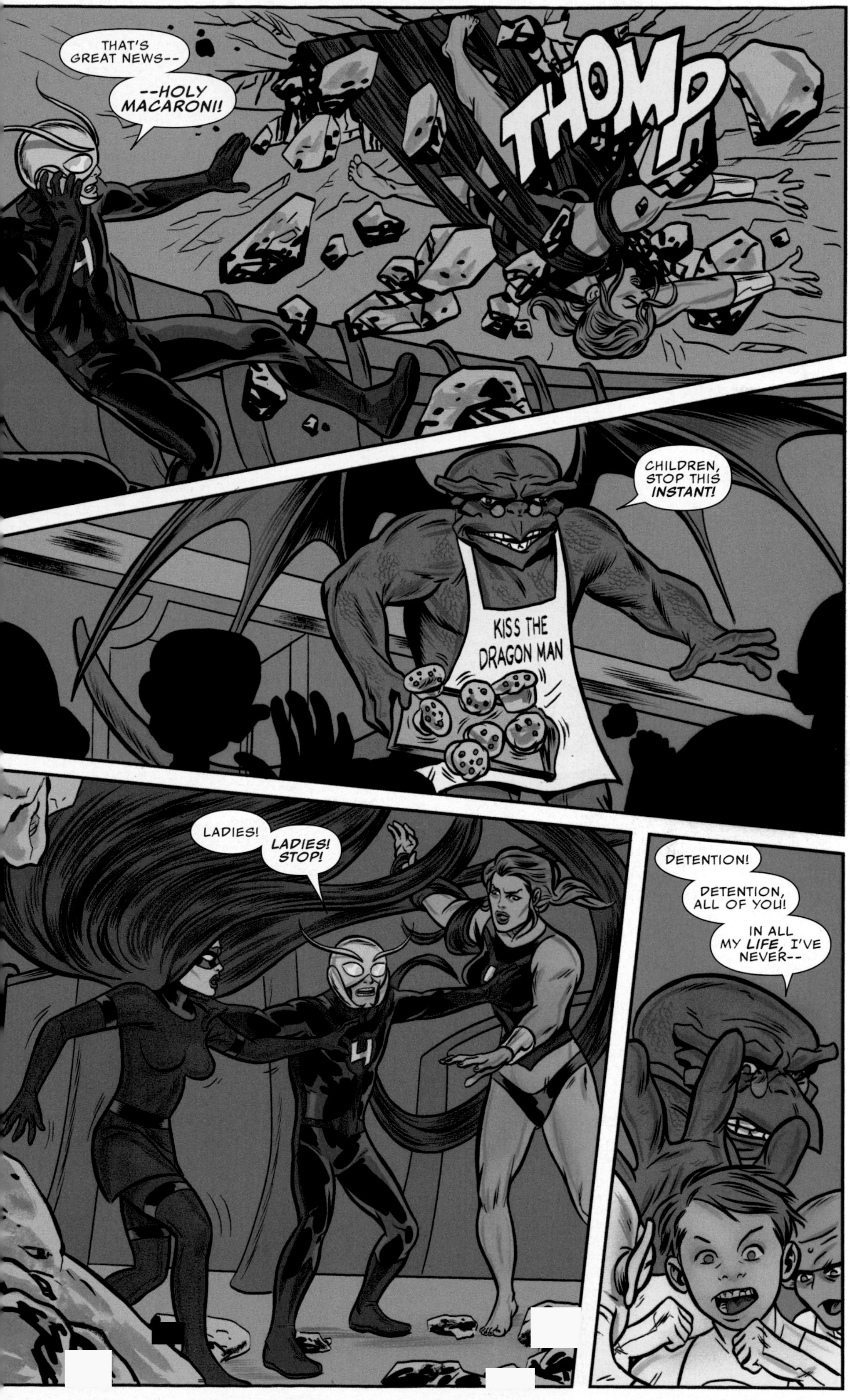
THAT'S GREAT NEWS--
--HOLY MACARONI!
THOMP
CHILDREN, STOP THIS INSTANT!
KISS THE DRAGON MAN
LADIES!
LADIES! STOP!
DETENTION!
DETENTION, ALL OF YOU!
IN ALL MY LIFE, I'VE NEVER--

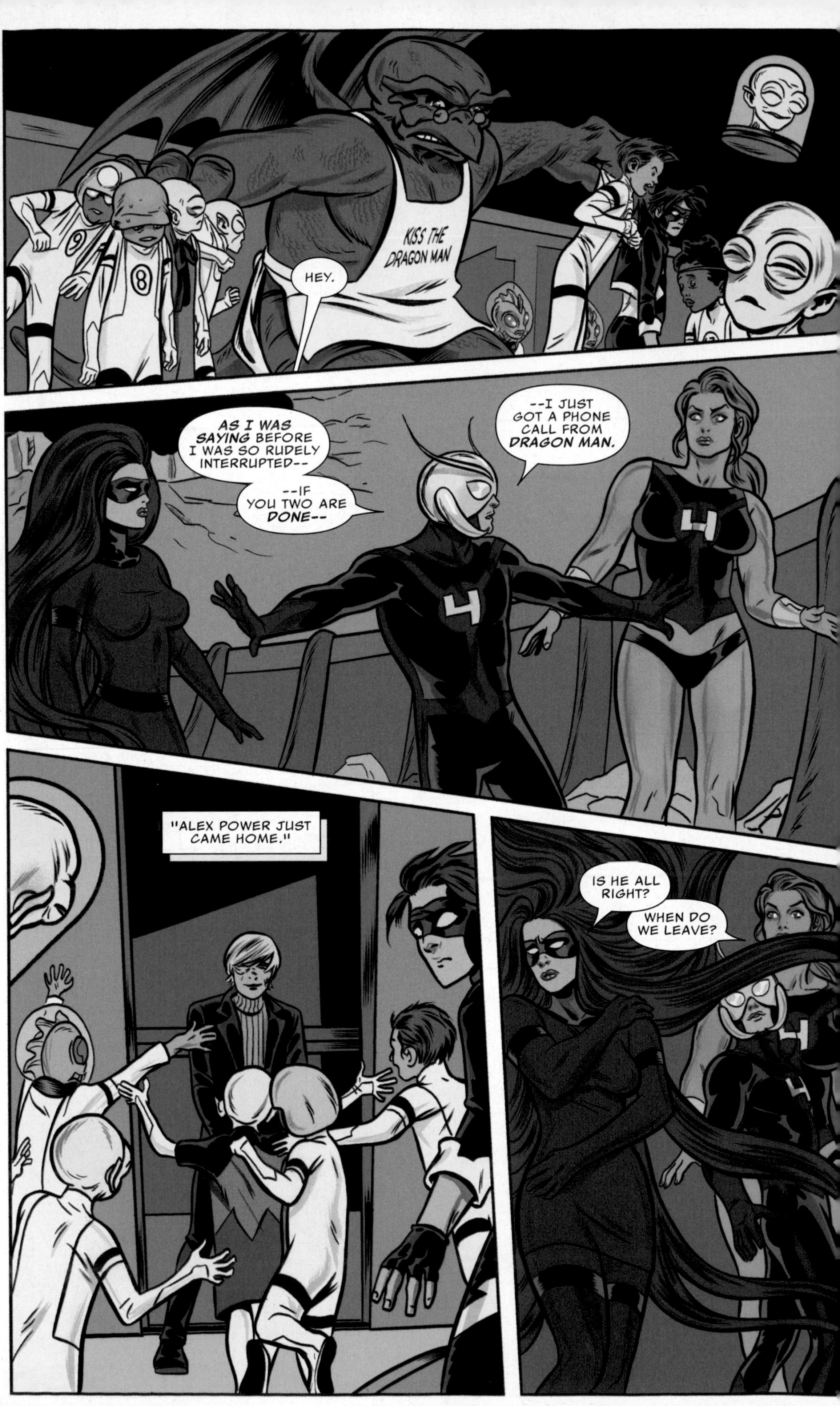
KISS THE DRAGON MAN
HEY.
AS I WAS SAYING BEFORE I WAS SO RUDELY INTERRUPTED--
--IF YOU TWO ARE DONE--
--I JUST GOT A PHONE CALL FROM DRAGON MAN.
"ALEX POWER JUST CAME HOME."
IS HE ALL RIGHT?
WHEN DO WE LEAVE?

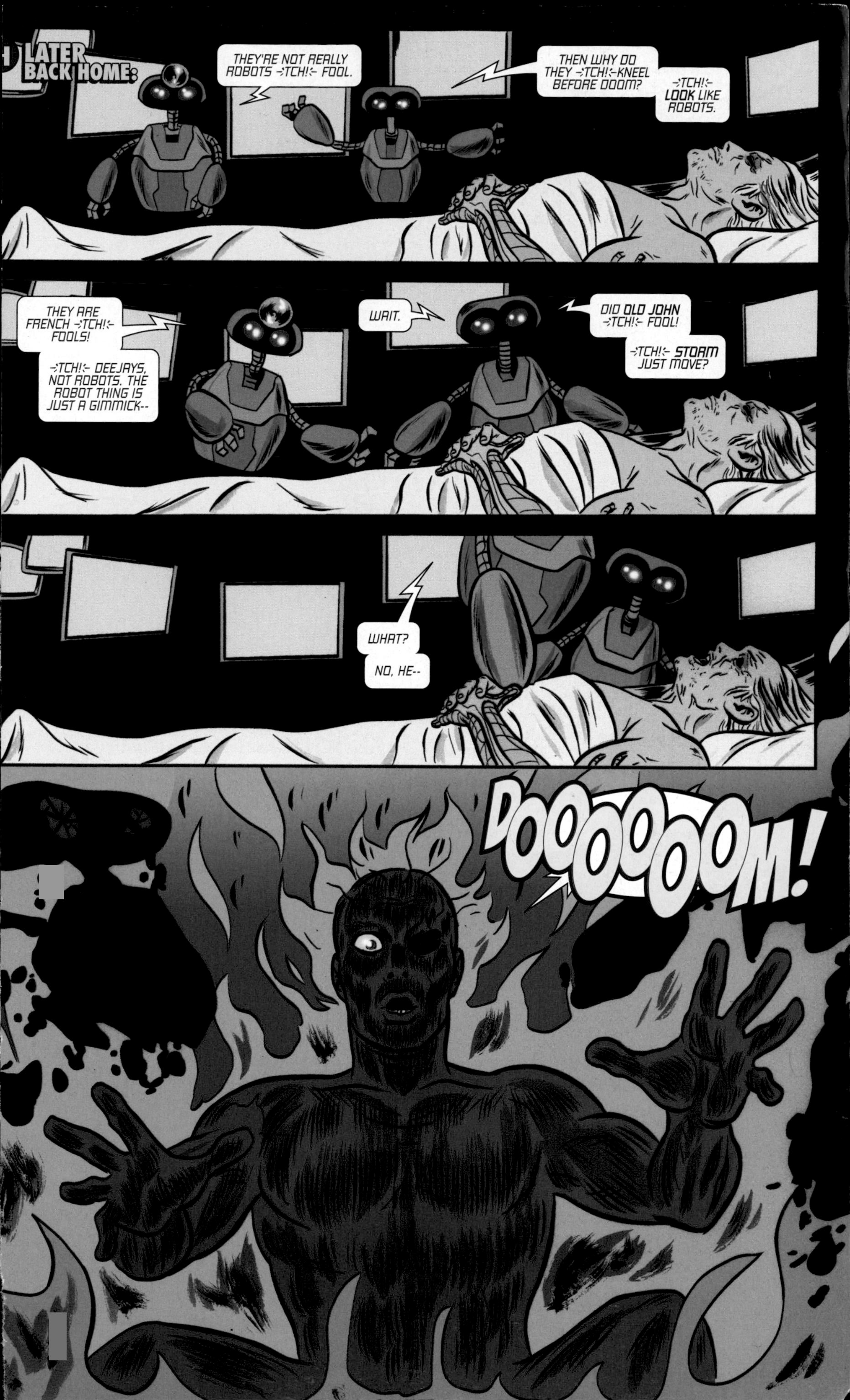
LATER BACK HOME:
THEY'RE NOT REALLY ROBOTS -TCH!- FOOL.
THEN WHY DO THEY -TCH!- KNEEL BEFORE DOOM?
-TCH!- LOOK LIKE ROBOTS.
THEY ARE FRENCH -TCH!- FOOLS!
-TCH!- DEEJAYS, NOT ROBOTS. THE ROBOT THING IS JUST A GIMMICK--
WAIT.
DID OLD JOHN -TCH!- FOOL!
-TCH!- STORM JUST MOVE?
WHAT?
NO, HE--
DOOOOOOOM!

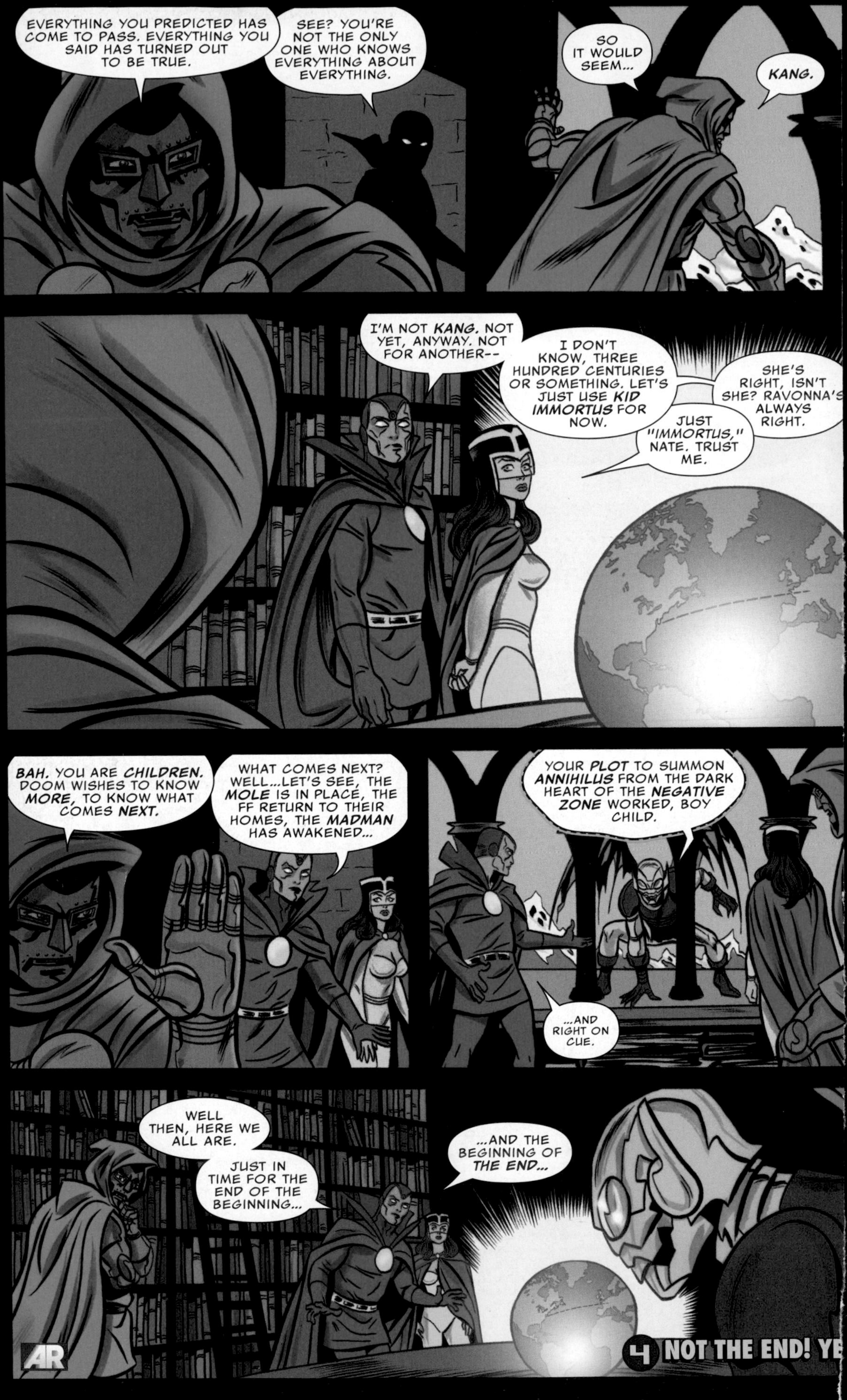
EVERYTHING YOU PREDICTED HAS COME TO PASS. EVERYTHING YOU SAID HAS TURNED OUT TO BE TRUE.
SEE? YOU'RE NOT THE ONLY ONE WHO KNOWS EVERYTHING ABOUT EVERYTHING.
SO IT WOULD SEEM...
KANG.
I'M NOT KANG. NOT YET, ANYWAY. NOT FOR ANOTHER--
I DON'T KNOW, THREE HUNDRED CENTURIES OR SOMETHING. LET'S JUST USE KID IMMORTUS FOR NOW.
JUST "IMMORTUS," NATE. TRUST ME.
SHE'S RIGHT, ISN'T SHE? RAVONNA'S ALWAYS RIGHT.
BAH. YOU ARE CHILDREN. DOOM WISHES TO KNOW MORE, TO KNOW WHAT COMES NEXT.
WHAT COMES NEXT? WELL...LET'S SEE, THE MOLE IS IN PLACE, THE FF RETURN TO THEIR HOMES, THE MADMAN HAS AWAKENED...
YOUR PLOT TO SUMMON ANNIHILUS FROM THE DARK HEART OF THE NEGATIVE ZONE WORKED, BOY CHILD.
...AND RIGHT ON CUE.
WELL THEN, HERE WE ALL ARE.
JUST IN TIME FOR THE END OF THE BEGINNING...
...AND THE BEGINNING OF THE END...
4 NOT THE END! YE

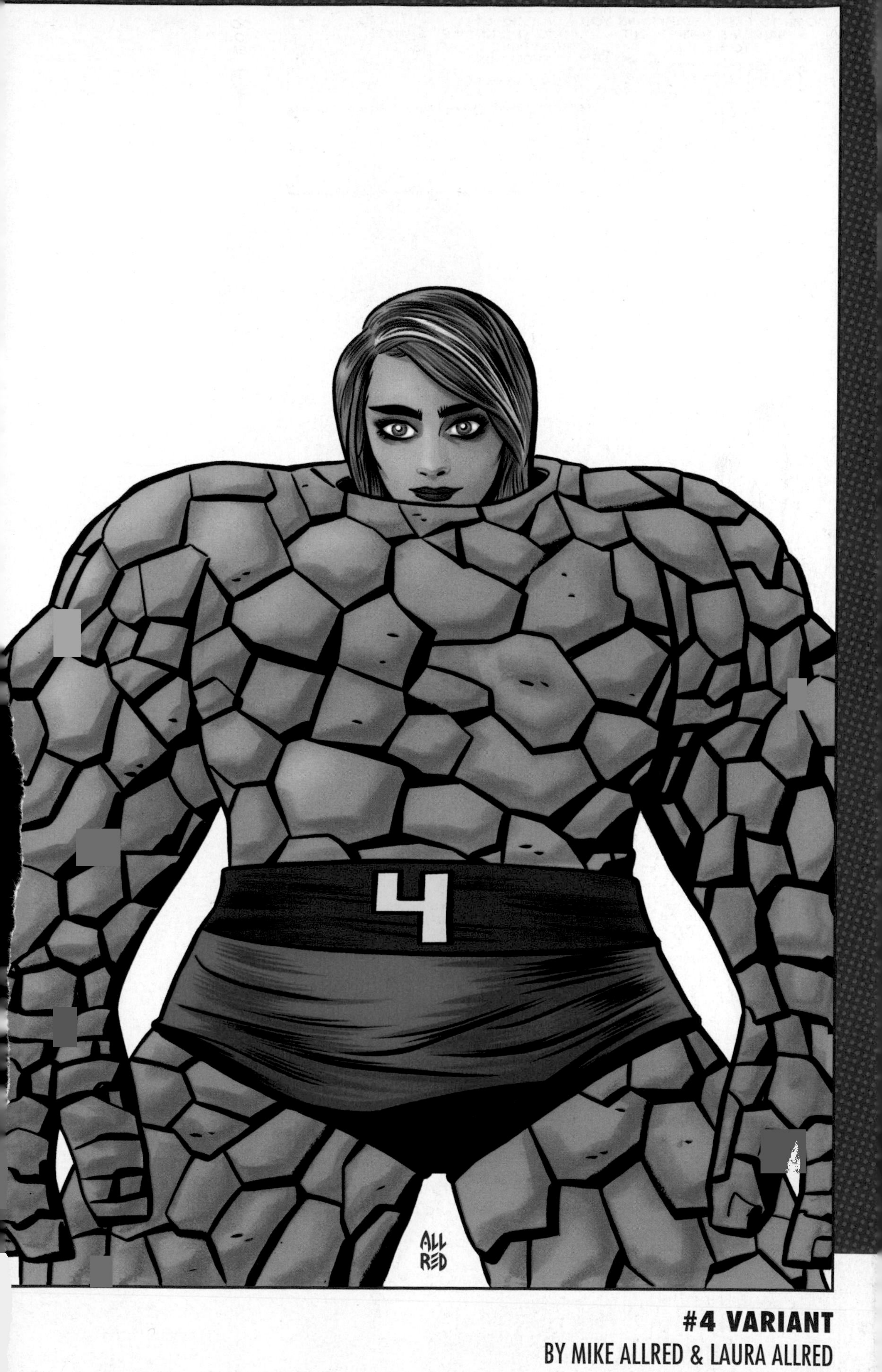
4
ALL
RED

#4 VARIANT
BY MIKE ALLRED & LAURA ALLRED

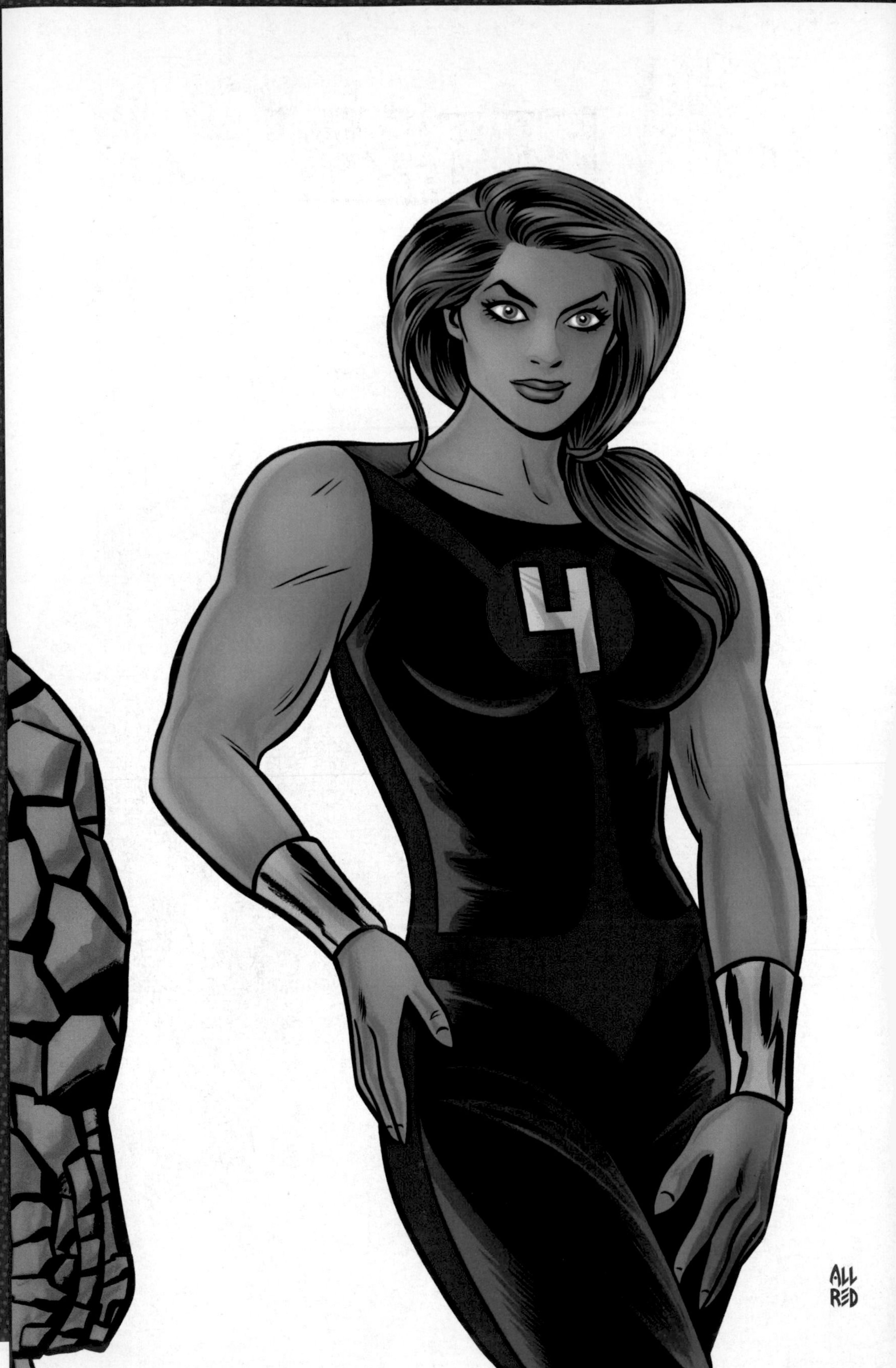

ALL
RED

#5 VARIANT
BY MIKE ALLRED & LAURA ALLRED

TO ACCESS THE FREE *MARVEL AUGMENTED REALITY APP*
THAT ENHANCES AND CHANGES THE WAY YOU EXPERIENCE COMIC

1. **Download the app for free via**
   marvel.com/ARapp
2. **Launch the app on your camera-enabled**
   Apple iOS® or Android™ device*

3. **Hold your mobile device's camera ov**
   any cover or panel with the **AR** grap
4. **Sit back and see the future of comics**
   in action!

*Available on most camera-enabled Apple iOS® and Android™ devices. Content subject to
change and availability.

INDEX